Edmund Burke

REFLECTIONS ON THE REVOLUTION IN FRANCE

〔英〕埃德蒙·伯克 著

评法国革命

林骧华 导读 任建国 注释

上海译文出版社

World Academic Classics
世界学术经典·英文版

总策划／总主编
庄智象　林骧华

上海时代教育出版研究中心 研发
Shanghai Epoch Education Publishing Research Center

编辑委员会

世界学术经典（英文版）
总　序

　　书之成为经典，乃人类在不同时代的思想、智慧与学术的结晶，优秀文化之积淀，具有不随时代变易的永恒价值。有道是读书须读经典，这是智者的共识。

　　对于中外经典著作中的思想表述，仅读外文书的中译本或文言著作的白话释文是不够的，尤其是当误译、误释发生的时候，读者容易被误导，或望文生义，或以讹传讹，使原有的文化差异变成更深的文化隔阂。因此，在"世界学术经典（英文版）"的选目中，大部分作品为英文原著；原作是其他语种的经典，则选用相对可靠的英文译本；至于中国古代经典，则采用汉英对照的方式呈现，旨在向西方阐释中国的思想和文化。其中，精选的中国经典是整个系列的重要组成部分。有了这一部分的经典，才真正体现出"世界性"。

　　以原典和英文方式出版，是为了使读者通过研读，准确理解以英文表达的思想、理论和方法，力求避免舛误，进而通过批判和接受，化为智慧力量。这有利于思想的传播，裨益于新思想的产生，同时亦可提高英语修养。

　　经典名著的重要性是不言而喻的，但是以下几点意义值得一再重申。

（一）学术经典提供思想源泉

两千六百年来的世界学术经典凝聚了人类思想的精华，世世代代的优秀思想家以他们独特的见识和智慧，留给后人取之不竭、用之不尽的思想源泉。从老子、孔子、柏拉图、亚里士多德以降，天才辈出，思想闪光，精彩纷呈。思想界的大师、名家们在人类思想史传统链条上的每一个环节，都启发后人开拓新的思想领域，探究生命的本质，直抵人性的深层。随着人类思想的不断成熟和完善，各个学科领域的理论从本体论、认识论、方法论、实践论、价值论等维度不断深化。后人继承前人的思想，借经典的滋养保持思想活力，丰富和发展前人的观点，使之形成一波又一波的思想洪流，从而改变人的思想和世界观，改变人类社会的进程。历史已经证明：人类社会的进步，思想的力量大于一切。

（二）学术经典传承精神力量

经典名著中蕴含的人类精神，传承的人类守望的共同价值原则和社会理想，在每一个具体领域里都有诸多丰富的表述，它们从整体上构成了推动人类进步的精神力量。研习和传承人类两千六百多年来的优秀思想，并将它化作求新求变的灵感，是人类文明的要义所在。仅有技术进步，还不足以表明人类的文明程度。若无优秀的思想底蕴，人类存在的意义将大打折扣。

中国思想传统中的基本理念和西方思想传统中的基本理念分别形成了东西方两大具有普遍价值的道德观念和价值系统。值得注意的是：（1）这两大道德系统应该是一个互补、互鉴的整体，两者都不可偏废，因为人类的思想是个多元整体。任何一个民族，缺少其中之一，在精神上都可能是不完整的；（2）这些基本理念都不是抽象概念，它们都具有很强的实践意义，并且必须由实践来考察，否则就很难体现其价值。

精神传承必然是一种自觉的过程，它靠习得，不靠遗传，因此我们需要研读经典。

（三）学术经典构成文化积淀

"文化"包含三大部分：（1）思想与精神现象；（2）制度与习俗；（3）有形的事物。学术经典是对思想与精神现象的归纳和提炼，对制度与习俗的探究和设计，对有形事物的形而上思考和描述。

每一个学科领域的经典著作中都会提出一些根本性的问题，这些问题直面人的困惑，思考人类社会的疑难，在新思想和新知识中展现人类的智慧。当这些思想成果积淀下来，就构成人类文化的主要组成部分。文化不只是制度或器物的外在形式，更重要的是凝结在其背后的精神与思想。

每一个学科的学术本身都要面对一些形而上的（超越性的、纯理论性的）文化问题。在很多人看来，理性的思考和理论的表述都是很枯燥的，但是热爱真理并且对思想情有独钟的人会从学术经典的理论中发现无限生动的天地，从而产生获得真理的快乐，这才是我们追求的真正文化。

大量阅读经典名著是一种学习、积累文化的根本方法，深度阅读和深刻记忆能使文化积淀在人的身上，并且代代相传。假如这一过程中断了，人世间只剩下花天酒地、歌舞升平，文化也就湮灭了。

（四）学术经典推动社会进步

毫无疑问，凡属学术经典，都必须含有新的学术成果——新思想、新理论、新方法，或者新探索。这样的原创性学术成果越多，人类的思想就越深邃，视野越开阔，理论更全面、完美，方法更先进、有效，社会的进步才能获得新的动力和保障。

人文主义推翻神学，理性主义旨在纠正人的偏激，启蒙精神主张打破思想束缚，多元主义反抗绝对理念。各种新思想层出不穷，带来了学术的进步，启发并推动了更大的社会变革。这些原创思想在历史长河中经过漫长的时间考验，成为经典，在任何一种文明中都是社会进步和发展的动力。

当我们研读完一部学术经典，分析和归纳其原创的思想观点时，可以很清晰地理解和感悟它在同时代的环境里对于社会的变革和进步有着何种意义，以及它对当下有哪些启迪。

相比技术的发展，思想并不浮显在社会的表层，它呈现在书本的字里行间，渗透于人的心智，在人的灵魂中闪光。每当社会需要时，它能让我们看到无形的巨大力量。

温故而知新。今日世界纷乱依旧，但时代已不再朦胧。人类思想史上的各种主张，在实践中都已呈现清晰的面貌。当我们重新梳理各种思想和理论时，自然不会再返回到"全盘接受"或者"全盘否定"的幼稚阶段。二十一世纪人类正确的世界观、人生观、价值观需要优秀思想传统的支撑，并通过批判继承，不断推陈出新，滋衍出磅礴之推力。

我们所选的这些学术经典，成书于不同的时代，代表了不同的思想与理论主张。有些著作带有时代烙印，有其局限性或片面性；有些观点不一定正确，但从另一个方面显示出人类思想的丰富性和复杂性。各门学科建立、各种主张提出之后，都曾经在历代思想的实验场上经受碰撞和检验，被接受或者被批判。我们的学者需要研读这些书，而青年学生们的思想成长更需要读这些书。当然，批评与分析是最有效和最有益的阅读方法。

有鉴于此，我们希望"世界学术经典（英文版）"能够真正做到"开卷有益"，使我们自己在潜移默化中都成长为有思想、有理想、有品位的人。

上海时代教育出版研究中心

2018 年 10 月

目 录

导　读

林骧华

埃德蒙·伯克（Edmund Burke，1729—1797），英国政论家、美学理论家。一生从政，所著《评法国革命》（1790）代表当时欧洲的保守主义思潮，是世界政治思想史上保守主义的重要著作。[注]

一、生平与著作

埃德蒙·伯克出生在爱尔兰都柏林一个中产阶级律师家庭，他的终生宗教信仰与派别是基督教新教，属于英国国教会，即圣

[注] 本书的原书名很长：《评法国革命，兼评伦敦与那一时间相关的某些社团的活动，意在以书信方式寄给在巴黎的一位绅士》（*Reflections on Revolution in France and on the Proceedings in Certain Societies in London Relative to That Event in a Letter Intended to Have Been Sent to a Gentleman in Paris*）。书名的中文译法已有《法国大革命反思录》《法国革命论》《法国革命感想录》等。本书导读作者和注释作者反复讨论，改作《评法国革命》。因为译成《法国革命论》，其意思会显得偏向于宣传法国革命；而若译成《法国大革命反思录》，"反思"一词在汉语习惯上是指对参与过的事件作深刻的思考和检讨，但伯克的立场是反对法国革命的，与"反思"无关。（英文 reflections 的原意是 an opinion arrived at after consideration；adverse criticism。）他在书中从保守主义立场出发，主张维护旧制度，提倡渐进式的改良道路，一方面为英国的"光荣革命"张目，另一方面以英国为标准而编派法国革命的种种不是，其意并不在给法国革命作总结，故译成《评法国革命》比较恰当。

公会。他毕业于都柏林的三一学院，随即参与爱尔兰下议院的政治斗争，争取立法使爱尔兰获得独立，间或充当政界人物的秘书。

27 岁时，他匿名出版了《论自然社会的合理性》(*The Vindication of Natural Society*，1756) 一书，抨击鲍林波洛克 (Bolingbroke，1678—1751，英国托利党政治家，自然神论哲学家) 的自然宗教 (natural religion) 理论。他断言，"如果所有的道德责任、社会基础都依靠它们的理由向每一个人说明和表达清楚，"结果必定是一片混乱。更主要的是，他认清了一个重要事实：在哲学领域的智性动荡和神学领域的喧嚣背后，静静地蔓延着一种可以动摇整个公民社会自身建构的力量。当人们发现他就是《论自然社会的合理性》的真正作者时，他开始出名了。1757 年，伯克出版了第二本著作《对崇高与美理念的哲学探源》(*A Philosophical Inquiry into the Origin of Our Ideas of the Sublime and Beautiful*)。这本美学著作在德国大获成功，其中运用的心理学方法在德国比在英国更吸引人，尤其受到它影响的是莱辛和康德。同时在 1757 年出版的第三本书是《欧洲在美洲的殖民地》(*An Account of the European Settlements in America*)。他的第四本书是《英格兰史》(*History of England*，1758)。他担任了世界事务评论刊物《年鉴》(*Annual Register*) 的主编，也成为当时英国消息最灵通的人物之一。在议会里他的知名度不断上升，成为全国拔尖的政治家。

1769 年，伯克出版了《评新书〈国家近况〉》(*Observations on a Late Publication Entitled "The Present State of the Nation"*)，表明自己反对议会改革，反对扩大选举权，理由是当时选民的情况很腐败，增加选民人数只会使事情更糟。他主张精简选民人数，希望留下来的选民能够珍视特权，约束自己的选举权。关于给北美殖民地在议会的席位问题，他声称地理问题使之不可能。关于法国的财政状况，伯克说他做过仔细研究，发现它非常令人沮丧，所以他时常期望"某种非同寻常的激变，对法国乃至对全欧洲的整个制度产生影响，但很难说得准"。1770 年，伯克出版了他的名著之一《对目前不满情绪原因的思考》（*Thoughts on the Causes of the Present Discontents*）。伯克在抨击法国革命及其原则时说："我并非那种认为人民绝不会错的人。他们一向如此大胆，既在别的国家，也在这个国家。但我要说的是，在他们与统治者之间的一切冲突中，可以推测，至少有一点相同，即赞同人民。……在伟大的国家里发生的革命不是偶然的结果，也不是流行的异想天开的结果。……至于民众，绝不是出于一种激情要攻讦它要反抗的对象，而是出于不再忍受所遭受的苦难。"关于法律，他认为："法律只达很少之处。无论你有多么赞同宪政政府，它大多必须依靠行使权力，权力最终依靠国家的大臣们的精明和正直。甚至法律的一切使用和权威也取决于他们。没有他们，你们的国家只不过是纸上的计划，也不会有活生生的、积极的、有效的宪法。"伯克对法国革命始终抱着激烈谴责的态度，并且宣布"对公民社会的最可怕、最残酷的打击是通过无神论。……无神论者不顾宪法，不光是在这个国家，全人类都是这样。他们绝不会得到支持，绝不会得到容忍。"

伯克的其他著作还有：《论趣味》（*Discourse Concerning Taste*，1757），《关于美洲税收的演讲》（*Speech on American Taxation*，1774），《关于同美洲调解的演讲》（*Speech on Conciliation with American*，1775，1778），《新辉格党人向老辉格党人的呼吁》（*Appeal from the New to the Old Whigs*，1791），《关于弹劾沃伦·黑斯廷斯的演讲，附

导言》(*Speeches on the Impeachment of Warren Hastings，with Introduction*，1792)。1901 年，美国波士顿比肯斯菲尔德（Beaconsfield）出版公司出版了 12 卷本《埃德蒙·伯克著作与演讲集》(*The Writings and Speeches of Edmund Burke*)。

二、《评法国革命》的写作背景

伯克成了旧制度的坚定维护者、启蒙运动的主要敌人，因为他认为启蒙运动严重侵犯了欧洲传统的政府与宗教。1774 年，他当选国会议员。他在议会里的一系列演讲揭示了他对政府地位的看法。他认为英国对殖民地拥有主权，只要英国认为合适，就有权对殖民地人课税。有人说这是权利问题，他认为权利不能同情势分开。1775 年 3 月，在关于同美洲殖民地之间调停的演讲中，他宣称"我认为问题不在于你是否有权让你的人民身处苦难，而在于你的兴趣是否让他们幸福。不应该由一位律师来告诉我可以做什么，而应该由人性、理性、正义来告诉我应该做什么"。他还说，"我在这里不是要区别各种权利，不是试图标出各种权利的界线，我对它们不做形而上的区分。我不想听到这些。对于关涉人、关涉人的事务的各种理论而言，这是真正的试金石——在整体上是否符合人性？是否符合他的各种习惯所限定的人性？"这次高超的演讲充分揭示了他的政治智慧，其中令人印象最深刻的两句话是："我不知道如何构想意在反对全体人民的方法。""政治上宽宏大量往往是最纯真的智慧；而一个大帝国同没有头脑结合在一起就是病态。"

不久后发生了美国独立战争，伯克相信，殖民地人的战斗是为了英国的自由事业，假如他们失败的话，其必然的结果就是英国人自己也相应地失去了那种自由。但是他并不清楚独立战争激进的一面。随着 1781 年英军在约克敦战败，北美战争结束，罗金厄姆出任英国首相，伯克被任命为枢密顾问官兼军队的总军需官，他改革制度，遏制滥用职权现象。不久后，他又弹劾沃伦·黑斯廷斯（Warren Hastings，1732—1818，英国首任孟加拉总督）的政策与行为，努力代表"败落的几百万印度人"，这场斗争一直持续到伯克在国会的生涯结束，迎来对黑斯廷斯的著名审判。弹劾过程涉及国会的各个机构，从 1788 年开始，持续了 7 年。期间小威廉·皮特组阁，伯克丢失了在总军需处的职务，但得到的安慰是在这段时间里的几项荣誉，其中包括担任为期一年的格拉斯哥大学名誉校长。

当 1789 年法国革命爆发时，英国人普遍热忱地接受这个消息，而令人瞩目的例外是埃德蒙·伯克。他警告英国，同时也警告欧洲其他国家：法国革命中建立的秩序是危险的。在巴士底监狱被攻占后，他写信给爱尔兰贵族查尔蒙勋爵说，暴力的发生很可能只是一场突如其来的爆发。但是"假如它是必然特性（character）而不是偶然事件（accident），那么，那里的人民就不配有自由"。10 月里，他写信给一位法国朋友说，他赞同法国的自由，而所有的人也确实希望自由。但他的"自由"理念是"社会的自由"。他所说的那种事物状态，指"自由是由有约束的平等来保障的。确实，这种自由只不过是另一种名称'正义'（justice）的代名词。自由与正义一旦分离，两者都是不安全的。"

伯克写作《评法国革命》，就像他反对英国对待美国革命的态度一样，主要的动机是为了英国："无论什么时候，邻居的房子着火了，不要忘记用救火车来照看自己的房子。"从表面上看，《评法国革命》是伯克写给一位法国记者的信，实际上是对不信奉国教的理查德·普莱斯（Richard Price）牧师于 1789 年 11 月 4 日在伦敦对"革命协会（The Revolution Society）"成员所作的布道中称赞法国革命原则一事的回应。

伯克宣称，从政治角度看，法国十分卑劣，而且失去了一切，甚至是她的国家名称。法国人表现出自己是世界上迄今为止最能干的废墟制造者。法国人做出的榜样中最坏的部分是由军队来设定公民资格。重要的是，要防止法国式的骚乱在英国发生。他认为英国有一些可恶之人已经显示出强烈的愿望，宣扬要仿照法国的改革精神。他强烈反对任何意图引进法国式民主的倾向及其目标，反对一切创新精神所夹带的暴力行为，因为暴力行为远离了真正安全改革的全部原则，处心积虑要推翻国家，而恰恰没有能力帮助国家。为此，他同支持法国思想的老朋友谢立丹彻底决裂。不久后，他又同另一个老朋友福克斯发生了分歧，他坚持维护关于审查的法令，感到在一两年内，英国国教将会比法国教会面临更严重的危险。英国的不信国教者主张议会改革，赞同法国革命，热烈赞扬民主，他们希望保障英国政治的世俗化，寻求财富与阶级地位"平等化"，这些都使伯克愤怒，也使他产生极大的厌恶。伯克在那些人的目标中看到了潜在的革命种子，认为其结果会推翻现有秩序，推翻一切在他看来使英国得以伟大和自由的事物。

于是他竭尽全力要把计划中评法国革命的著作写好。他充满热情，而且写得很小心仔细。1790 年 11 月，《评法国革命》出版了。初版定价 5 先令，很快售罄。一年之内，又重印了 10 次。这种反应是令人惊讶的。对于他的这部著作，有些人冷淡，但是有很多人积极赞同他的观点，因为大多数先前赞同法国革命的英国人现在产生了新的感觉，他们深切关注和意识到其中潜在的危险。英国诗人威廉·华兹华斯一开始对法国革命兴高采烈地表示支持，但随着法国革命形势的进展，他也感到很失望。英国国王原先是伯克的宿敌，此刻他也称《评法国革命》是一本非常好的书，并且推荐说，每一个绅士都应该读这本书。这部著作也给全欧洲统治阶级留下深刻印象，路易十六亲自将它翻译成法文。

三、《评法国革命》的主要内容

伯克认为法国革命是一场可怕的革命，是破坏社会秩序的罪恶行为。他猛烈抨击法国革命的原则，认为那些原则表面上维护人权和自由，实质上空洞而危险，是对真正的人权、自由、宪政和欧洲文明传统的践踏。他说，法国大革命的根本症结在于不懂得良好的秩序是一切良好事物的基础；"自由"只是一种抽象原则，滥用自由，迫使政客们的行为往往同他们的愿望不一致；借口人权没收财产，引起反感，制造了冲突与不满；一切邪恶归根结底是对人权概念的错误理解。他认为，法国人那种重新改组政府的行为，既背弃了人的本性，也背弃了历史。一个国家的民众并不是如《人权与公民权利宣言》所说的那样，被赋予一些宪法上的抽象概念，例如天赋权利。他说，权利，还有义务，是民众出生的那个国家的单个历史的产物。所有的国家，它们的历史将民众同它们的过去联系在一起，并赋予他们以现今的和未来的任务。所以法国人无权在没有参照过去的经验、没有考虑到未来的情况下，就去重新改建他们的国家和宪法。法国人的这种做法，是对传统与习俗的不尊重，这就破坏了世世代代以来由法国的历史构建起来的宝贵文明。

对于伯克而言，法国革命是"一场原则和理论教条的革命"，它建立的国家是"一所狂热的武装学院，所宣传的原则是谋杀、抢劫、欺骗、内讧、压迫、不敬神"的产物。国家突然陷入一大群腐败的无神论者之手，他们渴望权力，并且因为拥有权力而变得更加腐败。他们的理智动机是由形而上学理论家提供的，深奥难解；他们只不过是"强盗和凶手：从来没有一帮歹徒和土匪会在外表和腔调上假装成一个哲学家的学院"。当时欧洲许多第一流的思想家都赞同法国革命，因为它发誓拥护那些抽象原则。伯克却宣称说，各种情况（有些人对此视而不见）实际上赋予每一种政治原则以鲜明的色彩和有明显特点的效果；每一种民事和政治计划都必须对人类有益，否则就应该受到谴责。

伯克认为，在"无情地、盲目地摧毁现存秩序"和"在任何情况下都反对变革"的立场之间有一种快乐的中间道路："一个充满热情的、深思熟虑的仁慈之心的人会希望他所处的社会比他所见的社会要组织得更好些；但是一个优秀的爱国者，一个真正的政治家，总是考虑他的国家现有的大多数事物应该如何造成。既有守望的气质，也有推动进步的能力，两者相结合，这是我对作为一名国务活动家提出的标准。其余的一切在观念上都不重要，在行动中都是危险的。"他进一步指出："真正的立法人应该内心充满感受能力。他应该爱同类，尊敬同类，害怕自己。可能允许他的心情去抓住他的最终目标，只需要他的直觉一瞥；但是他朝向目标的动作应该是深思熟虑的。政治安排作为一种带社会目的之工作，只有靠社会手段才能完成。心智与心智必须共谋。心智的联合需要时间，只有它才能产生我们目标中的一切善。我们的耐心会比我们的力量获得更多的成绩。"

伯克的思想与当时主要思想家中间的流行意识是敌对的。他认识到，诉诸"自然"和"理性"从根本上来说是枯燥无味的。这些观念同他对国家的基督教观念底线是冲突的。"我们从内心感觉到宗教是公民社会的基础，也是一切善和一切舒适的来源。……人天生是宗教动物；因此无神论不仅反理性，而且违背我们的本能；所以它不可能长久流行。""以道德使我们的人性达到完美的人，也愿意采用使之完美的必要手段，所以他希望国家同它的来源、同一切完美的原型发生关联。"如此才能使人类尊崇国家，而且"社会实际上是一份契约。从属关系的契约，其纯粹兴趣的各种目标可能任意消散——但是国家不应该被认为只不过是贸易伙伴的协议，买卖胡椒和咖啡、白布、烟草或其他廉价的货物，……应该带着尊重来看待社会，因为社会不是事物的合作关系，不是粗劣的动物生存，短暂且容易死亡。社会的合作关系是全部科学、全部艺术、每一种美德、所有完美的事物。这类合作关系不可能在许多世代中达到目标，它变成合作关系，不仅在活着的人之间，而且在活着的人、死去的人、即将出生的人之间。每一个特定国家的每一份合约都不过是永恒社会的一份原始大合约中的一个条款，联结下层自然和上层自然，联结看得见的和看不见的世界，根据一种固定的协议，由神圣的誓言保护，包括所有的物质世界和精神世界，各自在指定的位置上。"他还认为，国家及其法律尊奉的主要原则之一是"为了避免（国家的）暂时拥有者和终身承担者漫不经心地对待他们从祖先那里接受的东西，或者漫不经心地对待子孙后代，他们应该表现得完全像个主人；

他们不应该认为自己有权切断限定继承权，或者浪费遗产，任意摧毁社会的整个原初结构，冒险留给后人一片废墟，而非栖居地——而且教后继者不尊重他们的计划，不像他们自己尊重先辈们的制度那样。以这种毫无原则的方法来经常地、大幅度地、用许多各种各样的方式改变国家，就像漂浮不定的想象或时尚风气，整个共同体的全部链条和连续性就会断裂。没有哪一代人能够同另一代人相连。人类就变得和夏天的苍蝇差不多了。"

为维护既有的政治制度，伯克解释了与英国王位有关的宪法原则。关于人民有权选择自己的统治者这一点上，他说，《权利宣言》也坚持世袭君主政体，但许可在紧急状态下，在有限范围内变更世袭原则；人们拥戴某一位君主，这就是他们的选择。关于人民有权罢黜他们的"渎职"统治者，他认为，没有哪一种永久统治可以建立在这样模糊的观点之上，国王是拥有最高权力的君主，不是人民的公仆。除了英国 1688 年"光荣革命"，世界上很少有革命能被认为是正当的。英国式自由并不是从 1688 年的"光荣革命"才产生的，它是一种英国传统，在光荣革命中得到保留，而本质上它是一种防御性的革命，维护了君主制度和"阶层照旧，秩序照旧，特权照旧，豁免权照旧，财产法则照旧，从属关系照旧"。"光荣革命"并不证明人民有权为自己组织一个政府，世袭君主政体是英国的传统遗产，是一种稳定社会的因素。从这一立场出发，伯克认为法国革命是错误的，法国人不应该摧毁旧制度，而应该在祖先留给他们的基础上建设国家。法国革命中实行的政策，其后果很严重，国民议会应该对邪恶的暴力政策负责。历史上有大人物滥用权力的例子，但同目前法国的暴行相比微不足道。"光荣革命"与法国革命之间存在巨大差异，光荣革命带来的是有序方式，而法国革命以失控方式上演的一幕，其特征是暴力，毁灭，无政府状态和恐怖。伯克反对法国革命的主要原因之一，恰恰是法国人激烈地同自己的以往分手，而不是像英国那样将自己的以往当作未来的基础。

关于人权的真实含义，伯克坚持认为，只有社会稳定才是真正原则；平均主义是虚假的平等原则；经过考验的美德和智慧是真正的领导原则；财产是使社会得以永存的不可缺少的因素，但是法国革命放弃了这些真正的原则。英国的危险在于"革命协会"的政治设计目标只不过是"为革命而革命"，会给英国带来同样的后果。真正的政府原则、政府的真实本质不可以用错误的人权概念来解释，自然法则的原理不适用于一个复杂的社会。伯克认为，在法国革命中，乌合之众统治了国民议会，暴民们反对王家、贵族、教士。启蒙运动带来的各种社会革命一方面表明骑士时代已经过去，诡辩家、经济学家、统计学家取而代之；另一方面，导致的后果是权力腐败和学术腐败，贸易衰落和制造业衰落，这在法国已经显而易见。英国的传统与法国的启蒙运动是相对立的，英国人不会像法国人一样行动。法国启蒙运动的特点是蔑视传统，而英国的启蒙运动对英国人民没有影响。

伯克极力为教会辩护，他说，在英国，教会是社会的基础之一。国家与教会无法分离；教育建立于传统，紧密附属于教会；国家和各个部门的领导人都需要宗教指导。教会和它的代表需要社会名声和财政独立，才能恰当地履行职责。但在法国，国民议会没收教会财产的政策缺乏法律基础，他们真正的目标是要摧毁基督教。国家的财政困境应该由那些对此负责的人来改善，教士是没有责任的。国民议会的政策对财产缺乏尊重，历史上很少有征服者会达到如此程度。国家的财政情况并不需要靠没收财产来挽救。教士和贵族税赋太重，他们为国家的财政需求而作贡献，但是教士的各种贡献都被否定了。国民议会以没收王室和教会的土地作为金融政策基础，使新纸币成为法定货币，这一政策的严重后果，一是破坏了与革命同情者的朋友关系，二是政策的失败迫使国民议会采取越来越残暴的政策，三是使"纯粹民主"的压迫显得和独裁君主的压迫一模一样。在法国的新秩序下，对教士的指控基于许多代人以前所犯的行为，这是错误的，不能让教士们为历史上洛林红衣大主教和1572年圣巴托洛谬大屠杀的行为负责。假如说教会人士也有错误的话，那是因为教会人士也是人，人的弱点不能混同于罪行；人类的激情是真正的罪恶，它不可能因毁灭社会领袖而被移除。国民议会建立的新的宗教体制实质上是被设计来废除宗教的，它推翻了原有的法规，导致无法无天的行为到处泛滥，也使无神论的疯狂威胁着英国和欧洲其他国家。

伯克还极力为法国君主制度与贵族制度辩护，认为君主制度具有它自身的优点，如果说法国君主滥用了权力，那么需要的是改革，而不是摧毁。他说，法国君主的业绩是明显的：增加了人口，增加了国民财富，提高了法国民众的总体文化水准，王室政府总体上思想是开放的。而革命建立的新政府，其业绩无法同旧政权相比，反而造成了大众的饥馑。因此，法国贵族的命运不该如此。旧制度要靠政治智慧来改善，而不是摧毁它。但是在法国，哲学推断压倒了政治智慧。国民议会侵犯了法国人民的天职，滥用武力取代政治智慧。没收土地、发行纸币，是为了解决新政权的财政困境，但是国民议会的政策是毁灭性的而不是建设性的，一时避开的困境，过后必定用武力解决。社会改革需要一定的时间、缓和的态度、同情式的理解，必须由占统治地位的原则来引导，但是相反，国民议会的政策虚弱无能，原因是它来自有害的观点。它的财政政策、金融政策完全是失败的，它的两难在于它的全部政策不一致。它缺乏政治智慧，税收制度缺乏政治判断，其中盐税是国民议会财政政策混乱的极好例子，任意征税，缺乏公正，整个制度显示出无能。它不遵循金融原则，不顾一切地花钱，早已破坏了国家信誉，将发行纸币当作最后的挽救措施，很值得怀疑，因为法国强行发行纸币同英国稳定可靠的纸币完全不可混淆。

在制度设计方面，伯克认为，在国民议会新立法的结构成分中，三条选举制度原则（基于地区；基于人口；基于贡献）与平等原则是相抵触的：它们相互之间不一致，各地区之间不存在可比性；它们导致政府去中心化，会破坏国家统一；共和国若持续下去，阶级对立将不可避免；人们希望宪法稳定，是出于一种恐惧，即改变宪法就会带来恐怖社会。新宪法使法国变成一个联盟而不是一个国家，国民议会的目标是建立一个由各独立部门组成的联盟，议员不再代表人民，而只代表他们的选区；议员们只考虑自己的共同利益。至于国家，没收财产和强制发行没有根底的纸币，都会摧毁权威，破坏已没收土地的价值，结果，法兰西王国变成了一张全国性的赌桌，懂得赌法的人大获其利，国家最终将被货币操纵者统治。新秩序下的行政部门存在严重的问题。国王的权力与其王室地位并不相称，留给国王的只有国民议会的脏活；王室内阁与国民议会宣布的主权不一致；政府部长们尽管对议会的决定不起作用，却要对议会的行为负责；这种二元体制迫使政府部长们要么背叛国王，要么背叛议会。司法部门要选择的是旧体系而不是新体系，但目前的法官们没有法律机构，只能服从国民议会的命令。国民议会认为没有法律的状态是合法的，它从自己的司法中取消了自己的治理机构，而计划中的最高法庭对于法国的最后一丝自由具有潜在的危险。法国军队状态不佳，军人屈从于政府当局；指派和提拔军官的制度对纪律和权威是破坏性的；所以到最后，法国只能依靠军队来维持秩序，虽说军队本身就是混乱的一个主要因素，但是当前情势需要一位强有力的独裁军事领袖，他将成为这个国家的新主人。后来果然革命的成果落到了拿破仑手里，人们将这一点看作伯克的精确预言。

在他原先的写作计划中，有 4 个关键词：教会，君主政治，贵族体制，民主。但实际上他主要强调了宗教，而民主却被省略了。他觉得对法国革命中建立的"国民议会（National Assembly）"很难下判断，这大概是因为在那个时代，"民主"的概念及其在政体方面的实践还比较难以解释吧。

四、分析与批评

在西方，伴随着由法国革命奠定的社会秩序和制度的延续和发展，研究法国革命的著作汗牛充栋，其中讴歌的多，批评的少，彻底否定的更是少见。但是伯克的《评法国革命》以彻底否定的态度，表现了他对这一喧闹纷乱的革命事件的思考。此书在出版后的 230 年里，有许多版本，被称作"反对法国革命及其原则的保守派杰作（the great conservative statement against the Revolution and its principles）"，倘若思考和研究革命事件、政治制度设计、保守主义政治，它到今天仍然是一部重要的参考著作。

《评法国革命》的出版在当时就引发了一批反驳文章，文章作者们纷纷抨击伯克的观点，其中最有名的是美国独立战争和法国革命的鼓动家托马斯·潘恩（Thomas Paine）写的思想宣传小册子《论人权》（*Rights of Man*，1792）。伯克被批评得最多的，是他未能认识到法国的旧制度在社会和经济方面的邪恶性质是需要彻底改变的。在这一点上，伯克无可否认是盲目的，原因在于他在政治和宗教方面的先入之见。人们一方面看到他在美国革命问题上的立场，另一方面看到他对法国革命的态度，于是不加思考地认为他的立场是从根本上无法调和的。其实伯克对这两场革命的看法，思维原则是同样的，推论方法也是相同的；然而尽管过程同样是合理的，但在不同情况下，得出的推论结果却几乎完全相反。伯克在书中提出的"守成与改良"主张，无疑是社会的一部分人从经济、政治、社会地位、文化传统出发的考量。至于对法国革命历史的评判，他断言 1790 年国民议会的行动是不公正的、轻率的、破坏性的、不稳定的，这一评判比较客观。

　　然而冷静地反思历史，应当想到，革命当然不是、也不应该是乌托邦。革命是复杂的。革命是为了建立一种新制度。被称为革命的，必然是社会的大动荡、大变革，是历史进程中的突变，它的思想、文化、政治制度、社会秩序必然发生质的变化，在渐进中突然显现，而使社会生活变得不同。在这一意义上，习称的"法国大革命"无须冠以"大"字，它是近代史上一场真正意义上的革命。与此相比，英国 1688 年的"光荣革命（Glorious Revolution）"只是一场改良式的妥协，而"美国革命（American Revolution）"只不过是一场抗税的造反，称之为"独立战争（The War of Independence）"才比较准确。

革命是社会历史进程的一种突变，以突然爆发为特征，它是对旧制度、旧政权的全面颠覆。当大多数人对公平、正义的强烈诉求长期不能得到满足，自由受到残酷压制时，对旧政权的集体愤懑达到了极限，这时革命就会爆发。然而在突变的同时，社会自身发展的逻辑又决定了它在某些方面（集体心理、文化习俗、社会转型等）是渐进变化的。旧的社会消失了，但旧思想还长期存在，其中也包括了文化传统的延续。所以在考察历史的时候，参阅不同观点可以产生更多的思考，获得更多的智慧；即使面对错误历史观的陈述，对之不一概视而不见，不只作笼统否定，也可以引发更深刻的反思。在研究政治革命和制度革命的历史时，可以将那些对立的具体观点当作自己的镜鉴和磨砺，从而使政治设计更臻完善。选读此书，可以引发我们对暴力革命的思考和对历史的反思。21 世纪的人面对现实和未来，检讨先人的足迹，应该从经验和教训中增长智慧，以能更好地肩负起历史与社会的责任。

Reflections
on
The Revolution in France

It may not be unnecessary to inform the reader that the following Reflections had their origin in a correspondence between the author and a very young gentleman at Paris[1], who did him the honour of desiring his opinion upon the important transactions which then, and ever since have, so much occupied the attention of all men. An answer was written some time in the month of October, 1789; but it was kept back upon prudential considerations. That letter is alluded to in the beginning of the following sheets. It has been since forwarded to the person to whom it was addressed. The reasons for the delay in sending it were assigned in a short letter to the same gentleman. This produced on his part a new and pressing application for the author's sentiments[2].

The author began a second and more full discussion on the subject. This he had some thoughts of publishing early in the last spring; but the matter gaining upon him, he found that what he had undertaken not only far exceeded the measure of a letter, but that its importance required rather a more detailed consideration than at that time he had any leisure to bestow upon it. However, having thrown down his first thoughts in the form of a letter, and indeed when he sat down to write, having intended it for a private letter, he found it difficult to change the form of address, when his sentiments had grown into a greater extent and had received another direction. A different plan, he is sensible, might be more favourable to a commodious[3] division and distribution of his matter.

---

1. *a very young gentleman at Paris*：指弗朗索瓦·杜邦（Charles-Jean Francois Depont），伯克认识的一位法国青年记者和国民议会代表。法国大革命爆发后，杜邦于 1789 年 11 月和 12 月两次写信给伯克，请他谈谈对此次革命的看法。伯克曾回信作答，不过直到 1790 年他才将该信寄出。与此同时，伯克开始以回函的形式写作本书。杜邦后来成为雅各宾党人。本书公开出版后，他在给伯克的回信中写道："如果当时我了解了你的观点，我不光不会征求你的想法，而且还一定会请求你不要将它们公之于众。"
2. *sentiments*：作者在书中使用这一词语时，显然是指自己的"感受（feelings）"。
3. *commodious*：宽敞的，广阔的

Dear Sir,

You are pleased to call again, and with some earnestness, for my thoughts on the late proceedings in France. I will not give you reason to imagine that I think my sentiments of such value as to wish myself to be solicited about them. They are of too little consequence to be very anxiously either communicated or withheld. It was from attention to you, and to you only, that I hesitated at the time when you first desired to receive them. In the first letter I had the honour to write to you, and which at length I send, I wrote neither for nor from any description[1] of men; nor shall I in this. My errors, if any, are my own. My reputation alone is to answer for them.

You see, Sir, by the long letter I have transmitted to you, that, though I do most heartily wish that France may be animated by a spirit of rational liberty, and that I think you bound, in all honest policy, to provide a permanent body in which that spirit may reside, and an effectual organ by which it may act, it is my misfortune to entertain great doubts concerning several material points in your late transactions.

You imagined, when you wrote last, that I might possibly be reckoned among the approvers of certain proceedings in France, from the solemn public seal of sanction they have received from two clubs of gentlemen in London, called the Constitutional Society[2], and the Revolution Society[3].

---

1. description：种类 (kind)，即同一类的人或事物。
2. Constitutional Society："宪制协会"，成立于 1780 年，其宗旨是促进英国议会改革。
3. Revolution Society："革命协会"，成立于 1788 年，目的是为了庆贺英国 1688 年的"光荣革命"。

I certainly have the honour to belong to more clubs than one in which the constitution of this kingdom and the principles[1] of the glorious Revolution[2] are held in high reverence; and I reckon myself among the most forward in my zeal for maintaining that constitution and those principles in their utmost purity and vigour. It is because I do so that I think it necessary for me that there should be no mistake. Those who cultivate the memory of our revolution, and those who are attached to the constitution of this kingdom, will take good care how they are involved with persons who, under the pretext of zeal towards the Revolution and Constitution, too frequently wander from their true principles, and are ready on every occasion to depart from the firm, but cautious and deliberate, spirit which produced the one and which presides in the other. Before I proceed to answer the more material particulars in your letter, I shall beg leave to give you such information as I have been able to obtain of the two clubs which have thought proper, as bodies, to interfere in the concerns of France; first assuring you that I am not, and that I have never been, a member of either of those societies.

The first, calling itself the Constitutional Society, or Society for Constitutional Information, or by some such title, is, I believe, of seven or eight years' standing. The institution of this society appears to be of a charitable, and so far of a laudable nature: it was intended for the circulation, at the expense of the members, of many books which few others would be at the expense of buying, and which might lie on the hands of the booksellers, to the great loss of an useful body of men. Whether the books so charitably circulated were ever as charitably read is more than I know. Possibly several of them have been exported to France, and, like goods not in request here, may with you have found a market. I have heard much talk of the lights to be drawn from books that are sent from hence. What improvements they have had in

---

1. principles：信念
2. glorious Revolution：光荣革命，详见“术语汇编与简释”。

their passage (as it is said some liquors are meliorated by crossing the sea) I cannot tell: But I never heard a man of common judgment or the least degree of information speak a word in praise of the greater part of the publications circulated by that society; nor have their proceedings been accounted, except by some of themselves, as of any serious consequence.

Your National Assembly seems to entertain much the same opinion that I do of this poor charitable club. As a nation, you reserved the whole stock of your eloquent acknowledgments for the Revolution Society, when their fellows in the Constitutional were in equity entitled to some share. Since you have selected the Revolution Society as the great object of your national thanks and praises, you will think me excusable in making its late conduct the subject of my observations. The National Assembly of France has given importance to these gentlemen by adopting them; and they return the favour by acting as a committee in England for extending the principles of the National Assembly. Henceforward we must consider them as a kind of privileged persons, as no inconsiderable members in the diplomatic body. This is one among the revolutions which have given splendour to obscurity and distinction to undiscerned merit. Until very lately I do not recollect to have heard of this club. I am quite sure that it never occupied a moment of my thoughts, nor, I believe, those of any person out of their own set. I find, upon inquiry, that on the anniversary of the Revolution in 1688, a club of Dissenters[1], but of what denomination I know not, have long had the custom of hearing a sermon in one of their churches, and that afterwards they spent the day cheerfully, as other clubs do, at the tavern. But I never heard that any public measure or political system, much less that the merits of the constitution of any foreign nation, had been the subject of a formal

---

1. Dissenters：指不顺从英国国教的新教徒。详见"术语汇编与简释"。

proceeding at their festivals, until, to my inexpressible surprise, I found them in a sort of public capacity, by a congratulatory address, giving an authoritative sanction to the proceedings of the National Assembly in France.

In the ancient principles and conduct of the club, so far at least as they were declared, I see nothing to which I could take exception. I think it very probable, that for some purpose, new members may have entered among them, and that some truly Christian politicians, who love to dispense benefits, but are careful to conceal the hand which distributes the dole[1], may have made them the instruments of their pious designs. Whatever I may have reason to suspect concerning private management, I shall speak of nothing as of a certainty but what is public.

For one, I should be sorry to be thought directly or indirectly concerned in their proceedings. I certainly take my full share, along with the rest of the world, in my individual and private capacity, in speculating on what has been done, or is doing, on the public stage, in any place, ancient or modern, in the republic of Rome, or the republic of Paris; but having no general apostolical mission, being a citizen of a particular state, and being bound up, in a considerable degree, by its public will, I should think it at least improper and irregular for me to open a formal public correspondence with the actual government of a foreign nation, without the express authority of the government under which I live.

I should be still more unwilling to enter into that correspondence under anything like an equivocal description, which to many, unacquainted with our usages, might make the address in which I joined appear as the act of persons in some sort of corporate capacity, acknowledged by the laws of this kingdom, and authorized to speak the sense of some part of it. On account of the ambiguity and

---

1. distributes the dole: 分发（政府的）救济

uncertainty of unauthorized general descriptions, and of the deceit which may be practised under them, and not from mere formality, the House of Commons would reject the most sneaking petition for the most trifling object, under that mode of signature to which you have thrown open the folding-doors of your presence-chamber[1], and have ushered into your National Assembly with as much ceremony and parade, and with as great a bustle of applause, as if you had been visited by the whole representative majesty of the whole English nation. If what this society has thought proper to send forth had been a piece of argument, it would have signified little whose argument it was. It would be neither the more nor the less convincing on account of the party it came from. But this is only a vote and resolution. It stands solely on authority; and in this case it is the mere authority of individuals, few of whom appear. Their signatures ought, in my opinion, to have been annexed to their instrument. The world would then have the means of knowing how many they are, who they are, and of what value their opinions may be, from their personal abilities, from their knowledge, their experience, or their lead and authority in this state. To me, who am but a plain man, the proceeding looks a little too refined and too ingenious; it has too much the air of a political stratagem, adopted for the sake of giving, under a high-sounding name, an importance to the public declarations of this club, which, when the matter came to be closely inspected, they did not altogether so well deserve. It is a policy that has very much the complexion of a fraud.

I flatter myself that I love a manly[2], moral, regulated liberty as well as any gentleman of that society, be he who he will; and perhaps I have given as good proofs of my attachment to that cause, in the whole course of my public conduct. I think I envy liberty as little as they do to any other nation. But I cannot stand forward, and give praise or blame

---

1. presence-chamber：（君主或政要）接见（他人的）大厅
2. manly：正直的

to anything which relates to human actions and human concerns on a simple view of the object, as it stands stripped of every relation, in all the nakedness and solitude of metaphysical abstraction. Circumstances (which with some gentlemen pass for nothing) give in reality to every political principle its distinguishing colour and discriminating effect. The circumstances are what render every civil and political scheme beneficial or noxious to mankind. Abstractedly speaking, government, as well as liberty, is good; yet could I, in common sense, ten years ago, have felicitated[1] France on her enjoyment of a government (for she then had a government) without inquiry what the nature of that government was, or how it was administered? Can I now congratulate the same nation upon its freedom? Is it because liberty in the abstract may be classed amongst the blessings of mankind, that I am seriously to felicitate a madman who has escaped from the protecting restraint and wholesome darkness of his cell on his restoration to the enjoyment of light and liberty? Am I to congratulate a highwayman and murderer, who has broke prison, upon the recovery of his natural rights? This would be to act over again the scene of the criminals condemned to the galleys, and their heroic deliverer, the metaphysic Knight of the Sorrowful Countenance.[2]

When I see the spirit of liberty in action, I see a strong principle[3] at work; and this, for a while, is all I can possibly know of it. The wild *gas*, the fixed air[4], is plainly broke loose: but we ought to suspend our judgment until the first effervescence[5] is a little subsided, till the liquor is cleared, and until we see something deeper than the agitation of a

---

1. felicitated：（正式）向……致贺
2. Knight of the Sorrowful Countenance：愁面苦脸的骑士（常用来形容西班牙作家塞万提斯同名小说中的人物堂·吉诃德）
3. principle：本书中这一词语用作单数名词时，作者多采用该词现今已废弃的词义：源泉 (source)、起因 (cause)、缘由 (driver) 等。
4. fixed air：碳酸的早期名称
5. effervescence：欢腾

troubled and frothy surface. I must be tolerably sure, before I venture publicly to congratulate men upon a blessing, that they have really received one. Flattery corrupts both the receiver and the giver; and adulation[1] is not of more service to the people than to kings. I should therefore suspend my congratulations on the new liberty of France, until I was informed how it had been combined with government; with public force; with the discipline and obedience of armies; with the collection of an effective and well-distributed revenue; with morality and religion; with solidity and property; with peace and order; with civil and social manners. All these (in their way) are good things, too; and without them, liberty is not a benefit whilst it lasts, and is not likely to continue long. The effect of liberty to individuals is, that they may do what they please: We ought to see what it will please them to do, before we risk congratulations, which may be soon turned into complaints. Prudence would dictate this in the case of separate, insulated, private men. But liberty, when men act in bodies, is *power*. Considerate people, before they declare themselves, will observe the use which is made of *power*, and particularly of so trying a thing as *new* power in *new* persons, of whose principles, tempers, and dispositions they have little or no experience, and in situations where those who appear the most stirring in the scene may possibly not be the real movers.

All these considerations, however, were below the transcendental dignity of the Revolution Society. Whilst I continued in the country, from whence I had the honour of writing to you, I had but an imperfect idea of their transactions. On my coming to town, I sent for an account of their proceedings, which had been published by their authority, containing a sermon of Dr. Price[2], with the Duke de

---

1. adulation: 奉承，谄媚
2. Dr. Price: 理查德·普赖斯博士（Richard Price, 1723—1791），英国牧师，以不顺从国教著称。他同情美国革命（即美国独立战争），与《独立宣言》起草和签署人之一的本杰明·富兰克林保持密切关系。

Rochefoucault's and the Archbishop of Aix's[1] letter and several other documents annexed. The whole of that publication, with the manifest design of connecting the affairs of France with those of England, by drawing us into an imitation of the conduct of the National Assembly, gave me a considerable degree of uneasiness. The effect of that conduct upon the power, credit, prosperity, and tranquillity of France became every day more evident. The form of constitution to be settled, for its future polity[2], became more clear. We are now in a condition to discern with tolerable exactness the true nature of the object held up to our imitation. If the prudence of reserve and decorum dictates silence in some circumstances, in others prudence of a higher order may justify us in speaking our thoughts. The beginnings of confusion with us in England are at present feeble enough; but with you we have seen an infancy still more feeble growing by moments into a strength to heap mountains upon mountains, and to wage war with Heaven itself. Whenever our neighbour's house is on fire, it cannot be amiss for the engines to play a little on our own. Better to be despised for too anxious apprehensions than ruined by too confident a security.

Solicitous chiefly for the peace of my own country, but by no means unconcerned for yours, I wish to communicate more largely what was at first intended only for your private satisfaction. I shall still keep your affairs in my eye, and continue to address myself to you. Indulging myself in the freedom of epistolary[3] intercourse, I beg leave to throw out my thoughts and express my feelings just as they arise in my mind, with very little attention to formal method. I set out with the proceedings

---

1. Duke de Rochefoucault and Archbishop of Aix：德拉罗什富科公爵（Louis-Alexandre de La Rochefoucauld，1743—1792），法国贵族，支持法国革命，赞同国民议会，并会同其他 47 名法国贵族加入第三等级；艾克斯区大主教（Jean de Dieu-Raymond de Cuce Boisgelin，1732—1804），时任法国国民议会主席。
2. polity：政体
3. epistolary：书信体的

of the Revolution Society; but I shall not confine myself to them. Is it possible I should? It looks to me as if I were in a great crisis, not of the affairs of France alone, but of all Europe, perhaps of more than Europe. All circumstances taken together, the French Revolution is the most astonishing that has hitherto happened in the world. The most wonderful things are brought about in many instances by means the most absurd and ridiculous, in the most ridiculous modes, and apparently by the most contemptible instruments. Everything seems out of nature in this strange chaos of levity and ferocity, and of all sorts of crimes jumbled together with all sorts of follies. In viewing this monstrous tragi-comic[1] scene, the most opposite passions necessarily succeed and sometimes mix with each other in the mind; alternate contempt and indignation; alternate laughter and tears; alternate scorn and horror.

It cannot, however, be denied that to some this strange scene appeared in quite another point of view. Into them it inspired no other sentiments than those of exultation and rapture. They saw nothing in what has been done in France but a firm and temperate exertion of freedom; so consistent, on the whole, with morals and with piety as to make it deserving not only of the secular applause of dashing Machiavellian politicians[2], but to render it a fit theme for all the devout effusions of sacred eloquence.

* * * * *

On the forenoon of the 4th of November last, Doctor Richard Price, a non-conforming minister of eminence, preached at the dissenting meeting-house of the Old Jewry[3], to his club or society, a very

---

1. tragi-comic：悲喜交集的
2. Machiavellian politicians：（意大利政治家）马基雅维利式的政客
3. Old Jewry：位于伦敦金融区的一条小街，当年不顺从国教的新教领袖们常在那儿的教堂布道。

extraordinary miscellaneous sermon, in which there are some good moral and religious sentiments, and not ill expressed, mixed up with a sort of porridge of various political opinions and reflections: but the revolution in France is the grand ingredient in the caldron. I consider the address transmitted by the Revolution Society to the National Assembly, through Earl Stanhope[1], as originating in the principles of the sermon, and as a corollary from them. It was moved by the preacher of that discourse. It was passed by those who came reeking from the effect of the sermon, without any censure or qualification, expressed or implied. If, however, any of the gentlemen concerned shall wish to separate the sermon from the resolution, they know how to acknowledge the one and to disavow the other. They may do it: I cannot.

For my part, I looked on that sermon as the public declaration of a man much connected with literary caballers and intriguing philosophers, with political theologians and theological politicians, both at home and abroad. I know they set him up as a sort of oracle; because, with the best intentions in the world, he naturally *philippizes*,[2] and chants his prophetic song in exact unison with their designs.

That sermon is in a strain which I believe has not been heard in this kingdom, in any of the pulpits which are tolerated or encouraged in it, since the year 1648, when a predecessor of Dr. Price, the Reverend Hugh Peters[3], made the vault of the king's own chapel at St. James's ring with the honour and privilege of the saints, who, with the "high praises of God in their mouths, and a *two*-edged sword in their hands,

---

1. Earl Stanhope：斯坦厄普伯爵（Earl Charles Stanhope III, 1753—1816），英国发明家，曾花费巨资用于科学和哲学实验。当时担任"革命协会"的会长。
2. *philippizes*：借神谕赐福。此词源于历史典故：当马其顿国王腓力二世兵临特尔斐城时，阿波罗的女祭司作出了偏袒腓力的神谕。
3. Reverend Hugh Peters：休·彼得斯牧师（1598—1660），英国独立宗教人士，著有若干檄文，因鼓动处死英王理查一世而被处以极刑。

were to execute judgment on the heathen, and punishments upon the *people*; to bind their *kings* with chains, and their nobles with fetters of iron." [1] Few harangues from the pulpit, except in the days of your League in France, or in the days of our Solemn League and Covenant[2] in England, have ever breathed less of the spirit of moderation than this lecture in the Old Jewry. Supposing, however, that something like moderation were visible in this political sermon, yet politics and the pulpit are terms that have little agreement. No sound ought to be heard in the church but the healing voice of Christian charity. The cause of civil liberty and civil government gains as little as that of religion by this confusion of duties. Those who quit their proper character to assume what does not belong to them are, for the greater part, ignorant both of the character they leave and of the character they assume. Wholly unacquainted with the world, in which they are so fond of meddling, and inexperienced in all its affairs, on which they pronounce with so much confidence, they have nothing of politics but the passions they excite. Surely the church is a place where one day's truce ought to be allowed to the dissensions and animosities of mankind.

This pulpit style, revived after so long a discontinuance, had to me the air of novelty, and of a novelty not wholly without danger. I do not charge this danger equally to every part of the discourse. The hint given to a noble and reverend lay-divine, who is supposed high in office in one of our universities[3], and other lay-divines "of *rank* and literature," may be proper and seasonable, though somewhat new. If

---

1. "high praises of God ... nobles with fetters of iron"：引自《圣经·旧约》诗篇。
2. Solemn League and Covenant：神圣盟约，指 1643 年英格兰与苏格兰的贵族代表和平民代表为反对查理一世、维护长老会制而签订的宗教统一盟约。
3. The hint given to a noble ... in one of our universities：引自普赖斯博士的《论热爱吾国》。

the noble *Seekers*[1] should find nothing to satisfy their pious fancies in the old staple of the national church, or in all the rich variety to be found in the well-assorted warehouses of the dissenting congregations, Dr. Price advises them to improve upon non-conformity, and to set up, each of them, a separate meeting-house upon his own particular principles. It is somewhat remarkable that this reverend divine should be so earnest for setting up new churches, and so perfectly indifferent concerning the doctrine which may be taught in them. His zeal is of a curious character. It is not for the propagation of his own opinions, but of any opinions. It is not for the diffusion of truth, but for the spreading of contradiction. Let the noble teachers but dissent, it is no matter from whom or from what. This great point once secured, it is taken for granted their religion will be rational and manly. I doubt whether religion would reap all the benefits which the calculating divine computes from this "great company of great preachers." It would certainly be a valuable addition of nondescripts to the ample collection of known classes, genera, and species, which at present beautify the *hortus siccus*[2] of dissent. A sermon from a noble duke, or a noble marquis, or a noble earl, or baron bold[3], would certainly increase and diversify the amusements of this town, which begins to grow satiated with the uniform round of its vapid dissipations. I should only stipulate that these new *Mess-Johns*[4] in robes and coronets should keep some sort of bounds in the democratic and levelling principles which are expected from their titled pulpits. The new evangelists will, I dare say, disappoint the hopes that are conceived of them. They will not become, literally as well as figuratively, polemic divines, nor be

---

1. *Seekers*：指 17 世纪基督教中追求宗教独立的教派，其中大部分人后来加入 "贵格会（Quakers）"。
2. *hortus siccus*：植物标本集，隐喻枯萎凋零的园林。
3. a noble duke ... baron bold：指英国贵族的各种头衔。详见 "术语汇编与简释"。
4. *Mess-Johns*："圣约翰"，苏格兰民谣诗歌中对牧师的戏称。

disposed so to drill their congregations, that they may, as in former blessed times, preach their doctrines to regiments of dragoons and corps of infantry and artillery. Such arrangements, however favourable to the cause of compulsory freedom, civil and religious, may not be equally conducive to the national tranquillity. These few restrictions I hope are no great stretches of intolerance, no very violent exertions of despotism.

But I may say of our preacher, "*Utinam nugis tota illa dedisset et tempora sævitiæ.*" [1] — All things in this his fulminating bull[2] are not of so innoxious a tendency. His doctrines affect our Constitution in its vital parts. He tells the Revolution Society, in this political sermon, that his Majesty "is almost the *only* lawful king in the world, because the *only* one who owes his crown to *the choice of his people.*" As to the kings of *the world*, all of whom (except one) this arch-pontiff of the *rights of men*, with all the plenitude and with more than the boldness of the Papal deposing power in its meridian fervour of the twelfth century, puts into one sweeping clause of ban and anathema[3], and proclaims usurpers by circles of longitude and latitude over the whole globe, it behoves them to consider how they admit into their territories these apostolic missionaries, who are to tell their subjects they are not lawful kings. That is their concern. It is ours, as a domestic interest of some moment, seriously to consider the solidity of the *only* principle upon which these gentlemen acknowledge a king of Great Britain to be entitled to their allegiance.

This doctrine, as applied to the prince now on the British throne, either is nonsense, and therefore neither true nor false, or it affirms

---

1. "*Utinam nugis ... tempora sævitiæ.*"：〈拉〉引自古罗马讽刺诗人尤维纳利斯的《讽刺诗集》第四卷。译成英文的大意为："and would that he had devoted all that time to these trifles rather than to cruelty"。
2. bull：教皇训谕；教皇诏书。作者在此嘲讽普拉斯的布道气势犹如教皇发布诏书一般。
3. anathema：诅咒

a most unfounded, dangerous, illegal, and unconstitutional position. According to this spiritual doctor of politics, if his Majesty does not owe his crown to the choice of his people, he is no *lawful* king. Now nothing can be more untrue than that the crown of this kingdom is so held by his Majesty. Therefore, if you follow their rule, the king of Great Britain, who most certainly does not owe his high office to any form of popular election, is in no respect better than the rest of the gang of usurpers, who reign, or rather rob, all over the face of this our miserable world, without any sort of right or title to the allegiance of their people. The policy of this general doctrine, so qualified, is evident enough. The propagators of this political gospel are in hopes their abstract principle (their principle that a popular choice is necessary to the legal existence of the sovereign magistracy) would be overlooked, whilst the king of Great Britain was not affected by it. In the mean time the ears of their congregations would be gradually habituated to it, as if it were a first principle admitted without dispute. For the present it would only operate as a theory, pickled in the preserving juices of pulpit eloquence, and laid by for future use. *Condo et compono quæ mox depromere passim.*[1] By this policy, whilst our government is soothed with a reservation in its favour, to which it has no claim, the security which it has in common with all governments, so far as opinion is security, is taken away.

Thus these politicians proceed, whilst little notice is taken of their doctrines; but when they come to be examined upon the plain meaning of their words and the direct tendency of their doctrines, then equivocations and slippery constructions come into play. When they say the king owes his crown to the choice of his people, and is therefore the only lawful sovereign in the world, they will perhaps tell

---

1. *Condo et compono ... depromere passim.*：〈拉〉引自古罗马诗人贺拉斯的《书札》。译成英文的大意为："I search and search, and when I find I lay | The wisdom up against a rainy day"。

us they mean to say no more than that some of the king's predecessors have been called to the throne by some sort of choice, and therefore he owes his crown to the choice of his people. Thus, by a miserable subterfuge, they hope to render their proposition safe by rendering it nugatory[1]. They are welcome to the asylum they seek for their offence, since they take refuge in their folly. For, if you admit this interpretation, how does their idea of election differ from our idea of inheritance? And how does the settlement of the crown in the Brunswick line[2], derived from James I, come to legalize our monarchy rather than that of any of the neighbouring countries? At some time or other, to be sure, all the beginners of dynasties were chosen by those who called them to govern. There is ground enough for the opinion that all the kingdoms of Europe were at a remote period elective, with more or fewer limitations in the objects of choice. But whatever kings might have been here or elsewhere a thousand years ago, or in whatever manner the ruling dynasties of England or France may have begun, the king of Great Britain is at this day king by a fixed rule of succession, according to the laws of his country; and whilst the legal conditions of the compact of sovereignty are performed by him (as they are performed) he holds his crown in contempt of the choice of the Revolution Society, who have not a single vote for a king amongst them, either individually or collectively: though I make no doubt they would soon erect themselves into an electoral college[3], if things were ripe to give effect to their claim. His Majesty's heirs and successors, each in his time and order, will come to the crown with the same contempt of their choice with which his Majesty has succeeded to that

---

1. nugatory：无价值的
2. the crown in the Brunswick line：指统治英国、具有日耳曼血统的布伦瑞克（亦称汉诺威）王朝。1714 年英国斯图亚特王朝女王安妮去世，依 1701 年的嗣位法，汉诺威公爵乔治·路易到英国即位称乔治一世，从而开始英国的汉诺威王朝。
3. electoral college：选举人团

he wears.

Whatever may be the success of evasion in explaining away the gross error *fact*, which supposes that his Majesty (though he holds it in concurrence with the wishes) owes his crown to the choice of his people, yet nothing can evade their full, explicit declaration concerning the principle of a right in the people to choose, which right is directly maintained, and tenaciously adhered to. All the oblique insinuations concerning election bottom in this proposition, and are referable to it. Lest the foundation of the king's exclusive legal title should pass for a mere rant of adulatory freedom, the political divine proceeds dogmatically to assert, that, by the principles of the Revolution, the people of England have acquired three fundamental rights, all of which, with him, compose one system, and lie together in one short sentence: namely, that we have acquired a right:

1. To choose our own governors.
2. To cashier them for misconduct.
3. To frame a government for ourselves.[1]

This new and hitherto unheard-of bill of rights, though made in the name of the whole people, belongs to those gentlemen and their faction only. The body of the people of England have no share in it. They utterly disclaim it. They will resist the practical assertion of it with their lives and fortunes. They are bound to do so by the laws of their country, made at the time of that very Revolution which is appealed to in favour of the fictitious rights claimed by the society which abuses its name.

These gentlemen of the Old Jewry, in all their reasonings on the Revolution of 1688, have a revolution which happened in England

---

1. To choose ... for ourselves：指普赖斯博士在《论热爱吾国》中倡导的三种权利。

about forty years before, and the late French Revolution, so much before their eyes and in their hearts, that they are constantly confounding all the three together. It is necessary that we should separate what they confound. We must recall their erring fancies to the *acts* of the Revolution which we revere, for the discovery of its true *principles*. If the *principles* of the Revolution of 1688 are anywhere to be found, it is in the statute called the *Declaration of Right*[1]. In that most wise, sober, and considerate declaration, drawn up by great lawyers and great statesmen, and not by warm and inexperienced enthusiasts, not one word is said, nor one suggestion made, of a general right "to choose our own *governors*, to cashier them for misconduct, and to *form* a government for *ourselves*."

This Declaration of Right (the act of the 1st of William and Mary, sess. 2, ch. 2) is the corner-stone of our Constitution, as reinforced, explained, improved, and in its fundamental principles forever settled. It is called "An act for declaring the rights and liberties of the subject, and for *settling* the *succession* of the crown." You will observe that these rights and this succession are declared in one body, and bound indissolubly together.

A few years after this period, a second opportunity offered for asserting a right of election to the crown. On the prospect of a total failure of issue from King William, and from the princess, afterwards Queen Anne[2], the consideration of the settlement of the Crown, and of a further security for the liberties of the people, again came before the legislature. Did they this second time make any provision for legalizing the crown on the spurious Revolution principles of the Old Jewry? No. They followed the principles which prevailed in the

---

1. *Declaration of Right*：通常指 1689 年英国议会向当时的国王威廉和女王玛丽宣布议会通过的《权利法》(Bill of Right)。
2. Queen Anne：英国女王安妮（1665—1714），为斯图亚特王朝最后一代君主。

Declaration of Right; indicating with more precision the persons who were to inherit in the Protestant line. This act also incorporated, by the same policy, our liberties and an hereditary succession in the same act. Instead of a right to choose our own governors, they declared that the *succession* in that line (the Protestant line drawn from James I) was absolutely necessary "for the peace, quiet, and security of the realm," and that it was equally urgent on them "to maintain a *certainty in the succession* thereof, to which the subjects may safely have recourse for their protection." Both these acts, in which are heard the unerring, unambiguous oracles of Revolution policy, instead of countenancing the delusive gypsy predictions of a "right to choose our governors," prove to a demonstration how totally adverse the wisdom of the nation was from turning a case of necessity into a rule of law.

Unquestionably there was at the Revolution, in the person of King William, a small and a temporary deviation from the strict order of a regular hereditary succession[1]; but it is against all genuine principles of jurisprudence to draw a principle from a law made in a special case and regarding an individual person. *Privilegium non transit in exemplum.*[2] If ever there was a time favourable for establishing the principle that a king of popular choice was the only legal king, without all doubt it was at the Revolution. Its not being done at that time is a proof that the nation was of opinion it ought not to be done at any time. There is no person so completely ignorant of our history as not to know that the majority in Parliament, of both parties, were so little disposed to anything resembling that principle, that at first they were determined

---

1. deviation from ... hereditary succession：指英王詹姆士二世 1688 年被废黜后，其王位由大女儿玛丽及其夫婿威廉共同继承。然而玛丽死后，威廉以国王的身份继续统治英国，这在英国王位继承史上可谓史无前例。

2. *Privilegium ... in exemplum.*：〈拉〉罗马法中的格言之一。英文的大意是：an individual's right does not translate into a general rule。

to place the vacant crown, not on the head of the Prince of Orange[1], but on that of his wife, Mary, daughter of King James, the eldest born of the issue of that king, which they acknowledged as undoubtedly his. It would be to repeat a very trite story, to recall to your memory all those circumstances which demonstrated that their accepting King William was not properly a *choice*; but to all those who did not wish in effect to recall King James, or to deluge their country in blood, and again to bring their religion, laws, and liberties into the peril they had just escaped, it was an act of *necessity*, in the strictest moral sense in which necessity can be taken.

In the very act in which, for a time, and in a single case, Parliament departed from the strict order of inheritance, in favour of a prince who, though not next, was, however, very near in the line of succession, it is curious to observe how Lord Somers[2], who drew the bill called the Declaration of Right, has comported himself on that delicate occasion. It is curious to observe with what address this temporary solution of continuity is kept from the eye; whilst all that could be found in this act of necessity to countenance the idea of an hereditary succession is brought forward, and fostered, and made the most of, by this great man, and by the legislature who followed him. Quitting the dry, imperative style of an act of parliament, he makes the lords and commons fall to a pious legislative ejaculation, and declare that they consider it "as a marvellous providence, and merciful goodness of God to this nation, to preserve their said majesties' *royal* persons most happily to reign over us *on the throne of their ancestors*, for which, from the bottom of their hearts, they return their humblest thanks and praises." The legislature plainly had in view the act of recognition of

---

1. Prince of Orange：威廉在继承英格兰王位、成为威廉三世之前是荷兰奥兰治亲王。
2. Lord Somers：约翰·萨默斯（John Somers, 1651—1716），英国辉格党政治家，1697年担任英国大法官。他是《权利宣言》起草委员会的主席。

the first of Queen Elizabeth, Chap. 3rd, and of that of James I, Chap. 1st, both acts strongly declaratory of the inheritable nature of the crown; and in many parts they follow, with a nearly literal precision, the words, and even the form of thanksgiving which is found in these old declaratory statutes.

The two houses, in the act of King William, did not thank God that they had found a fair opportunity to assert a right to choose their own governors, much less to make an election the *only lawful* title to the crown. Their having been in a condition to avoid the very appearance of it, as much as possible, was by them considered as a providential escape. They threw a politic, well-wrought veil over every circumstance tending to weaken the rights which in the meliorated order of succession they meant to perpetuate, or which might furnish a precedent for any future departure from what they had then settled forever. Accordingly, that they might not relax the nerves of their monarchy, and that they might preserve a close conformity to the practice of their ancestors, as it appeared in the declaratory statutes of Queen Mary and Queen Elizabeth, in the next clause they vest, by recognition, in their majesties *all* the legal prerogatives of the crown, declaring "that in them they are most *fully*, rightfully, and *entirely* invested, incorporated, united, and annexed." In the clause which follows, for preventing questions, by reason of any pretended titles to the crown, they declare (observing also in this the traditionary language, along with the traditionary policy of the nation, and repeating as from a rubric the language of the preceding acts of Elizabeth and James) that on the preserving "a *certainty* in the SUCCESSION thereof the unity, peace, and tranquillity of this nation doth, under God, wholly depend."

They knew that a doubtful title of succession would but too much resemble an election, and that an election would be utterly destructive of the "unity, peace, and tranquillity of this nation," which they thought to be considerations of some moment. To provide for these objects, and therefore to exclude forever the Old Jewry doctrine of "a right to choose our own governors," they follow with a clause containing a most solemn pledge, taken from the preceding act of Queen Elizabeth, as solemn a pledge as ever was or can be given in favour of an hereditary succession, and as solemn a renunciation as could be made of the principles by this society imputed to them. "The lords spiritual and temporal, and commons, do, in the name of all the people aforesaid, most humbly and faithfully submit *themselves, their heirs, and posterities forever*, and do faithfully promise that they will stand to, maintain, and defend their said Majesties, and also the *limitation of the crown*, herein specified and contained, to the utmost of their powers," &c., &c.

So far is it from being true that we acquired a right by the Revolution to elect our kings, that, if we had possessed it before, the English nation did at that time most solemnly renounce and abdicate it, for themselves, and for all their posterity forever. These gentlemen may value themselves as much as they please on their Whig[1] principles; but I never desire to be thought a better Whig than Lord Somers, or to understand the principles of the Revolution better than those by whom it was brought about, or to read in the Declaration of Right any mysteries unknown to those whose penetrating style has engraved in our ordinances, and in our hearts, the words and spirit of that immortal law.

It is true, that, aided with the powers derived from force and opportunity, the nation was at that time, in some sense, free to take what course it pleased for filling the throne; but only free to do so upon the same grounds on which they might have wholly abolished their monarchy, and every other part of their constitution. However, they did not think such bold changes within their commission. It

---

1. Whig：（英）辉格党，即英国自由党的前身。

is, indeed, difficult, perhaps impossible, to give limits to the mere *abstract* competence of the supreme power, such as was exercised by Parliament at that time; but the limits of a *moral* competence, subjecting, even in powers more indisputably sovereign, occasional will to permanent reason, and to the steady maxims of faith, justice, and fixed fundamental policy, are perfectly intelligible, and perfectly binding upon those who exercise any authority, under any name, or under any title, in the state. The House of Lords, for instance, is not morally competent to dissolve the House of Commons; no, nor even to dissolve itself, nor to abdicate, if it would, its portion in the legislature of the kingdom. Though a king may abdicate for his own person, he cannot abdicate for the monarchy. By as strong, or by a stronger reason, the House of Commons cannot renounce its share of authority. The engagement and pact of society, which generally goes by the name of the constitution, forbids such invasion and such surrender. The constituent parts of a state are obliged to hold their public faith with each other, and with all those who derive any serious interest under their engagements, as much as the whole state is bound to keep its faith with separate communities. Otherwise, competence and power would soon be confounded, and no law be left but the will of a prevailing force. On this principle, the succession of the crown has always been what it now is, an hereditary succession by law: in the old line it was a succession by the common law; in the new by the statute law[1], operating on the principles of the common law, not changing the substance, but regulating the mode and describing the persons. Both these descriptions of law are of the same force, and are derived from an equal authority, emanating from the common agreement and original compact of the state, *communi sponsione reipublicæ*[2], and as such

---

1. statute law：成文法，此处指由英国议会制定的法律。
2. *communi sponsione reipublicæ*：〈拉〉此句拉丁文短语为作者杜撰。英文的大意是：The consent of the entire commonwealth（获共同体一致同意）。

are equally binding on king, and people too, as long as the terms are observed, and they continue the same body politic.

It is far from impossible to reconcile, if we do not suffer ourselves to be entangled in the mazes of metaphysic sophistry[1], the use both of a fixed rule and an occasional deviation; the sacredness of an hereditary principle of succession in our government with a power of change in its application in cases of extreme emergency. Even in that extremity (if we take the measure of our rights by our exercise of them at the Revolution) the change is to be confined to the peccant part only; to the part which produced the necessary deviation; and even then it is to be effected without a decomposition of the whole civil and political mass, for the purpose of originating a new civil order out of the first elements of society.

A state without the means of some change is without the means of its conservation. Without such means it might even risk the loss of that part of the constitution which it wished the most religiously to preserve. The two principles of conservation and correction operated strongly at the two critical periods of the Restoration and Revolution, when England found itself without a king. At both those periods the nation had lost the bond of union in their ancient edifice; they did not, however, dissolve the whole fabric. On the contrary, in both cases they regenerated the deficient part of the old constitution through the parts which were not impaired. They kept these old parts exactly as they were, that the part recovered might be suited to them. They acted by the ancient organized states in the shape of their old organization, and not by the organic *moleculæ*[2] of a disbanded people. At no time, perhaps, did the sovereign legislature manifest a more tender regard to that fundamental principle of British constitutional policy than at the time of the Revolution, when it deviated from the direct line of

---

1. sophistry：诡辩
2. *moleculæ*：〈废〉molecule 的复数形式

hereditary succession. The crown was carried somewhat out of the line in which it had before moved; but the new line was derived from the same stock. It was still a line of hereditary descent; still an hereditary descent in the same blood, though an hereditary descent qualified with Protestantism. When the legislature altered the direction, but kept the principle, they showed that they held it inviolable.

On this principle, the law of inheritance had admitted some amendment in the old time, and long before the era of the Revolution. Some time after the Conquest great questions arose upon the legal principles of hereditary descent. It became a matter of doubt whether the heir *per capita* or the heir *per stirpes*[1] was to succeed; but whether the heir *per capita* gave way when the heirdom *per stirpes* took place, or the Catholic heir when the Protestant was preferred, the inheritable principle survived with a sort of immortality through all transmigrations — *multosque per annos stat fortuna domûs et avi numerantur avorum.*[2] This is the spirit of our constitution, not only in its settled course, but in all its revolutions. Whoever came in, or however he came in, whether he obtained the crown by law or by force, the hereditary succession was either continued or adopted.

The gentlemen of the Society for Revolutions see nothing in that of 1688 but the deviation from the constitution; and they take the deviation from the principle for the principle. They have little regard to the obvious consequences of their doctrine, though they may see that it leaves positive authority in very few of the positive institutions of this country. When such an unwarrantable maxim is once established, that no throne is lawful but the elective, no one act of the princes who preceded this era of fictitious election can be valid. Do these theorists

---

1. *per stirpes*：〈拉〉按家系（用于遗产分配）
2. *multosque ... numerantur avorum*：〈拉〉引自古罗马诗人维吉尔（Virgil，前 70—前 19）的《农事诗》第四卷。英文的大意是："Through many years, the fortune of the house stands, and grandfathers of grandfathers are counted"。

mean to imitate some of their predecessors, who dragged the bodies of our ancient sovereigns out of the quiet of their tombs? Do they mean to attaint and disable backwards all the kings that have reigned before the Revolution, and consequently to stain the throne of England with the blot of a continual usurpation? Do they mean to invalidate, annul, or to call into question, together with the titles of the whole line of our kings, that great body of our statute law which passed under those whom they treat as usurpers, to annul laws of inestimable value to our liberties — of as great value at least as any which have passed at or since the period of the Revolution? If kings, who did not owe their crown to the choice of their people, had no title to make laws, what will become of the statute *de tallagio non concedendo*[1]? — of the *petition of right*? — of the act of *habeas corpus*[2]? Do these new doctors of the rights of men presume to assert that King James II, who came to the crown as next of blood, according to the rules of a then unqualified succession, was not to all intents and purposes a lawful king of England, before he had done any of those acts which were justly construed into an abdication of his crown? If he was not, much trouble in Parliament might have been saved at the period these gentlemen commemorate. But King James was a bad king with a good title, and not an usurper. The princes who succeeded according to the act of Parliament which settled the crown on the Electress Sophia[3] and on her descendants, being Protestants, came in as much by a title of inheritance as King James did. He came in according to the law, as it stood at his accession to the crown; and the princes of the House of Brunswick came to the inheritance of the crown, not by election, but

---

1. *de tallagio non concedendo*：〈拉〉未经授权不许向佃户征收地租
2. *habeas corpus*：〈拉〉人身保护法（对被拘禁者的羁押期予以限制）
3. Electress Sophia：指英国王位继承人、德国汉诺威的索菲亚，其儿子后来成为英格兰国王乔治一世。Electress 为（神圣罗马帝国）有权选举或当选帝王的诸侯妻子或遗孀。

by the law, as it stood at their several accessions, of Protestant descent and inheritance, as I hope I have shown sufficiently.

The law by which this royal family is specifically destined to the succession is the act of the 12th and 13th of King William.[1] The terms of this act bind "us, and our *heirs*, and our *posterity*, to them, their *heirs*, and their *posterity*," being Protestants, to the end of time, in the same words as the Declaration of Right had bound us to the heirs of King William and Queen Mary. It therefore secures both an hereditary crown and an hereditary allegiance. On what ground, except the constitutional policy of forming an establishment to secure that kind of succession which is to preclude a choice of the people forever, could the legislature have fastidiously rejected the fair and abundant choice which our own country presented to them, and searched in strange lands for a foreign princess, from whose womb the line of our future rulers were to derive their title to govern millions of men through a series of ages?

The Princess Sophia was named in the act of settlement of the 12th and 13th of King William, for a *stock* and root of *inheritance* to our kings, and not for her merits as a temporary administratrix of a power which she might not, and in fact did not, herself ever exercise. She was adopted for one reason, and for one only, because, says the act, "the most excellent Princess Sophia, Electress and Duchess Dowager of Hanover, is *daughter* of the most excellent Princess Elizabeth, late Queen of Bohemia, *daughter* of our late *sovereign lord* King James I, of happy memory, and is hereby declared to be the next in *succession* in the Protestant line," &c., &c.; "and the crown shall continue to the *heirs* of her body, being Protestants." This limitation was made by Parliament, that through the Princess Sophia an inheritable line not only was to be continued in future, but (what they thought very

---

1. act of ... King William: 指英国 1701 年通过的《嗣位法》(Act of Settlement 1701)。

material) that through her it was to be connected with the old stock of inheritance in King James I; in order that the monarchy might preserve an unbroken unity through all ages, and might be preserved (with safety to our religion) in the old approved mode by descent, in which, if our liberties had been once endangered, they had often, through all storms and struggles of prerogative and privilege, been preserved. They did well. No experience has taught us that in any other course or method than that of an *hereditary crown* our liberties can be regularly perpetuated and preserved sacred as our *hereditary right*. An irregular, convulsive movement may be necessary to throw off an irregular, convulsive disease. But the course of succession is the healthy habit of the British constitution. Was it that the legislature wanted, at the act for the limitation of the crown in the Hanoverian line, drawn through the female descendants of James I, a due sense of the inconveniences of having two or three, or possibly more, foreigners in succession to the British throne? No! — they had a due sense of the evils which might happen from such foreign rule, and more than a due sense of them. But a more decisive proof cannot be given of the full conviction of the British nation that the principles of the Revolution did not authorize them to elect kings at their pleasure, and without any attention to the ancient fundamental principles of our government, than their continuing to adopt a plan of hereditary Protestant succession in the old line, with all the dangers and all the inconveniences of its being a foreign line full before their eyes, and operating with the utmost force upon their minds.

A few years ago I should be ashamed to overload a matter so capable of supporting itself by the then unnecessary support of any argument; but this seditious, unconstitutional doctrine is now publicly taught, avowed, and printed. The dislike I feel to revolutions, the signals for which have so often been given from pulpits; the spirit of change that is gone abroad; the total contempt which prevails with you, and may come to prevail with us, of all ancient institutions, when set in opposition to a present sense of convenience, or to the bent of a present inclination: all these considerations make it not unadvisable, in my opinion, to call back our attention to the true principles of our own domestic laws, that you, my French friend, should begin to know, and that we should continue to cherish them. We ought not, on either side of the water, to suffer ourselves to be imposed upon by the counterfeit wares which some persons, by a double fraud, export to you in illicit bottoms, as raw commodities of British growth, though wholly alien to our soil, in order afterwards to smuggle them back again into this country, manufactured after the newest Paris fashion of an improved liberty.

The people of England will not ape the fashions they have never tried, nor go back to those which they have found mischievous on trial. They look upon the legal hereditary succession of their crown as among their rights, not as among their wrongs; as a benefit, not as a grievance; as a security for their liberty, not as a badge of servitude. They look on the frame of their commonwealth, *such as it stands*, to be of inestimable value; and they conceive the undisturbed succession of the crown to be a pledge of the stability and perpetuity of all the other members of our constitution.

I shall beg leave, before I go any further, to take notice of some paltry artifices which the abettors of election as the only lawful title to the crown are ready to employ, in order to render the support of the just principles of our constitution a task somewhat invidious. These sophisters substitute a fictitious cause, and feigned personages, in whose favour they suppose you engaged, whenever you defend the inheritable nature of the crown. It is common with them to dispute as if they were in a conflict with some of those exploded fanatics of slavery who formerly maintained, what I believe no creature now maintains, "that the crown is held by divine, hereditary, and indefeasible right." — These old fanatics of single arbitrary power dogmatized as if hereditary royalty was the only lawful government in the world, just as our new fanatics of popular arbitrary power maintain that a popular election is the sole lawful source of authority. The old prerogative enthusiasts, it is true, did speculate foolishly, and perhaps impiously too, as if monarchy had more of a divine sanction than any other mode of government; and as if a right to govern by inheritance were in strictness *indefeasible* in every person, who should be found in the succession to a throne, and under every circumstance, which no civil or political right can be. But an absurd opinion concerning the king's hereditary right to the crown does not prejudice one that is rational, and bottomed upon solid principles of law and policy. If all the absurd theories of lawyers and divines were to vitiate the objects in which they are conversant, we should have no law, and no religion, left in the world. But an absurd theory on one side of a question forms no justification for alleging a false fact, or promulgating mischievous maxims on the other.

*   *   *   *   *

The second claim of the Revolution Society is "a right of cashiering their governors for *misconduct.*" Perhaps the apprehensions our ancestors entertained of forming such a precedent as that "of cashiering for misconduct" was the cause that the declaration of the act which implied the abdication of King James was, if it had any fault, rather too guarded and too circumstantial. But all this guard, and all this accumulation of circumstances, serves to show the spirit of caution which predominated in the national councils, in a situation in which men irritated by oppression, and elevated by a triumph over it, are apt to abandon themselves to violent and extreme courses; it shows the anxiety of the great men who influenced the conduct of affairs at that great event to make the Revolution a parent of settlement, and not a nursery of future revolutions.

No government could stand a moment, if it could be blown down with anything so loose and indefinite as an opinion of "*misconduct.*" They who led at the Revolution grounded their virtual abdication of King James upon no such light and uncertain principle. They charged him with nothing less than a design, confirmed by a multitude of illegal overt acts, to *subvert the Protestant Church and State,* and their *fundamental,* unquestionable laws and liberties: they charged him with having broken the *original contract* between king and people. This was more than *misconduct.* A grave and overruling necessity obliged them to take the step they took, and took with infinite reluctance, as under that most rigorous of all laws. Their trust for the future preservation of the constitution was not in future revolutions. The grand policy of all their regulations was to render it almost impracticable for any future sovereign to compel the states of the kingdom to have again recourse to those violent remedies. They left the crown, what in the eye and estimation of law it had ever been, perfectly irresponsible. In order to lighten the crown still further, they aggravated responsibility on ministers of state. By the statute of the first of King William, sess. 2d, called "*the act for declaring the rights and liberties of the subject, and for settling the succession of the crown,*" they enacted that the ministers should serve the crown on the terms of that declaration. They secured soon after the *frequent meetings of Parliament,* by which the whole government would be under the constant inspection and active control of the popular representative and of the magnates of the kingdom. In the next great constitutional act, that of the 12th and 13th of King William, for the further limitation of the crown, and *better* securing the rights and liberties of the subject, they provided "that no pardon under the great seal of England should be pleadable to an impeachment by the Commons in Parliament." The rule laid down for government in the Declaration of Right, the constant inspection of Parliament, the practical claim of impeachment, they thought infinitely a better security not only for their constitutional liberty, but against the vices of administration, than the reservation of a right so difficult in the practice, so uncertain in the issue, and often so mischievous in the consequences, as that "cashiering their governors."

Dr. Price, in this sermon, condemns, very properly, the practice of gross adulatory addresses to kings. Instead of this fulsome style, he proposes that his Majesty should be told, on occasions of congratulation, that "he is to consider himself as more properly the servant than the sovereign of his people." For a compliment, this new form of address does not seem to be very soothing. Those who are servants in name, as well as in effect, do not like to be told of their situation, their duty, and their obligations. The slave in the old play tells his master, "*Hæc commemeratio est quasi exprobratio.*" [1] It is not pleasant as compliment; it is not wholesome as instruction. After all, if the king were to bring himself to echo this new kind of address, to adopt it in terms, and even to take the appellation of Servant of the People as his royal style, how either he or we should be much mended by it I cannot imagine. I have seen very assuming letters signed, "Your most obedient, humble servant." The proudest domination that ever was endured on earth took a title of still greater humility than that which is now proposed for sovereigns by the Apostle of Liberty. Kings and nations were trampled upon by the foot of one calling himself "The Servant of Servants"; and mandates for deposing sovereigns were sealed with the signet of "the Fisherman." [2]

I should have considered all this as no more than a sort of flippant, vain discourse, in which, as in an unsavoury fume, several persons suffer the spirit of liberty to evaporate, if it were not plainly in

---

1. "*Hæc commemeratio est quasi exprobratio.*"：〈拉〉引自古罗马喜剧作家泰伦斯（Torence，前 190—前 159）的剧作《安得里亚》。英文的大意是：For this reminder is as it were a rebuke。
2. one calling ... "the Fisherman"：指罗马天主教教皇通常称自己是 "the Servant of Servants"。渔人权戒是一种印戒 (signet ring)，为教皇佩戴的王位标志之一。直到 1842 年，渔人权戒一直被用来封印教皇签署的官方文件。

support of the idea, and a part of the scheme, of "cashiering kings for misconduct." In that light it is worth some observation.

Kings, in one sense, are undoubtedly the servants of the people, because their power has no other rational end than that of the general advantage; but it is not true that they are, in the ordinary sense, (by our Constitution, at least,) anything like servants; the essence of whose situation is to obey the commands of some other, and to be removable at pleasure. But the king of Great Britain obeys no other person; all other persons are individually, and collectively too, under him, and owe to him a legal obedience. The law, which knows neither to flatter nor to insult, calls this high-magistrate, not our servant, as this humble divine calls him, but *"our sovereign Lord the King"* ; and we, on our parts, have learned to speak only the primitive language of the law, and not the confused jargon of their Babylonian pulpits.

As he is not to obey us, but we are to obey the law in him, our constitution has made no sort of provision towards rendering him, as a servant, in any degree responsible. Our constitution knows nothing of a magistrate like the *Justicia* of Aragon[1]; nor of any court legally appointed, nor of any process legally settled, for submitting the king to the responsibility belonging to all servants. In this he is not distinguished from the commons and the lords, who, in their several public capacities, can never be called to an account for their conduct; although the Revolution Society chooses to assert, in direct opposition to one of the wisest and most beautiful parts of our constitution, that "a king is no more than the first servant of the public, created by it, *and responsible to it.*"

Ill would our ancestors at the Revolution have deserved their fame for wisdom, if they had found no security for their freedom, but in rendering their government feeble in its operations and

---

1. *Justicia* of Aragon：Justicia 为中世纪阿拉贡王国的最高法官，他有权裁决贵族之间，甚至国王与贵族之间的纠纷。

precarious in its tenure; if they had been able to contrive no better remedy against arbitrary power than civil confusion. Let these gentlemen state who that *representative* public is to whom they will affirm the king, as a servant, to be responsible. It will be then time enough for me to produce to them the positive statute law which affirms that he is not.

The ceremony of cashiering kings, of which these gentlemen talk so much at their ease, can rarely, if ever, be performed without force. It then becomes a case of war, and not of constitution. Laws are commanded to hold their tongues amongst arms; and tribunals fall to the ground with the peace they are no longer able to uphold. The Revolution of 1688 was obtained by a just war, in the only case in which any war, and much more a civil war, can be just. *"Justa bella quibus necessaria."* [1] The question of dethroning, or, if these gentlemen, like the phrase better, "cashiering kings," will always be, as it has always been, an extraordinary question of state, and wholly out of the law: a question (like all other questions of state) of dispositions, and of means, and of probable consequences, rather than of positive rights. As it was not made for common abuses, so it is not to be agitated by common minds. The speculative line of demarcation, where obedience ought to end and resistance must begin, is faint, obscure, and not easily definable. It is not a single act or a single event which determines it. Governments must be abused and deranged indeed, before it can be thought of; and the prospect of the future must be as bad as the experience of the past. When things are in that lamentable condition, the nature of the disease is to indicate the remedy to those whom Nature has qualified to administer in extremities this critical, ambiguous, bitter potion to a distempered state. Times and

---

1. *"Justa bella quibus necessaria."*：〈拉〉引自古罗马历史学家李维（Livy，前59—公元17）所著《古罗马史》。译成英文的大意是：War is just to those for whom it is necessary。

occasions and provocations will teach their own lessons. The wise will determine from the gravity of the case; the irritable, from sensibility to oppression; the high-minded, from disdain and indignation at abusive power in unworthy hands; the brave and bold, from the love of honourable danger in a generous cause: but, with or without right, a revolution will be the very last resource of the thinking and the good.

*　*　*　*　*

The third head of right asserted by the pulpit of the Old Jewry, namely, the "right to form a government for ourselves," has, at least, as little countenance from anything done at the Revolution, either in precedent or principle, as the two first of their claims. The Revolution was made to preserve our *ancient* indisputable laws and liberties, and that *ancient* constitution of government which is our only security for law and liberty. If you are desirous of knowing the spirit of our constitution, and the policy which predominated in that great period which has secured it to this hour, pray look for both in our histories, in our records, in our acts of Parliament and journals of Parliament, and not in the sermons of the Old Jewry, and the after-dinner toasts of the Revolution Society. In the former you will find other ideas and another language. Such a claim is as ill-suited to our temper and wishes as it is unsupported by any appearance of authority. The very idea of the fabrication of a new government is enough to fill us with disgust and horror. We wished at the period of the Revolution, and do now wish, to derive all we possess as *an inheritance from our forefathers.* Upon that body and stock of inheritance we have taken care not to inoculate any scion alien to the nature of the original plant. All the reformations we have hitherto made have proceeded upon the principle of reference to antiquity; and I hope, nay, I am persuaded, that all those which possibly may be made hereafter will be carefully formed upon analogical precedent, authority, and example.

Our oldest reformation is that of Magna Charta[1]. You will see that Sir Edward Coke[2], that great oracle of our law, and indeed all the great men who follow him, to Blackstone[3], are industrious to prove the pedigree of our liberties. They endeavour to prove that the ancient charter, the Magna Charta of King John, was connected with another positive charter from Henry I, and that both the one and the other were nothing more than a re-affirmance of the still more ancient standing law of the kingdom. In the matter of fact, for the greater part, these authors appear to be in the right; perhaps not always: but if the lawyers mistake in some particulars, it proves my position still the more strongly; because it demonstrates the powerful prepossession towards antiquity with which the minds of all our lawyers and legislators, and of all the people whom they wish to influence, have been always filled, and the stationary policy of this kingdom in considering their most sacred rights and franchises as an *inheritance*.

In the famous law of the 3rd of Charles I. called the *Petition of Right*, the parliament says to the king, "Your subjects have *inherited* this freedom," claiming their franchises, not on abstract principles "as the rights of men," but as the rights of Englishmen, and as a patrimony derived from their forefathers. Selden[4], and the other profoundly learned men who drew this Petition of Right, were as well acquainted, at least, with all the general theories concerning the "rights of men" as any of the discoursers in our pulpits or on your tribune: full as

---

1. Magna Charta：〈史〉大宪章，指英格兰金雀花王朝国王约翰于 1215 年同贵族集团签署的、英国最早的一份宪法性文件。
2. Sir Edward Coke：爱德华·柯克爵士（1552—1634），英国法学家，曾任下院议长，协助起草 1628 年的《权利请愿书》，反对詹姆士一世的王室特权。
3. Blackstone：布莱克斯通（Sir William Blackstone, 1723—1780），英国法学家，其主要著作《英国法律评论》对英美法律体系之形成产生很大的影响。
4. Selden：约翰·塞尔登（John Selden, 1584—1654），英国著名律师，参与反对国王詹姆士一世和查理一世的政治活动。

well as Dr. Price, or as the Abbé Sièyes[1]. But, for reasons worthy of that practical wisdom which superseded their theoretic science, they preferred this positive, recorded, *hereditary* title to all which can be dear to the man and the citizen to that vague, speculative right which exposed their sure inheritance to be scrambled for and torn to pieces by every wild, litigious spirit.

The same policy pervades all the laws which have since been made for the preservation of our liberties. In the 1st of William and Mary, in the famous statute called the Declaration of Right, the two Houses utter not a syllable of "a right to frame a government for themselves." You will see that their whole care was to secure the religion, laws, and liberties that had been long possessed, and had been lately endangered. "Taking into their most serious consideration the *best* means for making such an establishment that their religion, laws, and liberties might not be in danger of being again subverted," they auspicate all their proceedings by stating as some of those *best* means, "in the *first place*," to do "as their *ancestors in like cases have usually* done for vindicating their *ancient* rights and liberties, to *declare*" ; and then they pray the king and queen "that it may be *declared* and enacted that *all and singular* the rights and liberties *asserted and declared* are the true *ancient* and indubitable rights and liberties of the people of this kingdom."

You will observe, that, from Magna Charta to the Declaration of Right, it has been the uniform policy of our constitution to claim and assert our liberties as an *entailed inheritance* derived to us from our forefathers, and to be transmitted to our posterity; as an estate specially belonging to the people of this kingdom, without any reference whatever to any other more general or prior right. By this means our constitution preserves an unity in so great a diversity of

---

1. the Abbé Sièyes：西耶斯牧师（Emanuel Joseph Sieyes, 1748—1836），法国革命时期的重要活动家，天主教牧师，参加起草《人权宣言》。

its parts. We have an inheritable crown, an inheritable peerage, and a house of commons and a people inheriting privileges, franchises, and liberties from a long line of ancestors.

This policy appears to me to be the result of profound reflection; or rather the happy effect of following nature, which is wisdom without reflection, and above it. A spirit of innovation is generally the result of a selfish temper and confined views. People will not look forward to posterity, who never look backward to their ancestors. Besides, the people of England well know that the idea of inheritance furnishes a sure principle of conservation, and a sure principle of transmission, without at all excluding a principle of improvement. It leaves acquisition free; but it secures what it acquires. Whatever advantages are obtained by a state proceeding on these maxims, are locked fast as in a sort of family settlement, grasped as in a kind of mortmain[1] forever. By a constitutional policy working after the pattern of nature, we receive, we hold, we transmit our government and our privileges, in the same manner in which we enjoy and transmit our property and our lives. The institutions of policy, the goods of fortune, the gifts of Providence, are handed down to us, and from us, in the same course and order. Our political system is placed in a just correspondence and symmetry with the order of the world, and with the mode of existence decreed to a permanent body composed of transitory parts; wherein, by the disposition of a stupendous wisdom, moulding together the great mysterious incorporation of the human race, the whole, at one time, is never old or middle-aged or young, but, in a condition of unchangeable constancy, moves on through the varied tenor of perpetual decay, fall, renovation, and progression. Thus, by preserving the method of Nature in the conduct of the state, in what we improve we are never wholly new, in what we retain we are never

---

1. mortmain:【法律】由教会或其他机构永久拥有的土地（或房屋）

wholly obsolete. By adhering in this manner and on those principles to our forefathers, we are guided, not by the superstition of antiquarians, but by the spirit of philosophic analogy. In this choice of inheritance we have given to our frame of polity the image of a relation in blood: binding up the constitution of our country with our dearest domestic ties; adopting our fundamental laws into the bosom of our family affections; keeping inseparable, and cherishing with the warmth of all their combined and mutually reflected charities, our state, our hearths, our sepulchres, and our altars.

Through the same plan of a conformity to nature in our artificial institutions, and by calling in the aid of her unerring and powerful instincts to fortify the fallible and feeble contrivances of our reason, we have derived several other, and those no small benefits, from considering our liberties in the light of an inheritance. Always acting as if in the presence of canonized forefathers, the spirit of freedom, leading in itself to misrule and excess, is tempered with an awful gravity. This idea of a liberal descent inspires us with a sense of habitual native dignity, which prevents that upstart insolence almost inevitably adhering to and disgracing those who are the first acquirers of any distinction. By this means our liberty becomes a noble freedom. It carries an imposing and majestic aspect. It has a pedigree and illustrating ancestors. It has its bearings and its ensigns armorial. It has its gallery of portraits, its monumental inscriptions, its records, evidences, and titles. We procure reverence to our civil institutions on the principle upon which Nature teaches us to revere individual men: on account of their age, and on account of those from whom they are descended. All your sophisters cannot produce anything better adapted to preserve a rational and manly freedom than the course that we have pursued, who have chosen our nature rather than our speculations, our breasts rather than our inventions, for the great conservatories and magazines of our rights and privileges.

* * * * *

You might, if you pleased, have profited of our example, and have given to your recovered freedom a correspondent dignity. Your privileges, though discontinued, were not lost to memory. Your constitution, it is true, whilst you were out of possession, suffered waste and dilapidation[1]; but you possessed in some parts the walls, and in all the foundations, of a noble and venerable castle. You might have repaired those walls; you might have built on those old foundations. Your constitution was suspended before it was perfected; but you had the elements of a constitution very nearly as good as could be wished. In your old states you possessed that variety of parts corresponding with the various descriptions of which your community was happily composed; you had all that combination and all that opposition of interests, you had that action and counteraction, which, in the natural and in the political world, from the reciprocal struggle of discordant powers draws out the harmony of the universe. These opposed and conflicting interests, which you considered as so great a blemish in your old and in our present constitution, interpose a salutary check to all precipitate resolutions. They render deliberation a matter, not of choice, but of necessity; they make all change a subject of *compromise*, which naturally begets moderation; they produce *temperaments*, preventing the sore evil of harsh, crude, unqualified reformations, and rendering all the headlong exertions of arbitrary power, in the few or in the many, forever impracticable. Through that diversity of members and interests, general liberty had as many securities as there were separate views in the several orders; whilst by pressing down the whole by the weight of a real monarchy, the separate parts would have been prevented from warping and starting from their allotted places.

---

1. dilapidation：浪费，挥霍；坍毁（状态）

You had all these advantages in your ancient states; but you chose to act as if you had never been moulded into civil society, and had everything to begin anew. You began ill, because you began by despising everything that belonged to you. You set up your trade without a capital. If the last generations of your country appeared without much lustre in your eyes, you might have passed them by, and derived your claims from a more early race of ancestors. Under a pious predilection for those ancestors, your imaginations would have realized in them a standard of virtue and wisdom beyond the vulgar practice of the hour; and you would have risen with the example to whose imitation you aspired. Respecting your forefathers, you would have been taught to respect yourselves. You would not have chosen to consider the French as a people of yesterday, as a nation of low-born, servile wretches until the emancipating year of 1789. In order to furnish, at the expense of your honour, an excuse to your apologists here for several enormities of yours, you would not have been content to be represented as a gang of Maroon slaves[1], suddenly broke loose from the house of bondage, and therefore to be pardoned for your abuse of the liberty to which you were not accustomed, and were ill fitted. Would it not, my worthy friend, have been wiser to have you thought, what I for one always thought you, a generous and gallant nation, long misled to your disadvantage by your high and romantic sentiments of fidelity, honour, and loyalty; that events had been unfavourable to you, but that you were not enslaved through any illiberal or servile disposition; that, in your most devoted submission, you were actuated by a principle of public spirit; and that it was your country you worshipped, in the person of your king? Had you made it to be understood, that, in the delusion of this amiable error, you had gone further than your wise ancestors; that you were resolved

---

1. Maroon slaves：逃亡黑奴

to resume your ancient privileges, whilst you preserved the spirit of your ancient and your recent loyalty and honour; or if, diffident of yourselves, and not clearly discerning the almost obliterated constitution of your ancestors, you had looked to your neighbours in this land, who had kept alive the ancient principles and models of the old common law of Europe, meliorated and adapted to its present state — by following wise examples you would have given new examples of wisdom to the world. You would have rendered the cause of liberty venerable in the eyes of every worthy mind in every nation. You would have shamed despotism from the earth, by showing that freedom was not only reconcilable, but, as, when well disciplined it is, auxiliary to law. You would have had an unoppressive but a productive revenue. You would have had a flourishing commerce to feed it. You would have had a free constitution, a potent monarchy, a disciplined army, a reformed and venerated clergy; a mitigated, but spirited nobility, to lead your virtue, not to overlay it; you would have had a liberal order of commons, to emulate and to recruit that nobility; you would have had a protected, satisfied, laborious, and obedient people, taught to seek and to recognize the happiness that is to be found by virtue in all conditions; in which consists the true moral equality of mankind, and not in that monstrous fiction which, by inspiring false ideas and vain expectations into men destined to travel in the obscure walk of laborious life, serves only to aggravate and embitter that real inequality which it never can remove, and which the order of civil life establishes as much for the benefit of those whom it must leave in an humble state as those whom it is able to exalt to a condition more splendid, but not more happy. You had a smooth and easy career of felicity and glory laid open to you, beyond anything recorded in the history of the world; but you have shown that difficulty is good for man.

Compute your gains: see what is got by those extravagant and presumptuous speculations which have taught your leaders to despise all their predecessors, and all their contemporaries, and even to despise themselves, until the moment in which they became truly despicable. By following those false lights, France has bought undisguised calamities at a higher price than any nation has purchased the most unequivocal blessings! France has bought poverty by crime! France has not sacrificed her virtue to her interest; but she has abandoned her interest, that she might prostitute her virtue. All other nations have begun the fabric of a new government, or the reformation of an old, by establishing originally, or by enforcing with greater exactness, some rites or other of religion. All other people have laid the foundations of civil freedom in severer manners, and a system of a more austere and masculine morality. France, when she let loose the reins of regal authority, doubled the license of a ferocious dissoluteness in manners, and of an insolent irreligion in opinions and practices; and has extended through all ranks of life, as if she were communicating some privilege, or laying open some secluded benefit, all the unhappy corruptions that usually were the disease of wealth and power. This is one of the new principles of equality in France.

France, by the perfidy[1] of her leaders, has utterly disgraced the tone of lenient council in the cabinets of princes, and disarmed it of its most potent topics. She has sanctified the dark, suspicious maxims of tyrannous distrust, and taught kings to tremble at (what will hereafter be called) the delusive plausibilities of moral politicians. Sovereigns will consider those who advise them to place an unlimited confidence in their people as subverters of their thrones; as traitors who aim at their destruction, by leading their easy good-nature, under specious pretences, to admit combinations of bold and faithless men into a participation of their power. This alone (if there were nothing else) is an irreparable calamity to you and to mankind. Remember that

---

1. perfidy: 背信弃义

your parliament of Paris[1] told your king, that in calling the states together, he had nothing to fear but the prodigal excess of their zeal in providing for the support of the throne. It is right that these men should hide their heads. It is right that they should bear their part in the ruin which their counsel has brought on their sovereign and their country. Such sanguine declarations tend to lull authority asleep; to encourage it rashly to engage in perilous adventures of untried policy; to neglect those provisions, preparations, and precautions which distinguish benevolence from imbecility; and without which no man can answer for the salutary effect of any abstract plan of government or of freedom. For want of these, they have seen the medicine of the state corrupted into its poison. They have seen the French rebel against a mild and lawful monarch, with more fury, outrage, and insult than ever any people has been known to rise against the most illegal usurper or the most sanguinary tyrant. Their resistance was made to concession; their revolt was from protection; their blow was aimed at a hand holding out graces, favours, and immunities.

This was unnatural. The rest is in order. They have found their punishment in their success. Laws overturned; tribunals subverted; industry without vigour; commerce expiring; the revenue unpaid, yet the people impoverished; a church pillaged, and a state not relieved; civil and military anarchy made the constitution of the kingdom; everything human and divine sacrificed to the idol of public credit, and national bankruptcy the consequence; and, to crown all, the paper securities of new, precarious, tottering power, the discredited paper securities of impoverished fraud and beggared rapine, held out as a currency for the support of an empire, in lieu of the two great recognized species that represent the lasting, conventional credit of

---

1. parliament of Paris：巴黎最高法院。详见“术语汇编与简释”。

mankind, which disappeared and hid themselves in the earth from whence they came, when the principle of property, whose creatures and representatives they are, was systematically subverted.

Were all these dreadful things necessary? Were they the inevitable results of the desperate struggle of determined patriots, compelled to wade through blood and tumult to the quiet shore of a tranquil and prosperous liberty? No! nothing like it. The fresh ruins of France, which shock our feelings wherever we can turn our eyes, are not the devastation of civil war; they are the sad, but instructive monuments of rash and ignorant counsel in time of profound peace. They are the display of inconsiderate and presumptuous, because unresisted and irresistible authority. The persons who have thus squandered away the precious treasure of their crimes, the persons who have made this prodigal and wild waste of public evils (the last stake reserved for the ultimate ransom of the state) have met in their progress with little, or rather with no opposition at all. Their whole march was more like a triumphal procession than the progress of a war. Their pioneers have gone before them, and demolished and laid everything level at their feet. Not one drop of *their* blood have they shed in the cause of the country they have ruined. They have made no sacrifices to their projects of greater consequence than their shoe-buckles[1], whilst they were imprisoning their king, murdering their fellow-citizens, and bathing in tears and plunging in poverty and distress thousands of worthy men and worthy families. Their cruelty has not even been the base result of fear. It has been the effect of their sense of perfect safety, in authorizing treasons, robberies, rapes, assassinations, slaughters, and burnings, throughout their harassed land. But the cause of all was plain from the beginning.

---

1. They have made ... shoe-buckles：指当时法国人民纷纷捐出值钱的物品，如银鞋扣等，力图帮助新生的革命政权渡过财政难关。

* * * * *

This unforced choice, this fond election of evil, would appear perfectly unaccountable, if we did not consider the composition of the National Assembly. I do not mean its formal constitution, which, as it now stands, is exceptionable enough, but the materials of which in a great measure it is composed, which is of ten thousand times greater consequence than all the formalities in the world. If we were to know nothing of this assembly but by its title and function, no colours could paint to the imagination anything more venerable. In that light, the mind of an inquirer, subdued by such an awful image as that of the virtue and wisdom of a whole people collected into one focus, would pause and hesitate in condemning things even of the very worst aspect. Instead of blameable, they would appear only mysterious. But no name, no power, no function, no artificial institution whatsoever, can make the men, of whom any system of authority is composed, any other than God, and nature, and education, and their habits of life have made them. Capacities beyond these the people have not to give. Virtue and wisdom may be the objects of their choice; but their choice confers neither the one nor the other on those upon whom they lay their ordaining hands. They have not the engagement of nature, they have not the promise of revelation for any such powers.

After I had read over the list of the persons and descriptions elected into the *Tiers État*[1], nothing which they afterwards did could appear astonishing. Among them, indeed, I saw some of known rank, some of shining talents; but of any practical experience in the state not one man was to be found. The best were only men of theory. But whatever the distinguished few may have been, it is the substance and mass of the body which constitutes its character, and must finally

---

1. *Tiers État*：〈法〉第三等级（Third Estate）。详见"术语汇编与简释"。

determine its direction. In all bodies, those who will lead must also, in a considerable degree, follow. They must conform their propositions to the taste, talent, and disposition of those whom they wish to conduct: therefore, if an Assembly is viciously or feebly composed in a very great part of it, nothing but such a supreme degree of virtue as very rarely appears in the world, and for that reason cannot enter into calculation, will prevent the men of talents disseminated through it from becoming only the expert instruments of absurd projects. If, what is the more likely event, instead of that unusual degree of virtue, they should be actuated by sinister ambition and a lust of meretricious glory, then the feeble part of the Assembly, to whom at first they conform, becomes, in its turn, the dupe and instrument of their designs. In this political traffic, the leaders will be obliged to bow to the ignorance of their followers, and the followers to become subservient to the worst designs of their leaders.

To secure any degree of sobriety in the propositions made by the leaders in any public assembly, they ought to respect, in some degree perhaps to fear, those whom they conduct. To be led any otherwise than blindly, the followers must be qualified, if not for actors, at least for judges; they must also be judges of natural weight and authority. Nothing can secure a steady and moderate conduct in such assemblies, but that the body of them should be respectably composed, in point of condition in life, of permanent property, of education, and of such habits as enlarge and liberalize the understanding.

In the calling of the States-General of France, the first thing that struck me was a great departure from the ancient course. I found the representation for the third estate composed of six hundred persons[1]. They were equal in number to the representatives of both the other

---

1. the third estate composed of six hundred persons: 1788 年 12 月，法兰西国王路易十六同意将第三等级的人数从 300 人增加到 600 人。

orders[1]. If the orders were to act separately, the number would not, beyond the consideration of the expense, be of much moment. But when it became apparent that the three orders were to be melted down into one, the policy and necessary effect of this numerous representation became obvious. A very small desertion from either of the other two orders must throw the power of both into the hands of the third[2]. In fact, the whole power of the state was soon resolved into that body. Its due composition became, therefore, of infinitely the greater importance.

Judge, Sir, of my surprise, when I found that a very great proportion of the Assembly (a majority, I believe, of the members who attended) was composed of practitioners in the law. It was composed, not of distinguished magistrates, who had given pledges to their country of their science, prudence, and integrity; not of leading advocates, the glory of the bar; not of renowned professors in universities; — but for the far greater part, as it must in such a number, of the inferior, unlearned, mechanical, merely instrumental members of the profession. There were distinguished exceptions; but the general composition was of obscure provincial advocates, of stewards of petty local jurisdictions, country attorneys, notaries, and the whole train of the ministers of municipal litigation, the fomenters and conductors of the petty war of village vexation. From the moment I read the list, I saw distinctly, and very nearly as it has happened, all that was to follow.

The degree of estimation in which any profession is held becomes the standard of the estimation in which the professors hold themselves. Whatever the personal merits of many individual lawyers might have

---

1. the representatives of both the other orders：另外两个等级的代表，指
"三级会议"中的第一和第二等级代表。
2. A very small desertion ... to the third：指 1789 年 6 月下旬，第一等级和
第二等级的代表纷纷跳槽，加入第三等级，最终形成国民议会。

been, and in many it was undoubtedly very considerable, in that military kingdom no part of the profession had been much regarded, except the highest of all, who often united to their professional offices great family splendour, and were invested with great power and authority. These certainly were highly respected, and even with no small degree of awe. The next rank was not much esteemed; the mechanical part was in a very low degree of repute.

Whenever the supreme authority is vested in a body so composed, it must evidently produce the consequences of supreme authority placed in the hands of men not taught habitually to respect themselves; who had no previous fortune in character at stake; who could not be expected to bear with moderation or to conduct with discretion a power which they themselves, more than any others, must be surprised to find in their hands. Who could flatter himself that these men, suddenly, and as it were by enchantment, snatched from the humblest rank of subordination, would not be intoxicated with their unprepared greatness? Who could conceive, that men who are habitually meddling, daring, subtle, active, of litigious dispositions and unquiet minds, would easily fall back into their old condition of obscure contention, and laborious, low, and unprofitable chicane? Who could doubt but that, at any expense to the state, of which they understood nothing, they must pursue their private interests, which they understood but too well? It was not an event depending on chance or contingency. It was inevitable; it was necessary; it was planted in the nature of things. They must *join* (if their capacity did not permit them to *lead*) in any project which could procure to them a *litigious constitution*; which could lay open to them those innumerable lucrative jobs which follow in the train of all great convulsions and revolutions in the state, and particularly in all great and violent permutations of property. Was it to be expected that they would attend to the stability of property, whose existence had always depended upon whatever rendered property questionable, ambiguous, and insecure? Their objects would be enlarged with their elevation; but their disposition, and habits, and mode of accomplishing their designs must remain the same.

Well! but these men were to be tempered and restrained by other descriptions, of more sober minds and more enlarged understandings. Were they, then, to be awed by the super-eminent authority and awful dignity of a handful of country clowns, who have seats in that Assembly, some of whom are said not to be able to read and write? and by not a greater number of traders, who, though somewhat more instructed, and more conspicuous in the order of society, had never known anything beyond their counting-house? No! both these descriptions were more formed to be overborne and swayed by the intrigues and artifices of lawyers than to become their counterpoise. With such a dangerous disproportion, the whole must needs be governed by them. To the faculty of law was joined a pretty considerable proportion of the faculty of medicine. This faculty had not, any more than that of the law, possessed in France its just estimation. Its professors, therefore, must have the qualities of men not habituated to sentiments of dignity. But supposing they had ranked as they ought to do, and as with us they do actually, the sides of sick-beds are not the academies for forming statesmen and legislators. Then came the dealers in stocks and funds, who must be eager, at any expense, to change their ideal paper wealth for the more solid substance of land. To these were joined men of other descriptions, from whom as little knowledge of or attention to the interests of a great state was to be expected, and as little regard to the stability of any institution; men formed to be instruments, not controls. Such, in general, was the composition of the *Tiers État* in the National Assembly; in which was scarcely to be perceived the slightest traces of what we call the natural landed interest of the country.

We know that the British house of commons, without shutting its doors to any merit in any class, is, by the sure operation of adequate causes, filled with everything illustrious in rank, in descent, in hereditary and in acquired opulence, in cultivated talents, in military, civil, naval, and politic distinction, that the country can afford. But supposing, what hardly can be supposed as a case, that the house of commons should be composed in the same manner with the *Tiers État* in France, would this dominion of chicane be borne with patience, or even conceived without horror? God forbid I should insinuate[1] anything derogatory to that profession, which is another priesthood, administering the rights of sacred justice! But whilst I revere men in the functions which belong to them, and would do as much as one man can do to prevent their exclusion from any, I cannot, to flatter them, give the lie to Nature. They are good and useful in the composition; they must be mischievous, if they preponderate so as virtually to become the whole. Their very excellence in their peculiar functions may be far from a qualification for others. It cannot escape observation, that, when men are too much confined to professional and faculty habits, and, as it were, inveterate[2] in the recurrent employment of that narrow circle, they are rather disabled than qualified for whatever depends on the knowledge of mankind, on experience in mixed affairs, on a comprehensive, connected view of the various, complicated, external, and internal interests which go to the formation of that multifarious thing called a state.

After all, if the house of commons were to have an wholly professional and faculty composition, what is the power of the house of commons, circumscribed and shut in by the immovable barriers of laws, usages, positive rules of doctrine and practice, counterpoised by the house of lords, and every moment of its existence at the discretion of the crown to continue, prorogue, or dissolve us? The power of the house of commons, direct or indirect, is, indeed, great: and long

---

1. insinuate：暗示
2. inveterate：积习的

may it be able to preserve its greatness, and the spirit belonging to true greatness, at the full; and it will do so, as long as it can keep the breakers of law in India from becoming the makers of law for England. The power, however, of the house of commons, when least diminished, is as a drop of water in the ocean, compared to that residing in a settled majority of your National Assembly. That Assembly, since the destruction of the orders, has no fundamental law, no strict convention, no respected usage to restrain it. Instead of finding themselves obliged to conform to a fixed constitution, they have a power to make a constitution which shall conform to their designs. Nothing in heaven or upon earth can serve as a control on them. What ought to be the heads, the hearts, the dispositions, that are qualified, or that dare, not only to make laws under a fixed constitution, but at one heat to strike out a totally new constitution for a great kingdom, and in every part of it, from the monarch on the throne to the vestry of a parish? But — *"Fools rush in where angels fear to tread.*[1]*"* In such a state of unbounded power, for undefined and undefinable purposes, the evil of a moral and almost physical inaptitude of the man to the function must be the greatest we can conceive to happen in the management of human affairs.

Having considered the composition of the third estate, as it stood in its original frame, I took a view of the representatives of the clergy. There too it appeared that full as little regard was had to the general security of property, or to the aptitude of the deputies for their public purposes, in the principles of their election. That election was so contrived as to send a very large proportion of mere country curates to the great and arduous work of new-modelling a state: men who never had seen the state so much as in a picture; men who knew nothing of the world beyond the bounds of an obscure village; who, immersed

---

1. *"Fools rush in where angels fear to tread"*: "天使踟蹰却步，而蠢人则勇往无前"，引自英国诗人亚历山大·蒲柏的《批评随笔》。

in hopeless poverty, could regard all property, whether secular or ecclesiastical, with no other eye than that of envy; among whom must be many who, for the smallest hope of the meanest dividend in plunder, would readily join in any attempts upon a body of wealth in which they could hardly look to have any share, except in a general scramble. Instead of balancing the power of the active chicaners in the other assembly, these curates must necessarily become the active coadjutors, or at best the passive instruments, of those by whom they had been habitually guided in their petty village concerns. They, too, could hardly be the most conscientious of their kind, who, presuming upon their incompetent understanding, could intrigue for a trust which led them from their natural relation to their flocks, and their natural spheres of action, to undertake the regeneration of kingdoms. This preponderating weight, being added to the force of the body of chicane in the *Tiers État*, completed that momentum of ignorance, rashness, presumption, and lust of plunder, which nothing has been able to resist.

To observing men it must have appeared from the beginning, that the majority of the Third Estate, in conjunction with such a deputation from the clergy as I have described, whilst it pursued the destruction of the nobility, would inevitably become subservient to the worst designs of individuals in that class. In the spoil and humiliation of their own order these individuals would possess a sure fund for the pay of their new followers. To squander away the objects which made the happiness of their fellows would be to them no sacrifice at all. Turbulent, discontented men of quality, in proportion as they are puffed up with personal pride and arrogance, generally despise their own order. One of the first symptoms they discover of a selfish and mischievous ambition is a profligate disregard of a dignity which they partake with others. To be attached to the subdivision, to love the little platoon we belong to in society, is the first principle (the germ as it were) of public affections. It is the first link in the series by which we proceed towards a love to our country and to mankind. The interest of that portion of social arrangement is a trust in the hands of all those who compose it; and as none but bad men would justify it in abuse, none but traitors would barter it away for their own personal advantage.

There were, in the time of our civil troubles in England (I do not know whether you have any such in your Assembly in France) several persons, like the then Earl of Holland[1], who by themselves or their families had brought an odium on the throne by the prodigal dispensation of its bounties towards them, who afterwards joined in the rebellions arising from the discontents of which they were themselves the cause: men who helped to subvert that throne to which they owed, some of them, their existence, others all that power which they employed to ruin their benefactor. If any bounds are set to the rapacious[2] demands of that sort of people, or that others are permitted to partake in the objects they would engross, revenge and envy soon fill up the craving void that is left in their avarice. Confounded by the complication of distempered passions, their reason is disturbed; their views become vast and perplexed; to others inexplicable, to themselves uncertain. They find, on all sides, bounds to their unprincipled ambition in any fixed order of things; but in the fog and haze of confusion all is enlarged, and appears without any limit.

When men of rank sacrifice all ideas of dignity to an ambition without a distinct object, and work with low instruments and for low ends, the whole composition becomes low and base. Does not something like this now appear in France? Does it not produce something ignoble and inglorious: a kind of meanness in all the prevalent policy; a tendency in all that is done to lower along with

---

1. Earl of Holland：指荷兰伯爵亨利·理奇（Henry Rich, 1590—1649）。他一度是英王查理一世的支持者，但在英国内战时期却多次变换阵营，最后被内战获胜方处死。
2. rapacious：贪婪的

individuals all the dignity and importance of the state? Other revolutions have been conducted by persons who, whilst they attempted or affected changes in the commonwealth, sanctified their ambition by advancing the dignity of the people whose peace they troubled. They had long views. They aimed at the rule, not at the destruction of their country. They were men of great civil and great military talents, and if the terror, the ornament of their age. They were not like Jew brokers contending with each other who could best remedy with fraudulent circulation and depreciated paper the wretchedness and ruin brought on their country by their degenerate councils. The compliment made to one of the great bad men of the old stamp (Cromwell[1]) by his kinsman, a favourite poet of that time, shows what it was he proposed, and what indeed to a great degree he accomplished in the success of his ambition:

Still as *you* rise, the *state*, exalted too,
Finds no distemper whilst 'tis chang'd by *you*;
Chang'd like the world's great scene, when without noise
The rising sun night's *vulgar* lights destroys.[2]

These disturbers were not so much like men usurping power as asserting their natural place in society. Their rising was to illuminate and beautify the world. Their conquest over their competitors was by outshining them. The hand, that, like a destroying angel, smote the country, communicated to it the force and energy under which it suffered. I do not say (God forbid!), I do not say that the virtues of

---

1. Cromwell: 奥利弗·克伦威尔（1599—1658），英国政治家、军事家、宗教领袖。17世纪英国资产阶级革命中曾逼迫英国君主退位，解散国会，建立英吉利共和国，出任护国公，成为英国事实上的国家元首。
2. Still ... lights destroys.：引自克伦威尔的远亲、英国诗人艾德蒙·沃勒（Edmund Waller，1606—1687）的诗歌《致护国公的颂歌》。

such men were to be taken as a balance to their crimes, but they were some corrective to their effects. Such was, as I said, our Cromwell. Such were your whole race of Guises, Condés, and Colignys[1]. Such the Richelieus[2], who in more quiet times acted in the spirit of a civil war. Such, as better men, and in a less dubious cause, were your Henry IV, and your Sully[3], though nursed in civil confusions, and not wholly without some of their taint. It is a thing to be wondered at, to see how very soon France, when she had a moment to respire, recovered and emerged from the longest and most dreadful civil war that ever was known in any nation. Why? Because, among all their massacres, they had not slain the *mind* in their country. A conscious dignity, a noble pride, a generous sense of glory and emulation, was not extinguished. On the contrary, it was kindled and inflamed. The organs also of the state, however shattered, existed. All the prizes of honour and virtue, all the rewards, all the distinctions, remained. But your present confusion, like a palsy, has attacked the fountain of life itself. Every person in your country, in a situation to be actuated by a principle of honour, is disgraced and degraded, and can entertain no sensation of life, except in a mortified and humiliated indignation. But this generation will quickly pass away. The next generation of the nobility will resemble the artificers and clowns, and money-jobbers, usurers, and Jews, who will be always their fellows, sometimes their masters. Believe me, Sir, those who attempt to level never equalize. In all societies consisting of various descriptions of citizens, some

---

1. Guises, Condés, and Colignys：三人都是 16 世纪法国宗教战争时期的重要人物。
2. the Richelieus：指法国红衣主教黎塞留（Armand-Jean du Plessis, 1550—1642），路易十三的首相。他在法国政务决策中具有主导性的影响力，在当时的欧洲政治和外交领域也起到极其重要的作用。
3. your Henry IV, and your Sully：指法兰西国王亨利四世（Henri IV, 1553—1610）及其重臣苏利公爵（Maximilien de Bethune, duc de Sully, 1560—1641）。

description must be uppermost. The levellers, therefore, only change and pervert the natural order of things: they load the edifice of society by setting up in the air what the solidity of the structure requires to be on the ground. The associations of tailors and carpenters, of which the republic (of Paris, for instance) is composed, cannot be equal to the situation into which, by the worst of usurpations, an usurpation on the prerogatives of nature, you attempt to force them.

The Chancellor of France, at the opening of the States, said, in a tone of oratorial flourish, that all occupations were honourable. If he meant only that no honest employment was disgraceful, he would not have gone beyond the truth. But in asserting that anything is honourable, we imply some distinction in its favour. The occupation of a hair-dresser, or of a working tallow-chandler, cannot be a matter of honour to any person — to say nothing of a number of other more servile employments. Such descriptions of men ought not to suffer oppression from the state; but the state suffers oppression, if such as they, either individually or collectively, are permitted to rule. In this you think you are combating prejudice, but you are at war with nature.[1]

I do not, my dear Sir, conceive you to be of that sophistical, captious spirit, or of that uncandid dullness, as to require, for every general observation or sentiment, an explicit detail of the correctives and exceptions which reason will presume to be included in all the general propositions which come from reasonable men. You do not imagine that I wish to confine power, authority, and distinction to blood and names and titles. No, Sir. There is no qualification for government but virtue and wisdom, actual or presumptive. Wherever they are actually found, they have, in whatever state, condition, profession, or trade, the passport of Heaven to human place and honour. Woe to the country which would madly and impiously reject the service of the talents and

---

1. 此段论述源自杜埃版《圣经》中的《德训篇》。

virtues, civil, military, or religious, that are given to grace and to serve it; and would condemn to obscurity everything formed to diffuse lustre and glory around a state! Woe to that country, too, that passing into the opposite extreme, considers a low education, a mean, contracted view of things, a sordid, mercenary occupation, as a preferable title to command! Everything ought to be open; but not indifferently to every man. No rotation, no appointment by lot[1], no mode of election operating in the spirit of sortition or rotation, can be generally good in a government conversant in extensive objects; because they have no tendency, direct or indirect, to select the man with a view to the duty, or to accommodate the one to the other. I do not hesitate to say that the road to eminence and power, from obscure condition, ought not to be made too easy, nor a thing too much of course. If rare merit be the rarest of all rare things, it ought to pass through some sort of probation. The temple of honour ought to be seated on an eminence. If it be opened through virtue, let it be remembered, too, that virtue is never tried but by some difficulty and some struggle.

Nothing is a due and adequate representation of a state, that does not represent its ability, as well as its property. But as ability is a vigorous and active principle, and as property is sluggish, inert, and timid, it never can be safe from the invasions of ability, unless it be, out of all proportion, predominant in the representation. It must be represented, too, in great masses of accumulation, or it is not rightly protected. The characteristic essence of property, formed out of the combined principles of its acquisition and conservation, is to be *unequal*. The great masses, therefore, which excite envy, and tempt rapacity, must be put out of the possibility of danger. Then they form a natural rampart about the lesser properties in all their gradations. The same quantity of property which is by the natural course of things divided among many

---

1. appointment by lot: 抽签任命

has not the same operation. Its defensive power is weakened as it is diffused. In this diffusion each man's portion is less than what, in the eagerness of his desires, he may flatter himself to obtain by dissipating the accumulations of others. The plunder of the few would, indeed, give but a share inconceivably small in the distribution to the many. But the many are not capable of making this calculation; and those who lead them to rapine never intend this distribution.

The power of perpetuating our property in our families is one of the most valuable and interesting circumstances belonging to it, and that which tends the most to the perpetuation of society itself. It makes our weakness subservient to our virtue; it grafts benevolence even upon avarice. The possessors of family wealth, and of the distinction which attends hereditary possession (as most concerned in it) are the natural securities for this transmission. With us the House of Peers[1] is formed upon this principle. It is wholly composed of hereditary property and hereditary distinction, and made, therefore, the third of the legislature, and, in the last event, the sole judge of all property in all its subdivisions. The House of Commons, too, though not necessarily, yet in fact, is always so composed, in the far greater part. Let those large proprietors be what they will (and they have their chance of being amongst the best); they are at the very worst, the ballast in the vessel of the commonwealth. For though hereditary wealth, and the rank which goes with it, are too much idolized by creeping sycophants[2], and the blind, abject admirers of power, they are too rashly slighted in shallow speculations of the petulant, assuming, short-sighted coxcombs of philosophy. Some decent, regulated pre-eminence, some preference (not exclusive appropriation) given to birth, is neither unnatural, nor unjust, nor impolitic.

---

1. House of Peers: 英国议会中的贵族院（上议院），通常称作 House of Lords。
2. sycophants: 谄媚者；奉承者

It is said that twenty-four millions ought to prevail over two hundred thousand. True; if the constitution of a kingdom be a problem of arithmetic. This sort of discourse does well enough with the lamp-post for its second: to men who *may* reason calmly it is ridiculous. The will of the many, and their interest, must very often differ; and great will be the difference when they make an evil choice. A government of five hundred country attorneys and obscure curates is not good for twenty-four millions of men, though it were chosen by eight-and-forty millions; nor is it the better for being guided by a dozen of persons of quality who have betrayed their trust in order to obtain that power. At present, you seem in everything to have strayed out of the high road of Nature. The property of France does not govern it. Of course property is destroyed, and rational liberty has no existence. All you have got for the present is a paper circulation, and a stock-jobbing constitution: and as to the future, do you seriously think that the territory of France, upon the republican system of eighty-three independent municipalities (to say nothing of the parts that compose them) can ever be governed as one body, or can ever be set in motion by the impulse of one mind? When the National Assembly has completed its work, it will have accomplished its ruin. These commonwealths will not long bear a state of subjection to the republic of Paris. They will not bear that this one body should monopolize the captivity of the king, and the dominion over the assembly calling itself national. Each will keep its own portion of the spoil of the church to itself; and it will not suffer either that spoil, or the more just fruits of their industry, or the natural produce of their soil, to be sent to swell the insolence or pamper the luxury of the mechanics of Paris. In this they will see none of the equality, under the pretence of which they have been tempted to throw off their allegiance to their sovereign, as well as the ancient constitution of their country. There can be no capital city in such a constitution as they have lately made. They have forgot, that, when they framed democratic governments, they had virtually dismembered their country. The person whom they persevere in calling king has not power left to him by the hundredth part sufficient to hold together this collection of republics. The republic of Paris will endeavour, indeed, to complete the debauchery of the army, and illegally to perpetuate the Assembly, without resort to its constituents, as the means of continuing its despotism. It will make efforts, by becoming the heart of a boundless paper circulation, to draw everything to itself; but in vain. All this policy in the end will appear as feeble as it is now violent.

*　*　*　*　*

If this be your actual situation, compared to the situation to which you were called, as it were by the voice of God and man, I cannot find it in my heart to congratulate you on the choice you have made, or the success which has attended your endeavours. I can as little recommend to any other nation a conduct grounded on such principles and productive of such effects. That I must leave to those who can see further into your affairs than I am able to do, and who best know how far your actions are favourable to their designs. The gentlemen of the Revolution Society, who were so early in their congratulations, appear to be strongly of opinion that there is some scheme of politics relative to this country, in which your proceedings may in some way be useful. For your Dr. Price, who seems to have speculated himself into no small degree of fervour upon this subject, addresses his auditors in the following very remarkable words: "I cannot conclude without recalling *particularly* to your recollection a consideration which I have *more than once alluded to*, and which probably your thoughts have *been all along anticipating*; a consideration with which my *mind is impressed more than can express*. I mean the consideration of the *favourableness of the present times to all exertions in the cause of liberty.*"

It is plain that the mind of this *political* preacher was at the time big with some extraordinary design; and it is very probable that the thoughts of his audience, who understood him better than I do, did all along run before him in his reflection, and in the whole train of consequences to which it led.

Before I read that sermon, I really thought I had lived in a free country; and it was an error I cherished, because it gave me a greater liking to the country I lived in. I was, indeed, aware that a jealous, ever-waking vigilance, to guard the treasure of our liberty, not only from invasion, but from decay and corruption, was our best wisdom and our first duty. However, I considered that treasure rather as a possession to be secured than as a prize to be contended for. I did not discern how the present time came to be so very favorable to all *exertions* in the cause of freedom. The present time differs from any other only by the circumstance of what is doing in France. If the example of that nation is to have an influence on this, I can easily conceive why some of their proceedings which have an unpleasant aspect, and are not quite reconcilable to humanity, generosity, good faith, and justice, are palliated with so much milky good-nature towards the actors, and borne with so much heroic fortitude towards the sufferers. It is certainly not prudent to discredit the authority of an example we mean to follow. But allowing this, we are led to a very natural question; — What is that cause of liberty, and what are those exertions in its favor, to which the example of France is so singularly auspicious? Is our monarchy to be annihilated, with all the laws, all the tribunals, and all the ancient corporations of the kingdom? Is every landmark of the country to be done away in favour of a geometrical and arithmetical constitution? Is the House of Lords to be voted useless? Is episcopacy to be abolished? Are the church lands to be sold to Jews and jobbers, or given to bribe new-invented municipal republics into a participation in sacrilege[1]? Are all the taxes to be

---

1. sacrilege：（对圣物或圣地的）亵渎

voted grievances, and the revenue reduced to a patriotic contribution or patriotic presents? Are silver shoe-buckles to be substituted in the place of the land-tax and the malt-tax, for the support of the naval strength of this kingdom? Are all orders, ranks, and distinctions to be confounded, that out of universal anarchy, joined to national bankruptcy, three or four thousand democracies should be formed into eighty-three, and that they may all, by some sort of unknown attractive power, be organized into one? For this great end is the army to be seduced from its discipline and its fidelity, first by every kind of debauchery, and then by the terrible precedent of a donative in the increase of pay? Are the curates to be seduced from their bishops by holding out to them the delusive hope of a dole out of the spoils of their own order? Are the citizens of London to be drawn from their allegiance by feeding them at the expense of their fellow-subjects? Is a compulsory paper currency to be substituted in the place of the legal coin of this kingdom? Is what remains of the plundered stock of public revenue to be employed in the wild project of maintaining two armies to watch over and to fight with each other? If these are the ends and means of the Revolution Society, I admit they are well assorted; and France may furnish them for both with precedents in point.

I see that your example is held out to shame us. I know that we are supposed a dull, sluggish race, rendered passive by finding our situation tolerable, and prevented by a mediocrity of freedom from ever attaining to its full perfection. Your leaders in France began by affecting to admire, almost to adore, the British constitution; but as they advanced, they came to look upon it with a sovereign contempt. The friends of your National Assembly amongst us have full as mean an opinion of what was formerly thought the glory of their country. The Revolution Society has discovered that the English nation is not free. They are convinced that the inequality in our representation is a "defect in our constitution *so gross and palpable* as to make it excellent chiefly in *form* and *theory*." [1] That a representation in the legislature of a kingdom is not only the basis of all constitutional liberty in it, but of "*all legitimate government*; that without it a *government* is nothing but an *usurpation*;" — that "when the representation is *partial*, the kingdom possesses liberty only *partially*; and if extremely partial, it gives only a *semblance*; and if not only extremely partial, but corruptly chosen, it becomes a *nuisance*." Dr. Price considers this inadequacy of representation as our *fundamental grievance*; and though, as to the corruption of this semblance of representation, he hopes it is not yet arrived to its full perfection of depravity, he fears that "nothing will be done towards gaining for us this *essential blessing*, until some *great abuse of power* again provokes our resentment, or some *great calamity* again alarms our fears, or perhaps till the acquisition of a *pure and equal representation by other countries*, whilst we are *mocked* with the *shadow*, kindles our shame." To this he subjoins a note in these words: "A representation, chosen chiefly by the Treasury, and a *few* thousands of the *dregs*[2] of the people, who are generally paid for their votes."

You will smile here at the consistency of those democratists[3] who, when they are not on their guard, treat the humbler part of the community with the greatest contempt, whilst, at the same time, they pretend to make them the depositories of all power. It would require a long discourse to point out to you the many fallacies that lurk in the generality and equivocal nature of the terms "inadequate representation." I shall only say here, in justice to that old-fashioned constitution under which we have long prospered, that our representation has been found perfectly adequate to all the purposes for which a representation of the people can be desired or devised. I defy the enemies of our constitution to show the contrary.

---

1. "defect in ... in *form* and *theory*"：引自普赖斯博士的《论热爱吾国》。
2. *dregs*：残渣，渣滓
3. democratists：尤指法国革命时期主张民主与共和的民主派或民主主义者。

To detail the particulars in which it is found so well to promote its ends would demand a treatise on our practical constitution. I state here the doctrine of the revolutionists, only that you and others may see what an opinion these gentlemen entertain of the constitution of their country, and why they seem to think that some great abuse of power, or some great calamity, as giving a chance for the blessing of a constitution according to their ideas, would be much palliated to their feelings; you see *why they* are so much enamoured of your fair and equal representation, which being once obtained, the same effects might follow. You see they consider our House of Commons as only "a semblance," "a form," "a theory," "a shadow," "a mockery," perhaps "a nuisance."

These gentlemen value themselves on being systematic, and not without reason. They must therefore look on this gross and palpable defect of representation, this fundamental grievance (so they call it) as a thing not only vicious in itself, but as rendering our whole government absolutely *illegitimate*, and not at all better than a downright *usurpation*. Another revolution, to get rid of this illegitimate and usurped government, would of course be perfectly justifiable, if not absolutely necessary. Indeed, their principle, if you observe it with any attention, goes much further than to an alteration in the election of the House of Commons; for, if popular representation, or choice, is necessary to the *legitimacy* of all government, the House of Lords is, at one stroke, bastardized and corrupted in blood. That house is no representative of the people at all, even in "semblance" or "in form." The case of the crown is altogether as bad. In vain the crown may endeavour to screen itself against these gentlemen by the authority of the establishment made on the Revolution. The Revolution, which is resorted to for a title, on their system, wants a title itself. The Revolution is built, according to their theory, upon a basis not more solid than our present formalities, as it was made by a House of Lords not representing any one but themselves, and by a House of Commons exactly such as the present, that is, as they term it, by a mere "shadow and mockery" of representation.

Something they must destroy, or they seem to themselves to exist for no purpose. One set is for destroying the civil power through the ecclesiastical; another for demolishing the ecclesiastic through the civil. They are aware that the worst consequences might happen to the public in accomplishing this double ruin of Church and State; but they are so heated with their theories, that they give more than hints that this ruin, with all the mischiefs that must lead to it and attend it, and which to themselves appear quite certain, would not be unacceptable to them, or very remote from their wishes. A man amongst them of great authority, and certainly of great talents[1], speaking of a supposed alliance between Church and State, says, "Perhaps *we must wait for the fall of the civil powers* before this most unnatural alliance be broken. Calamitous, no doubt, will that time be. But what convulsion in the political world ought to be a subject of lamentation, if it be attended with so desirable an effect?" You see with what a steady eye these gentlemen are prepared to view the greatest calamities which can befall their country!

It is no wonder therefore, that with these ideas of everything in their constitution and government at home, either in church or state, as illegitimate and usurped, or at best as a vain mockery, they look abroad with an eager and passionate enthusiasm. Whilst they are possessed by these notions, it is vain to talk to them of the practice of their ancestors, the fundamental laws of their country, the fixed form of a constitution whose merits are confirmed by the solid test of long experience and an increasing public strength and national prosperity. They despise experience as the wisdom of unlettered men; and as for

---

1. A man ... of great talents：指普赖斯博士的密友约瑟夫·普里斯特利 (Joseph Priestley, 1733—1804)。下文引自他于 1782 年出版的著作《基督教概念史》。

the rest, they have wrought under ground a mine that will blow up, at one grand explosion, all examples of antiquity, all precedents, charters, and acts of parliament. They have "the rights of men." Against these there can be no prescription[1]; against these no argument is binding: these admit no temperament and no compromise: anything withheld from their full demand is so much of fraud and injustice. Against these their rights of men let no government look for security in the length of its continuance, or in the justice and lenity of its administration. The objections of these speculatists, if its forms do not quadrate with their theories, are as valid against such an old and beneficent government as against the most violent tyranny or the greenest usurpation. They are always at issue with governments, not on a question of abuse, but a question of competency and a question of title. I have nothing to say to the clumsy subtilty of their political metaphysics. Let them be their amusement in the schools. — "*Illa se jactet in aula. — Æolus, et clauso ventorum carcere regnet.*" [2] — But let them not break prison to burst like a *Levanter*[3], to sweep the earth with their hurricane, and to break up the fountains of the great deep to overwhelm us!

Far am I from denying in theory; full as far is my heart from withholding in practice (if I were of power to give or to withhold) the *real* rights of men. In denying their false claims of right, I do not mean to injure those which are real, and are such as their pretended rights would totally destroy. If civil society be made for the advantage of man, all the advantages for which it is made become his right. It is an institution of beneficence; and law itself is only beneficence acting by a rule. Men have a right to live by that rule; they have a right to justice,

---

1. prescription: 由因袭成俗而取得的权利。详见"术语汇编与简释"。
2. "*Illa se jactet ... carcere regnet*": 〈拉〉引自维吉尔的名作《埃涅阿斯记》。译成英文的大意是: Let him flaunt himself in that hall — Aeolus, and let him rule the winds in his confined prison。
3. *Levanter*: 累范特季风, 尤指夏末时地中海西部地区强劲猛烈的东风。

as between their fellows, whether their fellows are in politic function or in ordinary occupation. They have a right to the fruits of their industry, and to the means of making their industry fruitful. They have a right to the acquisitions of their parents, to the nourishment and improvement of their offspring, to instruction in life and to consolation in death. Whatever each man can separately do, without trespassing upon others, he has a right to do for himself; and he has a right to a fair portion of all which society, with all its combinations of skill and force, can do in his favour. In this partnership all men have equal rights; but not to equal things. He that has but five shillings in the partnership has as good a right to it as he that has five hundred pounds has to his larger proportion; but he has not a right to an equal dividend in the product of the joint stock. And as to the share of power, authority, and direction which each individual ought to have in the management of the state, that I must deny to be amongst the direct original rights of man in civil society; for I have in my contemplation the civil social man, and no other. It is a thing to be settled by convention.

If civil society be the offspring of convention, that convention must be its law. That convention must limit and modify all the descriptions of constitution which are formed under it. Every sort of legislative, judicial, or executory power are its creatures. They can have no being in any other state of things; and how can any man claim, under the conventions of civil society, rights which do not so much as suppose its existence? Rights which are absolutely repugnant to it? One of the first motives to civil society, and which becomes one of its fundamental rules, is *that no man should be judge in his own cause*. By this each person has at once divested himself of the first fundamental right of uncovenanted man, that is, to judge for himself, and to assert his own cause. He abdicates all right to be his own governor. He inclusively, in a great measure, abandons the right of self-defence, the first law of Nature. Men cannot enjoy the rights of an uncivil and of a civil state together. That he may obtain justice, he gives up his right of determining what it is in points the most essential to him. That he may secure some liberty, he makes a surrender in trust of the whole of it.

Government is not made in virtue of natural rights, which may and do exist in total independence of it; and exist in much greater clearness, and in a much greater degree of abstract perfection: but their abstract perfection is their practical defect. By having a right to everything they want everything. Government is a contrivance of human wisdom to provide for human *wants*. Men have a right that these wants should be provided for by this wisdom. Among these wants is to be reckoned the want, out of civil society, of a sufficient restraint upon their passions. Society requires not only that the passions of individuals should be subjected, but that even in the mass and body, as well as in the individuals, the inclinations of men should frequently be thwarted, their will controlled, and their passions brought into subjection. This can only be done *by a power out of themselves;* and not, in the exercise of its function, subject to that will and to those passions which it is its office to bridle and subdue. In this sense the restraints on men, as well as their liberties, are to be reckoned among their rights. But as the liberties and the restrictions vary with times and circumstances, and admit of infinite modifications, they cannot be settled upon any abstract rule; and nothing is so foolish as to discuss them upon that principle.

The moment you abate anything from the full rights of men each to govern himself, and suffer any artificial, positive limitation upon those rights, from that moment the whole organization of government becomes a consideration of convenience. This it is which makes the constitution of a state, and the due distribution of its powers, a matter of the most delicate and complicated skill. It requires a deep knowledge of human nature and human necessities, and of the things which facilitate or obstruct the various ends which are to be pursued by the mechanism of civil institutions. The state is to have recruits to its strength and remedies to its distempers. What is the use of discussing a man's abstract right to food or medicine? The question is upon the method of procuring and administering them. In that deliberation I shall always advise to call in the aid of the farmer and the physician, rather than the professor of metaphysics.

The science of constructing a commonwealth, or renovating it, or reforming it, is, like every other experimental science, not to be taught *a priori*[1]. Nor is it a short experience that can instruct us in that practical science; because the real effects of moral causes are not always immediate, but that which in the first instance is prejudicial may be excellent in its remoter operation, and its excellence may arise even from the ill effects it produces in the beginning. The reverse also happens; and very plausible schemes, with very pleasing commencements, have often shameful and lamentable conclusions. In states there are often some obscure and almost latent causes, things which appear at first view of little moment, on which a very great part of its prosperity or adversity may most essentially depend. The science of government being, therefore, so practical in itself, and intended for such practical purposes, a matter which requires experience, and even more experience than any person can gain in his whole life, however sagacious[2] and observing he may be, it is with infinite caution that any man ought to venture upon pulling down an edifice which has answered in any tolerable degree for ages the common purposes of society, or on building it up again without having models and patterns of approved utility before his eyes.

These metaphysic rights entering into common life, like rays of light which pierce into a dense medium, are, by the laws of Nature, refracted from their straight line. Indeed, in the gross and complicated mass of human passions and concerns, the primitive rights of men

---

1. *a priori*：〈拉〉先验（的）
2. sagacious：睿智的，有洞察力的

undergo such a variety of refractions and reflections that it becomes absurd to talk of them as if they continued in the simplicity of their original direction. The nature of man is intricate; the objects of society are of the greatest possible complexity: and therefore no simple disposition or direction of power can be suitable either to man's nature or to the quality of his affairs. When I hear the simplicity of contrivance aimed at and boasted of in any new political constitutions, I am at no loss to decide that the artificers are grossly ignorant of their trade or totally negligent of their duty. The simple governments are fundamentally defective, to say no worse of them. If you were to contemplate society in but one point of view, all these simple modes of polity are infinitely captivating. In effect each would answer its single end much more perfectly than the more complex is able to attain all its complex purposes. But it is better that the whole, should be imperfectly and anomalously answered than that while some parts are provided for with great exactness, others might be totally neglected, or perhaps materially injured, by the over-care of a favourite member.

The pretended rights of these theorists are all extremes; and in proportion as they are metaphysically true, they are morally and politically false. The rights of men are in a sort of *middle*, incapable of definition, but not impossible to be discerned. The rights of men in governments are their advantages; and these are often in balances between differences of good; in compromises sometimes between good and evil, and sometimes between evil and evil. Political reason is a computing principle: adding, subtracting, multiplying, and dividing, morally, and not metaphysically or mathematically, true moral denominations.

By these theorists the right of the people is almost always sophistically confounded with their power. The body of the community, whenever it can come to act, can meet with no effectual resistance; but till power and right are the same, the whole body of them has no right inconsistent with virtue, and the first of all virtues, prudence. Men have no right to what is not reasonable, and to what is not for their benefit; for though a pleasant writer said, *"Liceat perire poetis,"* when one of them, in cold blood, is said to have leaped into the flames of a volcanic revolution, *"ardentem frigidus Ætnam insiluit,"* [1] I consider such a frolic rather as an unjustifiable poetic license than as one of the franchises of Parnassus[2]; and whether he were poet, or divine, or politician, that chose to exercise this kind of right, I think that more wise, because more charitable, thoughts would urge me rather to save the man than to preserve his brazen slippers as the monuments of his folly.

* * * * *

The kind of anniversary sermons to which a great part of what I write refers, if men are not shamed out of their present course, in commemorating the fact, will cheat many out of the principles and deprive them of the benefits of the Revolution they commemorate. I confess to you, Sir, I never liked this continual talk of resistance and revolution, or the practice of making the extreme medicine of the constitution its daily bread. It renders the habit of society dangerously valetudinary; it is taking periodical doses of mercury sublimate, and swallowing down repeated provocatives of cantharides[3] to our love of liberty.

This distemper of remedy, grown habitual, relaxes and wears out, by a vulgar and prostituted use, the spring of that spirit which is

---

1. *"Liceat perire poetis ... ardentem frigidus Ætnam insiluit."*: 〈拉〉这两段文字引自古罗马著名诗人贺拉斯（前 65—前 8）的《诗艺》。译成英文的大意是：Let poets have the right to perish if they please ... the cool-headed man [Empedocles] jumped into fiery Etna。
2. Parnassus：诗坛；帕纳塞斯山（位于希腊中部，古时被认为是太阳神和文艺女神们的灵地）。
3. cantharides：斑蝥，被认为可以用作利尿药。

to be exerted on great occasions. It was in the most patient period of Roman servitude that themes of tyrannicide made the ordinary exercise of boys at school — *cum perimit sævos classis numerosa tyrannos.*[1] In the ordinary state of things, it produces in a country like ours the worst effects, even on the cause of that liberty which it abuses with the dissoluteness of an extravagant speculation. Almost all the high-bred republicans of my time have, after a short space, become the most decided, thorough-paced courtiers; they soon left the business of a tedious, moderate, but practical resistance, to those of us whom, in the pride and intoxication of their theories, they have slighted as not much better than Tories[2]. Hypocrisy, of course, delights in the most sublime speculations; for, never intending to go beyond speculation, it costs nothing to have it magnificent. But even in cases where rather levity than fraud was to be suspected in these ranting speculations, the issue has been much the same. These professors, finding their extreme principles not applicable to cases which call only for a qualified, or, as I may say, civil and legal resistance, in such cases employ no resistance at all. It is with them a war or a revolution, or it is nothing. Finding their schemes of politics not adapted to the state of the world in which they live, they often come to think lightly of all public principle, and are ready, on their part, to abandon for a very trivial interest what they find of very trivial value. Some, indeed, are of more steady and persevering natures; but these are eager politicians out of parliament, who have little to tempt them to abandon their favourite projects. They have some change in the church or state, or both, constantly in their view. When that is the case, they are always bad citizens, and perfectly unsure connections. For, considering their speculative designs as of infinite value, and the actual arrangement of the state as of no

---

1. *cum perimit ... tyrannos*：〈拉〉引自古罗马诗人尤维纳利斯的《讽刺诗集》。英文的大意是：While a crowded class kills savage tyrants。
2. Tories：英国托利派；保守党

estimation, they are, at best, indifferent about it. They see no merit in the good, and no fault in the vicious management of public affairs; they rather rejoice in the latter, as more propitious to revolution. They see no merit or demerit in any man, or any action, or any political principle, any further than as they may forward or retard their design of change; they therefore take up, one day, the most violent and stretched prerogative, and another time the wildest democratic ideas of freedom, and pass from the one to the other without any sort of regard to cause, to person, or to party.

In France you are now in the crisis of a revolution, and in the transit from one form of government to another — you cannot see that character of men exactly in the same situation in which we see it in this country. With us it is militant, with you it is triumphant; and you know how it can act, when its power is commensurate to its will. I would not be supposed to confine those observations to any description of men, or to comprehend all men of any description within them — No, far from it! I am as incapable of that injustice as I am of keeping terms with those who profess principles of extremes, and who, under the name of religion, teach little else than wild and dangerous politics. The worst of these politics of revolution is this: they temper and harden the breast, in order to prepare it for the desperate strokes which are sometimes used in extreme occasions. But as these occasions may never arrive, the mind receives a gratuitous taint; and the moral sentiments suffer not a little, when no political purpose is served by the depravation. This sort of people are so taken up with their theories about the rights of man, that they have totally forgot his nature. Without opening one new avenue to the understanding, they have succeeded in stopping up those that lead to the heart. They have perverted in themselves, and in those that attend to them, all the well-placed sympathies of the human breast.

This famous sermon of the Old Jewry breathes nothing but this spirit through all the political part. Plots, massacres, assassinations, seem to some people a trivial price for obtaining a revolution. A cheap, bloodless reformation, a guiltless liberty, appear flat and vapid to their taste. There must be a great change of scene; there must be a magnificent stage effect; there must be a grand spectacle to rouse the imagination, grown torpid with the lazy enjoyment of sixty years' security, and the still unanimating repose of public prosperity. The preacher found them all in the French Revolution. This inspires a juvenile warmth through his whole frame. His enthusiasm kindles as he advances; and when he arrives at his peroration[1], it is in a full blaze. Then viewing, from the Pisgah[2] of his pulpit, the free, moral, happy, flourishing, and glorious state of France, as in a bird-eye landscape of a promised land, he breaks out into the following rapture:

"What an eventful period is this! I am *thankful* that I have lived to it; I could almost say, *Lord, now lettest thou thy servant depart in peace, for mine eyes have seen thy salvation.* — I have lived to see a *diffusion* of knowledge which has undermined superstition and error. — I have lived to see the *rights of men* better understood than ever, and nations panting for liberty which seemed to have lost the idea of it. — I have lived to see *Thirty Millions of People*, indignant and resolute, spurning at slavery, and demanding liberty with an irresistible voice. *Their King led in triumph, and an arbitrary monarch surrendering himself to his subjects.*"

Before I proceed further, I have to remark that Dr. Price seems rather to overvalue the great acquisitions of light which he has obtained and diffused in this age. The last century appears to me to have been quite as much enlightened. It had, though in a different place, a triumph as memorable as that of Dr. Price; and some of the great preachers of that period partook of it as eagerly as he has done in the triumph of France. On the trial of the Rev. Hugh Peters for

---

1. peroration：演讲的结束语
2. Pisgah：毗斯迦山（在现今的约旦附近）。《圣经》上说，摩西就是站在那儿的山顶首次眺望迦南。

high treason, it was deposed, that, when King Charles was brought to London for his trial[1], the Apostle of Liberty in that day conducted the *triumph.* "I saw," says the witness, "his Majesty in the coach with six horses, and Peters riding before the king *triumphing.*" Dr. Price, when he talks as if he had made a discovery, only follows a precedent; for, after the commencement of the king's trial, this precursor, the same Dr. Peters, concluding a long prayer at the royal chapel at Whitehall, (he had very triumphantly chosen his place) said, "I have prayed and preached these twenty years; and now I may say with old Simeon, *Lord, now lettest thou thy servant depart in peace, for mine eyes have seen thy salvation.*" Peters had not the fruits of his prayer; for he neither departed so soon as he wished, nor in peace. He became (what I heartily hope none of his followers may be in this country) himself a sacrifice to the triumph which he led as pontiff. They dealt at the Restoration[2], perhaps, too hardly with this poor good man. But we owe it to his memory and his sufferings, that he had as much illumination and as much zeal, and had as effectually undermined all *the superstition and error* which might impede the great business he was engaged in, as any who follow and repeat after him in this age, which would assume to itself an exclusive title to the knowledge of the rights of men, and all the glorious consequences of that knowledge.

After this sally of the preacher of the Old Jewry, which differs only in place and time, but agrees perfectly with the spirit and letter of the rapture of 1648, the Revolution Society, the fabricators of governments, the heroic band of *cashierers* of *monarchs*[3], electors of sovereigns, and leaders of kings in triumph, strutting with a proud

---

1. King Charles … for his trial：指英格兰国王查理一世因叛国罪受审并被判处死刑一事。
2. the Restoration：〈英史〉王政复辟。指克伦威尔死后，斯图亚特王朝卷土重来，把查理一世流亡在法国的长子接回英伦，并于 1660 年加冕为王，即查理二世。
3. *cashierers* of *monarchs*：君主制的废除者

consciousness of the diffusion of knowledge, of which every member had obtained so large a share in the donative, were in haste to make a generous diffusion of the knowledge they had thus gratuitously received. To make this bountiful communication, they adjourned from the church in the Old Jewry to the London Tavern, where the same Dr. Price, in whom the fumes of his oracular tripod were not entirely evaporated, moved and carried the resolution, or address of congratulation, transmitted by Lord Stanhope to the National Assembly of France.

I find a preacher of the Gospel profaning the beautiful and prophetic ejaculation, commonly called *"Nunc dimittis[1],"* made on the first presentation of our Saviour in the temple, and applying it, with an inhuman and unnatural rapture, to the most horrid, atrocious, and afflicting spectacle that perhaps ever was exhibited to the pity and indignation of mankind. This *"leading in triumph,"* a thing in its best form unmanly and irreligious, which fills our preacher with such unhallowed transports, must shock, I believe, the moral taste of every well-born mind. Several English were the stupefied and indignant spectators of that triumph. It was (unless we have been strangely deceived) a spectacle more resembling a procession of American savages entering into Onondaga[2] after some of their murders called victories, and leading into hovels hung round with scalps their captives overpowered with the scoffs and buffets of women as ferocious as themselves, much more than it resembled the triumphal pomp of a civilized martial nation; — if a civilized nation, or any men who had a sense of generosity, were capable of a personal triumph over the fallen and afflicted.

This, my dear Sir, was not the triumph of France. I must believe,

---

1. *"Nunc dimittis"*：〈拉〉"西蒙歌"。公元 4 世纪以来此曲一直被基督教教会用作晚间祈祷时的颂歌。
2. Onondaga：在安大略湖南部布道的耶稣会使团

that, as a nation, it overwhelmed you with shame and horror. I must believe that the National Assembly find themselves in a state of the greatest humiliation in not being able to punish the authors of this triumph or the actors in it, and that they are in a situation in which any inquiry they may make upon the subject must be destitute even of the appearance of liberty or impartiality. The apology of that assembly is found in their situation; but when we approve what they *must* bear, it is in us the degenerate choice of a vitiated mind.

With a compelled appearance of deliberation, they vote under the dominion of a stern necessity. They sit in the heart, as it were, of a foreign republic: they have their residence in a city whose constitution has emanated neither from the charter of their king nor from their legislative power. There they are surrounded by an army not raised either by the authority of their crown or by their command, and which, if they should order to dissolve itself, would instantly dissolve them. There they sit, after a gang of assassins had driven away some hundreds of the members[1]; whilst those who held the same moderate principles, with more patience or better hope, continued every day exposed to outrageous insults and murderous threats. There a majority, sometimes real, sometimes pretended, captive itself, compels a captive king to issue as royal edicts, at third hand, the polluted nonsense of their most licentious and giddy coffee-houses. It is notorious that all their measures are decided before they are debated. It is beyond doubt, that, under the terror of the bayonet, and the lamp-post, and the torch to their houses, they are obliged to adopt all the crude and desperate measures suggested by clubs composed of a monstrous medley of all conditions, tongues, and nations. Among these are found persons in comparison of whom Catiline would be

---

1. hundreds of the members: 指到 1789 年 10 月，因国民议会嘈杂纷乱的公开辩论，无休无止的请愿，以及以代表身份作陈词所带来的压力，有近 300 名国民议会的代表提出了辞呈。

thought scrupulous, and Cethegus[1] a man of sobriety and moderation. Nor is it in these clubs alone that the public measures are deformed into monsters. They undergo a previous distortion in academies, intended as so many seminaries for these clubs, which are set up in all the places of public resort. In these meetings of all sorts, every counsel, in proportion as it is daring and violent and perfidious, is taken for the mark of superior genius. Humanity and compassion are ridiculed as the fruits of superstition and ignorance. Tenderness to individuals is considered as treason to the public. Liberty is always to be estimated perfect as property is rendered insecure. Amidst assassination, massacre, and confiscation, perpetrated or meditated, they are forming plans for the good order of future society. Embracing in their arms the carcasses of base criminals, and promoting their relations on the title of their offences, they drive hundreds of virtuous persons to the same end, by forcing them to subsist by beggary or by crime.

The Assembly, their organ, acts before them the farce of deliberation with as little decency as liberty. They act like the comedians of a fair, before a riotous audience; they act amidst the tumultuous cries of a mixed mob of ferocious men, and of women lost to shame, who, according to their insolent fancies, direct, control, applaud, explode them, and sometimes mix and take their seats amongst them; domineering over them with a strange mixture of servile petulance and proud, presumptuous authority. As they have inverted order in all things, the gallery is in the place of the house. This Assembly, which overthrows kings and kingdoms, has not even the physiognomy and aspect of a grave legislative body — *nec color imperii, nec frons*

---

1. Catiline ... Cethegus：喀提林（Lucius Sergius Catiline，前 108—前 62），在罗马共和国末期企图发动武装政变，计划败露后被杀；西第古斯（Publius Cornelius Cethegus，生卒不详）是公元前 1 世纪古罗马的另一位擅长阴谋诡计的政客。

erat ulla senatûs.[1] They have a power given to them, like that of the evil principle, to subvert and destroy; but none to construct, except such machines as may be fitted for further subversion and further destruction.

Who is it that admires, and from the heart is attached to national representative assemblies, but must turn with horror and disgust from such a profane burlesque and abominable perversion of that sacred institute? Lovers of monarchy, lovers of republics, must alike abhor it. The members of your Assembly must themselves groan under the tyranny of which they have all the shame, none of the direction, and little of the profit. I am sure many of the members who compose even the majority of that body must feel as I do, notwithstanding the applauses of the Revolution Society. — Miserable king! miserable Assembly! How must that assembly be silently scandalized with those of their members who could call a day which seemed to blot the sun out of Heaven, "*un beau jour!*" [2] How must they be inwardly indignant at hearing others who thought fit to declare to them, "that the vessel of the state would fly forward in her course towards regeneration with more speed than ever," from the stiff gale of treason and murder which preceded our preacher's triumph! What must they have felt, whilst, with outward patience and inward indignation, they heard of the slaughter of innocent gentlemen in their houses, that "the blood spilled was not the most pure!" What must they have felt, when they were besieged by complaints of disorders which shook their country to its foundations, at being compelled coolly to tell the complainants that they were under the protection of the law, and that they would

---

1. *nec color imperii, nec frons erat ulla senatûs*：〈拉〉引自罗马诗人卢坎（Lucan, 39—65）最著名的史诗《法沙利亚》。英文的大意是：nor will there be the external form of government nor any appearance of a legislative authority。
2. "*un beau jour*"：〈法〉美好的一天。此处指 1789 年 10 月 6 日。那天清晨，数百名饥肠辘辘的法国男女平民有史以来首次涌入凡尔赛宫，迫使路易十六当晚搬出了作为王宫的凡尔赛宫。

address the king (the captive king) to cause the laws to be enforced for their protection, when the enslaved ministers of that captive king had formally notified to them that there were neither law nor authority nor power left to protect! What must they have felt at being obliged, as a felicitation on the present new year, to request their captive king to forget the stormy period of the last, on account of the great good which *he* was likely to produce to his people; to the complete attainment of which good they adjourned the practical demonstrations of their loyalty, assuring him of their obedience when he should no longer possess any authority to command!

This address was made with much good-nature and affection, to be sure. But among the revolutions in France must be reckoned a considerable revolution in their ideas of politeness. In England we are said to learn manners at second-hand from your side of the water, and that we dress our behaviour in the frippery of France. If so, we are still in the old cut, and have not so far conformed to the new Parisian mode of good breeding as to think it quite in the most refined strain of delicate compliment (whether in condolence or congratulation) to say, to the most humiliated creature that crawls upon the earth, that great public benefits are derived from the murder of his servants, the attempted assassination of himself and of his wife, and the mortification, disgrace, and degradation that he has personally suffered. It is a topic of consolation which our ordinary of Newgate[1] would be too humane to use to a criminal at the foot of the gallows. I should have thought that the hangman of Paris, now that he is liberalized by the vote of the National Assembly, and is allowed his rank and arms in the Herald's College of the rights of men, would be too generous, too gallant a man, too full of the sense of his new dignity, to employ that cutting consolation to any of the persons whom

---

1. ordinary of Newgate：（位于伦敦西门著名的）纽盖特监狱的神职人员

the *lèze-nation*[1] might bring under the administration of his *executive powers.*

A man is fallen indeed, when he is thus flattered. The anodyne draught of oblivion, thus drugged, is well calculated to preserve a galling wakefulness, and to feed the living ulcer of a corroding memory. Thus to administer the opiate potion of amnesty, powdered with all the ingredients of scorn and contempt, is to hold to his lips, instead of "the balm of hurt minds," the cup of human misery full to the brim, and to force him to drink it to the dregs.

Yielding to reasons, at least as forcible as those which were so delicately urged in the compliment on the new year, the king of France will probably endeavour to forget these events and that compliment. But history, who keeps a durable record of all our acts, and exercises her awful censure over the proceedings of all sorts of sovereigns, will not forget either those events, or the era of this liberal refinement in the intercourse of mankind. History will record, that, on the morning of the 6th of October 1789, the king and queen of France, after a day of confusion, alarm, dismay, and slaughter, lay down, under the pledged security of public faith, to indulge nature in a few hours of respite, and troubled, melancholy repose. From this sleep the queen was first startled by the voice of the sentinel at her door, who cried out to her to save herself by flight — that this was the last proof of fidelity he could give — that they were upon him, and he was dead. Instantly he was cut down. A band of cruel ruffians[2] and assassins, reeking with his blood, rushed into the chamber of the queen, and pierced with a hundred strokes of bayonets and poniards[3] the bed, from whence this persecuted woman had but just time to fly almost naked, and through

---

1. *lèze-nation*：冒犯国家罪。按照英国的法律，"冒犯君主（*lèze majeste*）"等同叛国，作者仿造该词自创"冒犯国家罪"这一罪名。
2. ruffians：恶棍，流氓
3. bayonets and poniards：刺刀和短剑

ways unknown to the murderers, had escaped to seek refuge at the feet of a king and husband not secure of his own life for a moment.[1]

This king, to say no more of him, and this queen, and their infant children (who once would have been the pride and hope of a great and generous people) were then forced to abandon the sanctuary of the most splendid palace in the world, which they left swimming in blood, polluted by massacre, and strewed with scattered limbs and mutilated carcasses. Thence they were conducted into the capital of their kingdom. Two had been selected from the unprovoked, unresisted, promiscuous slaughter which was made of the gentlemen of birth and family who composed the king's body-guard. These two gentlemen, with all the parade of an execution of justice, were cruelly and publicly dragged to the block, and beheaded in the great court of the palace. Their heads were stuck upon spears, and led the procession; whilst the royal captives who followed in the train were slowly moved along, amidst the horrid yells, and shrilling screams, and frantic dances, and infamous contumelies, and all the unutterable abominations of the furies of hell, in the abused shape of the vilest of women. After they had been made to taste, drop by drop, more than the bitterness of death, in the slow torture of a journey of twelve miles, protracted to six hours, they were, under a guard composed of those very soldiers who had thus conducted them through this famous triumph, lodged in one of the old palaces of Paris, now converted into a Bastille[2] for kings.

Is this a triumph to be consecrated at altars, to be commemorated with grateful thanksgiving, to be offered to the divine humanity with fervent prayer and enthusiastic ejaculation? — These Theban and

---

1. History will record ... moment：作者对 10 月 6 日所发生的事件之描述可谓绘声绘色，但后来证明他的说词并不确切。英裔美国思想家、法国革命宣传鼓动家托马斯·潘恩在其《人权》一书中称伯克的叙述为"戏剧性的表演"。
2. Bastille：法国巴黎的巴士底狱

Thracian Orgies[1], acted in France, and applauded only in the Old Jewry, I assure you, kindle prophetic enthusiasm in the minds but of very few people in this kingdom: although a saint and apostle, who may have revelations of his own, and who has so completely vanquished all the mean superstitions of the heart, may incline to think it pious and decorous to compare it with the entrance into the world of the Prince of Peace, proclaimed in an holy temple by a venerable sage, and not long before not worse announced by the voice of angels to the quiet innocence of shepherds.

At first I was at a loss to account for this fit of unguarded transport. I knew, indeed, that the sufferings of monarchs make a delicious repast to some sort of palates. There were reflections which might serve to keep this appetite within some bounds of temperance. But when I took one circumstance into my consideration, I was obliged to confess that much allowance ought to be made for the society, and that the temptation was too strong for common discretion; I mean, the circumstance of the *Io Pæan*[2] of the triumph, the animating cry which called for "*all* the BISHOPS to be hanged on the lamp-posts," might well have brought forth a burst of enthusiasm on the foreseen consequences of this happy day. I allow to so much enthusiasm some little deviation from prudence. I allow this prophet to break forth into hymns of joy and thanksgiving on an event which appears like the precursor of the Millennium, and the projected Fifth Monarchy[3], in the destruction of all church establishments. There was, however (as in all human affairs there is) in the midst of this joy, something to exercise the patience of these worthy gentlemen, and to try the long-

---

1. Theban and Thracian Orgies：古希腊时期的一些宗教狂欢活动
2. *Io Pæan*：爱娥潘，赞美、称颂阿波罗的赞歌。英语通常称为"胜利之歌"。
3. Fifth Monarchy：第五王国，又称千年王国，其信徒为 17 世纪英国清教徒中最激进的一派。

suffering of their faith. The actual murder of the king and queen, and their child, was wanting to the other auspicious circumstances of this "*beautiful day*." The actual murder of the bishops, though called for by so many holy ejaculations, was also wanting. A group of regicide and sacrilegious slaughter was indeed boldly sketched, but it was only sketched. It unhappily was left unfinished, in this great history-piece of the massacre of innocents. What hardy pencil of a great master, from the school of the rights of men, will finish it, is to be seen hereafter. The age has not yet the complete benefit of that diffusion of knowledge that has undermined superstition and error; and the king of France wants another object or two to consign to oblivion, in consideration of all the good which is to arise from his own sufferings, and the patriotic crimes of an enlightened age.

Although this work of our new light and knowledge did not go to the length that in all probability it was intended it should be carried, yet I must think that such treatment of any human creatures must be shocking to any but those who are made for accomplishing revolutions. But I cannot stop here. Influenced by the inborn feelings of my nature, and not being illuminated by a single ray of this new-sprung modern light, I confess to you, Sir, that the exalted rank of the persons suffering, and particularly the sex, the beauty, and the amiable qualities of the descendant of so many kings and emperors, with the tender age of royal infants, insensible only through infancy and innocence of the cruel outrages to which their parents were exposed, instead of being a subject of exultation, adds not a little to my sensibility on that most melancholy occasion.

I hear that the august person who was the principal object of our preacher's triumph, though he supported himself, felt much on that shameful occasion. As a man, it became him to feel for his wife and his children, and the faithful guards of his person that were massacred in cold blood about him; as a prince, it became him to feel for the strange and frightful transformation of his civilized subjects, and to be more grieved for them than solicitous for himself. It derogates little from his fortitude, while it adds infinitely to the honour of his humanity. I am very sorry to say it, very sorry indeed, that such personages are in a situation in which it is not unbecoming in us to praise the virtues of the great.

I hear, and I rejoice to hear, that the great lady, the other object of the triumph, has borne that day (one is interested that beings made for suffering should suffer well) and that she bears all the succeeding days, that she bears the imprisonment of her husband, and her own captivity, and the exile of her friends, and the insulting adulation of addresses, and the whole weight of her accumulated wrongs, with a serene patience, in a manner suited to her rank and race, and becoming the offspring of a sovereign distinguished for her piety and her courage; that, like her, she has lofty sentiments; that she feels with the dignity of a Roman matron; that in the last extremity she will save herself from the last disgrace; and that, if she must fall, she will fall by no ignoble hand.

It is now sixteen or seventeen years since I saw the queen of France, then the dauphiness[1], at Versailles[2]; and surely never lighted on this orb, which she hardly seemed to touch, a more delightful vision. I saw her just above the horizon, decorating and cheering the elevated sphere she just began to move in, — glittering like the morning-star, full of life and splendour and joy. Oh! what a revolution! and what an heart must I have, to contemplate without emotion that elevation and that fall! Little did I dream, when she added titles of veneration to those of enthusiastic, distant, respectful love, that she should ever be obliged to carry the sharp antidote against disgrace concealed in that bosom! Little did I dream that I should have lived to see such disasters fallen upon her in a nation of gallant men, in a nation of men

---

1. dauphiness：法国王太子妃
2. Versailles：凡尔赛（法国城市），法国王宫所在地。

of honour, and of cavaliers! I thought ten thousand swords must have leaped from their scabbards to avenge even a look that threatened her with insult. — But the age of chivalry is gone. — That of sophisters, economists, and calculators has succeeded; and the glory of Europe is extinguished forever. Never, never more, shall we behold that generous loyalty to rank and sex, that proud submission, that dignified obedience, that subordination of the heart, which kept alive, even in servitude itself, the spirit of an exalted freedom! The unbought grace of life, the cheap defence of nations, the nurse of manly sentiment and heroic enterprise, is gone! It is gone, that sensibility of principle, that chastity of honour, which felt a stain like a wound, which inspired courage whilst it mitigated ferocity, which ennobled whatever it touched, and under which vice itself lost half its evil by losing all its grossness!

This mixed system of opinion and sentiment had its origin in the ancient chivalry; and the principle, though varied in its appearance by the varying state of human affairs, subsisted and influenced through a long succession of generations, even to the time we live in. If it should ever be totally extinguished, the loss, I fear, will be great. It is this which has given its character to modern Europe. It is this which has distinguished it under all its forms of government, and distinguished it to its advantage, from the states of Asia, and possibly from those states which flourished in the most brilliant periods of the antique world. It was this, which, without confounding ranks, had produced a noble equality, and handed it down through all the gradations of social life. It was this opinion which mitigated kings into companions, and raised private men to be fellows with kings. Without force or opposition, it subdued the fierceness of pride and power; it obliged sovereigns to submit to the soft collar of social esteem, compelled stern authority to submit to elegance, and gave a domination vanquisher of laws, to be subdued by manners.

But now all is to be changed. All the pleasing illusions which made power gentle and obedience liberal, which harmonized the different shades of life, and which by a bland assimilation incorporated into politics the sentiments which beautify and soften private society, are to be dissolved by this new conquering empire of light and reason. All the decent drapery of life is to be rudely torn off. All the superadded ideas, furnished from the wardrobe of a moral imagination, which the heart owns and the understanding ratifies, as necessary to cover the defects of our naked, shivering nature, and to raise it to dignity in our own estimation, are to be exploded, as a ridiculous, absurd, and antiquated fashion.

On this scheme of things, a king is but a man; a queen is but a woman; a woman is but an animal; and an animal not of the highest order. All homage paid to the sex in general as such, and without distinct views, is to be regarded as romance and folly. Regicide, and parricide, and sacrilege, are but fictions of superstition, corrupting jurisprudence by destroying its simplicity. The murder of a king, or a queen, or a bishop, or a father, are only common homicide; and if the people are by any chance or in any way gainers by it, a sort of homicide much the most pardonable, and into which we ought not to make too severe a scrutiny.

On the scheme of this barbarous philosophy, which is the offspring of cold hearts and muddy understandings and which is as void of solid wisdom as it is destitute of all taste and elegance, laws are to be supported only by their own terrors, and by the concern which each individual may find in them from his own private speculations, or can spare to them from his own private interests. In the groves of *their* academy, at the end of every vista, you see nothing but the gallows. Nothing is left which engages the affections on the part of the commonwealth. On the principles of this mechanic philosophy, our institutions can never be embodied, if I may use the expression, in persons; so as to create in us love, veneration, admiration, or attachment. But that sort of reason which banishes the affections is incapable of filling their place. These public affections, combined with manners, are required sometimes as supplements, sometimes as correctives, always as aids to law. The precept given by a wise man, as well as a great critic, for the construction of poems, is equally true as to states. *Non satis est pulchra esse poemata, dulcia sunto.*[1] There ought to be a system of manners in every nation which a well-formed mind would be disposed to relish. To make us love our country, our country ought to be lovely.

But power, of some kind or other, will survive the shock in which manners and opinions perish; and it will find other and worse means for its support. The usurpation, which, in order to subvert ancient institutions, has destroyed ancient principles, will hold power by arts similar to those by which it has acquired it. When the old feudal and chivalrous spirit of *Fealty*, which, by freeing kings from fear, freed both kings and subjects from the precautions of tyranny, shall be extinct in the minds of men, plots and assassinations will be anticipated by preventive murder and preventive confiscation, and that long roll of grim and bloody maxims which form the political code of all power not standing on its own honour and the honour of those who are to obey it. Kings will be tyrants from policy, when subjects are rebels from principle.

When ancient opinions and rules of life are taken away, the loss cannot possibly be estimated. From that moment we have no compass to govern us, nor can we know distinctly to what port we steer. Europe, undoubtedly, taken in a mass, was in a flourishing condition the day on which your Revolution was completed. How much of that prosperous state was owing to the spirit of our old manners and opinions is not easy to say; but as such causes cannot be indifferent in their operation, we must presume, that, on the whole, their operation

---

1. *Non satis ... dulcia sunto.* 〈拉〉引自贺拉斯的《诗艺》，译成英文的大意是：
It is not enough for poems to be beautiful; they must also be sweet。

was beneficial.

We are but too apt to consider things in the state in which we find them, without sufficiently adverting to the causes by which they have been produced, and possibly may be upheld. Nothing is more certain than that our manners, our civilization, and all the good things which are connected with manners and with, civilization, have, in this European world of ours, depended for ages upon two principles, and were indeed the result of both combined: I mean the spirit of a gentleman, and the spirit of religion. The nobility and the clergy, the one by profession, and the other by patronage, kept learning in existence, even in the midst of arms and confusions, and whilst governments were rather in their causes than formed. Learning paid back what it received to nobility and to priesthood, and paid it with usury, by enlarging their ideas, and by furnishing their minds. Happy, if they had all continued to know their indissoluble union, and their proper place! Happy, if learning, not debauched[1] by ambition, had been satisfied to continue the instructor, and not aspired to be the master! Along with its natural protectors and guardians, learning will be cast into the mire and trodden down under the hoofs of a swinish multitude.

If, as I suspect, modern letters owe more than they are always willing to own to ancient manners, so do other interests which we value full as much as they are worth. Even commerce, and trade, and manufacture, the gods of our economical politicians, are themselves perhaps but creatures; are themselves but effects, which, as first causes, we choose to worship. They certainly grew under the same shade in which learning flourished. They, too, may decay with their natural protecting principles. With you, for the present at least, they all threaten to disappear together. Where trade and manufactures are wanting to

---

1. debauched: 堕落的

a people, and the spirit of nobility and religion remains, sentiment supplies, and not always ill supplies, their place; but if commerce and the arts should be lost in an experiment to try how well a state may stand without these old fundamental principles, what sort of a thing must be a nation of gross, stupid, ferocious, and at the same time poor and sordid barbarians, destitute of religion, honour, or manly pride, possessing nothing at present, and hoping for nothing hereafter?

I wish you may not be going fast, and by the shortest cut, to that horrible and disgustful situation. Already there appears a poverty of conception, a coarseness and vulgarity in all the proceedings of the Assembly and of all their instructors. Their liberty is not liberal. Their science is presumptuous ignorance. Their humanity is savage and brutal.

It is not clear whether in England we learned those grand and decorous principles and manners, of which considerable traces yet remain, from you, or whether you took them from us. But to you, I think, we trace them best. You seem to me to be – *gentis incunabula nostræ.*[1] France has always more or less influenced manners in England; and when your fountain is choked up and polluted, the stream will not run long or not run clear with us, or perhaps with any nation. This gives all Europe, in my opinion, but too close and connected a concern in what is done in France. Excuse me, therefore, if I have dwelt too long on the atrocious spectacle of the 6th of October 1789, or have given too much scope to the reflections which have arisen in my mind on occasion of the most important of all revolutions, which may be dated from that day: I mean a revolution in sentiments, manners, and moral opinions. As things now stand, with everything respectable destroyed without us, and an attempt to destroy within us every principle of respect, one is almost forced to apologize for harbouring

---

1. *gentis incunabula nostræ*：〈拉〉引自维吉尔的名作《埃涅阿斯记》。英文的大意是：the cradle of our people。

the common feelings of men.

* * * * *

Why do I feel so differently from the Reverend Dr. Price, and those of his lay flock who will choose to adopt the sentiments of his discourse? — For this plain reason — because it is *natural* I should; because we are so made as to be affected at such spectacles with melancholy sentiments upon the unstable condition of mortal prosperity, and the tremendous uncertainty of human greatness; because in those natural feelings we learn great lessons; because in events like these our passions instruct our reason; because when kings are hurled from their thrones by the Supreme Director of this great drama, and become the objects of insult to the base and of pity to the good, we behold such disasters in the moral as we should behold a miracle in the physical order of things. We are alarmed into reflection; our minds (as it has long since been observed) are purified by terror and pity; our weak, unthinking pride is humbled under the dispensations of a mysterious wisdom. Some tears might be drawn from me, if such a spectacle were exhibited on the stage. I should be truly ashamed of finding in myself that superficial, theatric sense of painted distress, whilst I could exult over it in real life. With such a perverted mind, I could never venture to show my face at a tragedy. People would think the tears that Garrick formerly, or that Siddons[1] not long since, have extorted from me, were the tears of hypocrisy; I should know them to be the tears of folly.

Indeed, the theatre is a better school of moral sentiments than churches where the feelings of humanity are thus outraged. Poets

---

1. Garrick ... Siddons：指大卫·盖里克 (David Garrick, 1717—1779) 和萨拉·西登斯 (Sarah Siddons, 1755—1831)，两人是英国当时很出名的舞台表演艺术家。

who have to deal with an audience not yet graduated in the school of the rights of men, and who must apply themselves to the moral constitution of the heart, would not dare to produce such a triumph as a matter of exultation. There, where men follow their natural impulses, they would not bear the odious maxims of a Machiavellian policy, whether applied to the attainment of monarchical or democratic tyranny. They would reject them on the modern, as they once did on the ancient stage, where they could not bear even the hypothetical proposition of such wickedness in the mouth of a personated tyrant, though suitable to the character he sustained. No theatric audience in Athens would bear what has been borne in the midst of the real tragedy of this triumphal day: a principal actor weighing, as it were in scales hung in a shop of horrors, — so much actual crime against so much contingent advantage, — and after putting in and out weights, declaring that the balance was on the side of the advantages. They would not bear to see the crimes of new democracy posted as in a ledger against the crimes of old despotism, and the book-keepers of politics finding democracy still in debt, but by no means unable or unwilling to pay the balance. In the theatre, the first intuitive glance, without any elaborate process of reasoning, would show that this method of political computation would justify every extent of crime. They would see, that on these principles, even where the very worst acts were not perpetrated, it was owing rather to the fortune of the conspirators than to their parsimony in the expenditure of treachery and blood. They would soon see that criminal means, once tolerated, are soon preferred. They present a shorter cut to the object than through the highway of the moral virtues. Justifying perfidy and murder for public benefit, public benefit would soon become the pretext, and perfidy and murder the end; until rapacity, malice, revenge, and fear more dreadful than revenge, could satiate their insatiable appetites. Such must be the consequences of losing, in the splendour of these triumphs of the rights of men, all natural sense of wrong and right.

But the reverend pastor exults in this "leading in triumph," because, truly, Louis XVI was "an arbitrary monarch" : that is, in other words, neither more nor less than because he was Louis XVI, and because he had the misfortune to be born king of France, with the prerogatives of which a long line of ancestors, and a long acquiescence of the people, without any act of his, had put him in possession. A misfortune it has indeed turned out to him, that he was born king of France. But misfortune is not crime, nor is indiscretion always the greatest guilt. I shall never think that a prince, the acts of whose whole reign were a series of concessions to his subjects, who was willing to relax his authority, to remit his prerogatives, to call his people to a share of freedom not known, perhaps not desired, by their ancestors; such a prince, though he should be subject to the common frailties attached to men and to princes, though he should have once thought it necessary to provide force against the desperate designs manifestly carrying on against his person and the remnants of his authority; though all this should be taken into consideration, I shall be led with great difficulty to think he deserves the cruel and insulting triumph of Paris, and of Dr. Price. I tremble for the cause of liberty, from such an example to kings. I tremble for the cause of humanity, in the unpunished outrages of the most wicked of mankind. But there are some people of that low and degenerate fashion of mind that they look up with a sort of complacent awe and admiration to kings who know to keep firm in their seat, to hold a strict hand over their subjects, to assert their prerogative, and, by the awakened vigilance of a severe despotism, to guard against the very first approaches of freedom. Against such as these they never elevate their voice. Deserters from principle, listed with fortune, they never see any good in suffering virtue, nor any crime in prosperous usurpation.

If it could have been made clear to me that the king and queen of France (those I mean who were such before the triumph) were inexorable and cruel tyrants, that they had formed a deliberate scheme for massacring the National Assembly (I think I have seen something like the latter insinuated in certain publications) I should think their captivity just. If this be true, much more ought to have been done, but done, in my opinion, in another manner. The punishment of real tyrants is a noble and awful act of justice; and it has with truth been said to be consolatory[1] to the human mind. But if I were to punish a wicked king, I should regard the dignity in avenging the crime. Justice is grave and decorous, and in its punishments rather seems to submit to a necessity than to make a choice. Had Nero[2], or Agrippina[3], or Louis XI[4], or Charles IX[5] been the subject, — if Charles XII of Sweden, after the murder of Patkul[6], or his predecessor, Christina, after the murder of Monaldeschi[7], had fallen into your hands, Sir, or into mine, I am sure our conduct would have been different.

If the French King, or King of the French[8], (or by whatever name he is known in the new vocabulary of your Constitution) has in his own person and that of his queen really deserved these unavowed, but unavenged, murderous attempts, and those frequent indignities more cruel than murder, such a person would ill deserve even that

---

1. consolatory: 慰藉；安慰的
2. Nero: 尼禄，罗马皇帝（公元 54—68 年在位）。
3. Agrippina: 尤利亚·维普桑尼亚·阿格里皮娜（15—59），古罗马皇后，尼禄的母亲。
4. Louis XI: 法兰西国王路易十一（1461—1483 年在位）
5. Charles IX: 指法兰西国王查理九世（1560—1574 年在位）
6. Charles ... after the murder of Patkul: 指瑞典国王查理十二以车轮刑处死立陶宛贵族约翰·莱因哈德·冯·帕特克尔（Johann Reinhold Patkul, 1660—1707）一事。
7. Christina, after the murder of Monaldeschi: 指瑞典女王克里斯蒂娜（1632—1654 年在位）处死其情人、意大利贵族吉安·里纳尔多·莫纳尔斯基一事。
8. King of the French: 从 King of France 到 King of the French 之转变应该说具有重大的象征意义，显示法兰西国王事实上与法国人民达成了某种契约，已不仅是拥有国家的君主。

subordinate executory trust which I understand is to be placed in him; nor is he fit to be called chief in a nation which he has outraged and oppressed. A worse choice for such an office in a new commonwealth than that of a deposed tyrant could not possibly be made. But to degrade and insult a man as the worst of criminals, and afterwards to trust him in your highest concerns, as a faithful, honest, and zealous servant, is not consistent in reasoning, nor prudent in policy, nor safe in practice. Those who could make such an appointment must be guilty of a more flagrant breach of trust than any they have yet committed against the people. As this is the only crime in which your leading politicians could have acted inconsistently, I conclude that there is no sort of ground for these horrid insinuations. I think no better of all the other calumnies.

In England, we give no credit to them. We are generous enemies; we are faithful allies. We spurn from us with disgust and indignation the slanders of those who bring us their anecdotes with the attestation of the flower-de-luce on their shoulder.[1] We have Lord George Gordon fast in Newgate;[2] and neither his being a public proselyte to Judaism, nor his having, in his zeal against Catholic priests and all sorts of ecclesiastics, raised a mob (excuse the term, it is still in use here) which pulled down all our prisons, have preserved to him a liberty of which he did not render himself worthy by a virtuous use of it. We have rebuilt Newgate, and tenanted the mansion. We have prisons almost as strong as the Bastille, for those who dare to libel the queens of France.

---

1. flower-de-luce on their shoulder：指肩章上的花瓣纹章。法国王室最先以百合花瓣作为王室纹章，此举后来为欧洲各王族所效仿。
2. We have Lord George Gordon fast in Newgate：乔治·戈登勋爵（Lord George Gordon, 1751—1793），英国新教徒协会会长。1780 年 6 月 2 日他组织 6 万名新教徒来到英国下院，请愿废除 1778 年的《天主教救济法》，结果在伦敦引起反天主教暴乱，焚烧民宅和教堂，袭击监狱和银行，招致国王乔治三世派军队镇压。戈登被捕并在法庭受审，但被判无罪后获释。之后他又因诽谤法国王后被关押，最终死在纽盖特监狱。

In this spiritual retreat let the noble libeller remain. Let him there meditate on his Talmud[1], until he learns a conduct more becoming his birth and parts, and not so disgraceful to the ancient religion to which he has become a proselyte; or until some persons from your side of the water, to please your new Hebrew brethren, shall ransom him. He may then be enabled to purchase, with the old hoards of the synagogue, and a very small poundage, on the long compound interest of the thirty pieces of silver (Dr. Price has shown us what miracles compound interest will perform in 1790 years) the lands which are lately discovered to have been usurped by the Gallican Church[2]. Send us your popish Archbishop of Paris, and we will send you our protestant Rabbin[3]. We shall treat the person you send us in exchange like a gentleman and an honest man, as he is; but pray let him bring with him the fund of his hospitality, bounty, and charity; and, depend upon it, we shall never confiscate a shilling of that honourable and pious fund, nor think of enriching the Treasury with the spoils of the poor-box[4].

To tell you the truth, my dear Sir, I think the honour of our nation to be somewhat concerned in the disclaimer of the proceedings of this society of the Old Jewry and the London Tavern. I have no man's proxy. I speak only from myself, when I disclaim, as I do with all possible earnestness, all communion with the actors in that triumph, or with the admirers of it. When I assert anything else, as concerning the people of England, I speak from observation, not from authority; but I speak from the experience I have had in a pretty extensive and mixed communication with the inhabitants of this kingdom, of all descriptions and ranks, and after a course of attentive observation,

---

1. Talmud：《塔木德》，犹太法典
2. Gallican Church：高卢教会，指法国天主教秉持教会不受梵蒂冈直接领导的自主精神。
3. we will send you our protestant Rabbin：指此时关押在纽盖特监狱、已放弃新教皈依犹太教的戈登。
4. poor-box：（教堂里的济贫）募捐箱

begun in early life, and continued for near forty years. I have often been astonished, considering that we are divided from you but by a slender dike of about twenty-four miles, and that the mutual intercourse between the two countries has lately been very great, to find how little you seem to know of us. I suspect that this is owing to your forming a judgment of this nation from certain publications, which do, very erroneously, if they do at all, represent the opinions and dispositions generally prevalent in England. The vanity, restlessness, petulance, and spirit of intrigue of several petty cabals, who attempt to hide their total want of consequence in bustle and noise, and puffing and mutual quotation of each other, makes you imagine that our contemptuous neglect of their abilities is a general mark of acquiescence in their opinions. No such thing, I assure you. Because half a dozen grasshoppers under a fern make the field ring with their importunate chink, whilst thousands of great cattle reposed beneath the shadow of the British oak chew the cud and are silent, pray do not imagine that those who make the noise are the only inhabitants of the field; that, of course, they are many in number; or that, after all, they are other than the little shrivelled, meagre, hopping, though loud and troublesome insects of the hour.

I almost venture to affirm that not one in a hundred amongst us participates in the "triumph" of the Revolution Society. If the king and queen of France and their children were to fall into our hands by the chance of war, in the most acrimonious of all hostilities (I deprecate such an event, I deprecate such hostility) they would be treated with another sort of triumphal entry into London. We formerly have had a king of France in that situation[1]; you have read how he was treated by the victor in the field, and in what manner he was afterwards received in England. Four hundred years have gone over us;

---

1. a king of France in that situation: 指法兰西国王约翰二世 (Jean II, 1319—1364) 于英法百年战争期间在伦敦被囚一事。

but I believe we are not materially changed since that period. Thanks to our sullen resistance to innovation, thanks to the cold sluggishness of our national character, we still bear the stamp of our forefathers. We have not (as I conceive) lost the generosity and dignity of thinking of the fourteenth century; nor as yet have we subtilized ourselves into savages. We are not the converts of Rousseau[1]; we are not the disciples of Voltaire[2]; Helvetius[3] has made no progress amongst us. Atheists are not our preachers; madmen are not our lawgivers. We know that *we* have made no discoveries, and we think that no discoveries are to be made, in morality; nor many in the great principles of government, nor in the ideas of liberty, which were understood long before we were born altogether as well as they will be after the grave has heaped its mould upon our presumption, and the silent tomb shall have imposed its law on our pert loquacity. In England we have not yet been completely embowelled of our natural entrails; we still feel within us, and we cherish and cultivate, those inbred sentiments which are the faithful guardians, the active monitors of our duty, the true supporters of all liberal and manly morals. We have not been drawn and trussed, in order that we may be filled, like stuffed birds in a museum, with chaff and rags, and paltry, blurred shreds of paper about the rights of man. We preserve the whole of our feelings still native and entire, unsophisticated by pedantry and infidelity. We have real hearts of flesh and blood beating in our bosoms. We fear God; we look up with awe to kings, with affection to parliaments, with duty to magistrates, with reverence to priests, and with respect to nobility. Why? Because, when such ideas are brought before our minds, it is *natural* to be so

---

1. Rousseau：卢梭 (Jean-Jacques Rousseau, 1712—1778)，18 世纪法国启蒙运动代表人物之一。
2. Voltaire：伏尔泰 (François-Marie Arouet, 1694—1778)，法国启蒙思想家、文学家、哲学家。
3. Helvetius：爱尔维修 (Claude Adrien Helvetius, 1715—1771)，法国启蒙思想家、唯物主义哲学家。

affected; because all other feelings are false and spurious, and tend to corrupt our minds, to vitiate our primary morals, to render us unfit for rational liberty; and by teaching us a servile, licentious, and abandoned insolence, to be our low sport for a few holidays, to make us perfectly fit for and justly deserving of slavery through the whole course of our lives.

You see, Sir, that in this enlightened age I am bold enough to confess that we are generally men of untaught feelings; that instead of casting away all our old prejudices, we cherish them to a very considerable degree; and, to take more shame to ourselves, we cherish them because they are prejudices; and the longer they have lasted, and the more generally they have prevailed, the more we cherish them. We are afraid to put men to live and trade each on his own private stock of reason; because we suspect that the stock in each man is small, and that the individuals would do better to avail themselves of the general bank and capital of nations and of ages. Many of our men of speculation, instead of exploding general prejudices, employ their sagacity to discover the latent wisdom which prevails in them. If they find what they seek, and they seldom fail, they think it more wise to continue the prejudice, with the reason involved, than to cast away the coat of prejudice, and to leave nothing but the naked reason; because prejudice, with its reason, has a motive to give action to that reason, and an affection which will give it permanence. Prejudice is of ready application in the emergency; it previously engages the mind in a steady course of wisdom and virtue, and does not leave the man hesitating in the moment of decision, sceptical, puzzled, and unresolved. Prejudice renders a man's virtue his habit, and not a series of unconnected acts. Through just prejudice, his duty becomes a part of his nature.

Your literary men, and your politicians, and so do the whole clan of the enlightened among us, essentially differ in these points. They have no respect for the wisdom of others; but they pay it off by a very full measure of confidence in their own. With them it is a sufficient motive to destroy an old scheme of things, because it is an old one. As to the new, they are in no sort of fear with regard to the duration of a building run up in haste; because duration is no object to those who think little or nothing has been done before their time, and who place all their hopes in discovery. They conceive, very systematically, that all things which give perpetuity are mischievous, and therefore they are at inexpiable[1] war with all establishments. They think that government may vary like modes of dress, and with as little ill effect; that there needs no principle of attachment, except a sense of present conveniency, to any constitution of the state. They always speak as if they were of opinion that there is a singular species of compact between them and their magistrates, which binds the magistrate, but which has nothing reciprocal in it, but that the majesty of the people has a right to dissolve it without any reason but its will. Their attachment to their country itself is only so far as it agrees with some of their fleeting projects: it begins and ends with that scheme of polity which falls in with their momentary opinion.

These doctrines, or rather sentiments, seem prevalent with your new statesmen. But they are wholly different from those on which we have always acted in this country.

I hear it is sometimes given out in France, that what is doing among you is after the example of England. I beg leave to affirm that scarcely anything done with you has originated from the practice or the prevalent opinions of this people, either in the act or in the spirit of the proceeding. Let me add, that we are as unwilling to learn these lessons from France as we are sure that we never taught them to that nation. The cabals here who take a sort of share in your transactions as yet consist of but a handful of people. If, unfortunately, by their

---

1. inexpiable：无法救赎的

intrigues, their sermons, their publications, and by a confidence derived from an expected union with the counsels and forces of the French nation, they should draw considerable numbers into their faction, and in consequence should seriously attempt anything here in imitation of what has been done with you, the event, I dare venture to prophesy, will be, that, with some trouble to their country, they will soon accomplish their own destruction. This people refused to change their law in remote ages from respect to the infallibility of Popes, and they will not now alter it from a pious implicit faith in the dogmatism of philosophers; though the former was armed with the anathema and crusade, and though the latter should act with the libel and the lamp-iron.

Formerly your affairs were your own concern only. We felt for them as men; but we kept aloof from them, because we were not citizens of France. But when we see the model held up to ourselves, we must feel as Englishmen, and feeling, we must provide as Englishmen. Your affairs, in spite of us, are made a part of our interest; so far at least as to keep at a distance your panacea or your plague. If it be a panacea, we do not want it. We know the consequences of unnecessary physic. If it be a plague, it is such a plague that the precautions of the most severe quarantine ought to be established against it.

I hear on all hands that a cabal, calling itself philosophic, receives the glory of many of the late proceedings, and that their opinions and systems are the true actuating spirit of the whole of them. I have heard of no party in England, literary or political, at any time, known by such a description. It is not with you composed of those men, is it? whom the vulgar, in their blunt, homely style, commonly call Atheists and Infidels? If it be, I admit that we too have had writers of that description, who made some noise in their day. At present they repose in lasting oblivion. Who, born within the last forty years, has read one word of Collins, and Toland, and Tindal, and Chubb, and Morgan, and that whole race who called themselves Freethinkers[1]? Who now reads Bolingbroke[2]? Who ever read him through? Ask the booksellers of London what is become of all these lights of the world. In as few years their few successors will go to the family vault of "all the Capulets." [3] But whatever they were, or are, with us they were and are wholly unconnected individuals. With us they kept the common nature of their kind, and were not gregarious. They never acted in corps, nor were known as a faction in the state, nor presumed to influence in that name or character, or for the purposes of such a faction, on any of our public concerns. Whether they ought so to exist, and so be permitted to act, is another question. As such cabals have not existed in England, so neither has the spirit of them had any influence in establishing the original frame of our constitution, or in any one of the several reparations and improvements it has undergone. The whole has been done under the auspices, and is confirmed by the sanctions, of religion and piety. The whole has emanated from the simplicity of our national character, and from a sort of native plainness and directness of understanding, which for a long time characterized those men who have successively obtained authority among us. This disposition still remains, at least in the great body of the people.

We know, and what is better, we feel inwardly, that religion is the basis of civil society, and the source of all good, and of all comfort. In England we are so convinced of this, that there is no rust of superstition, with which the accumulated absurdity of the human mind might have crusted it over in the course of ages, that ninety-nine in a hundred of the people of England would not prefer to impiety. We

---

1. Who ... called themselves Freethinkers：句中提到的那几个人都是自然神论的倡导者。
2. Bolingbroke：博林布鲁克子爵（Henry St John, 1ˢᵗ Viscount Bolingbroke, 1678—1751），英国政治家，1714 年逃到法国，1723 年返回英国。
3. "all the Capulets"："凯普莱特家族的所有人"，见莎士比亚的悲剧《罗密欧和朱丽叶》。

shall never be such fools as to call in an enemy to the substance of any system to remove its corruptions, to supply its defects, or to perfect its construction. If our religious tenets should ever want a further elucidation[1], we shall not call on atheism to explain them. We shall not light up our temple from that unhallowed fire. It will be illuminated with other lights. It will be perfumed with other incense than the infectious stuff which is imported by the smugglers of adulterated metaphysics. If our ecclesiastical establishment should want a revision, it is not avarice or rapacity, public or private, that we shall employ for the audit or receipt or application of its consecrated revenue. Violently condemning neither the Greek nor the Armenian, nor, since heats are subsided, the Roman system of religion, we prefer the Protestant: not because we think it has less of the Christian religion in it, but because, in our judgment, it has more. We are Protestants, not from indifference, but from zeal.

We know, and it is our pride to know, that man is by his constitution a religious animal; that atheism is against, not only our reason, but our instincts; and that it cannot prevail long. But if, in the moment of riot, and in a drunken delirium from the hot spirit drawn out of the alembic of hell, which in France is now so furiously boiling, we should uncover our nakedness, by throwing off that Christian religion which has hitherto been our boast and comfort, and one great source of civilization amongst us, and among many other nations, we are apprehensive (being well aware that the mind will not endure a void) that some uncouth, pernicious, and degrading superstition might take place of it.

For that reason, before we take from our establishment the natural, human means of estimation, and give it up to contempt, as you have done, and in doing it have incurred the penalties you well deserve to

---

1. elucidation: 说明，阐明

suffer, we desire that some other may be presented to us in the place of it. We shall then form our judgment.

On these ideas, instead of quarrelling with establishments, as some do, who have made a philosophy and a religion of their hostility to such institutions, we cleave closely to them. We are resolved to keep an established church, an established monarchy, an established aristocracy, and an established democracy, each in the degree it exists, and in no greater. I shall show you presently how much of each of these we possess.

It has been the misfortune (not as these gentlemen think it, the glory) of this age, that everything is to be discussed, as if the constitution of our country were to be always a subject rather of altercation than enjoyment. For this reason, as well as for the satisfaction of those among you (if any such you have among you) who may wish to profit of examples, I venture to trouble you with a few thoughts upon each of these establishments. I do not think they were unwise in ancient Rome, who, when they wished to new-model their laws, sent commissioners to examine the best-constituted republics within their reach.

* * * * *

First, I beg leave to speak of our church establishment, which is the first of our prejudices, not a prejudice destitute of reason, but involving in it profound and extensive wisdom. I speak of it first. It is first, and last, and midst in our minds. For, taking ground on that religious system of which we are now in possession, we continue to act on the early received and uniformly continued sense of mankind. That sense not only, like a wise architect, hath built up the august fabric of states, but like a provident proprietor, to preserve the structure from profanation and ruin, as a sacred temple, purged from all the impurities of fraud and violence and injustice and tyranny, hath solemnly and forever consecrated the commonwealth, and all that officiate in it. This consecration is made, that all who administer in the government of men, in which they stand in the person of God himself, should have high and worthy notions of their function and destination; that their hope should be full of immortality; that they should not look to the paltry pelf of the moment, nor to the temporary and transient praise of the vulgar, but to a solid, permanent existence, in the permanent part of their nature, and to a permanent fame and glory, in the example they leave as a rich inheritance to the world.

Such sublime principles ought to be infused into persons of exalted situations, and religious establishments provided that may continually revive and enforce them. Every sort of moral, every sort of civil, every sort of politic institution, aiding the rational and natural ties that connect the human understanding and affections to the divine, are not more than necessary, in order to build up that wonderful structure, Man; whose prerogative it is, to be in a great degree a creature of his own making, and who, when made as he ought to be made, is destined to hold no trivial place in the creation. But whenever man is put over men, as the better nature ought ever to preside, in that case more particularly he should as nearly as possible be approximated to his perfection.

The consecration[1] of the state by a state religious establishment is necessary also to operate with a wholesome awe upon free citizens; because, in order to secure their freedom, they must enjoy some determinate portion of power. To them, therefore, a religion connected with the state, and with their duty towards it, becomes even more necessary than in such societies where the people, by the terms of their subjection, are confined to private sentiments, and the management of their own family concerns. All persons possessing any portion of power ought to be strongly and awfully impressed with an idea that they act

---

1. consecration: 神圣化

in trust, and that they are to account for their conduct in that trust to the one great master, author, and founder of society.

This principle ought even to be more strongly impressed upon the minds of those who compose the collective sovereignty than upon those of single princes. Without instruments, these princes can do nothing. Whoever uses instruments, in finding helps, finds also impediments. Their power is therefore by no means complete; nor are they safe in extreme abuse. Such persons, however elevated by flattery, arrogance, and self-opinion, must be sensible that, whether covered or not by positive law, in some way or other they are accountable even here for the abuse of their trust. If they are not cut off by a rebellion of their people, they may be strangled by the very janissaries[1] kept for their security against all other rebellion. Thus we have seen the king of France sold by his soldiers for an increase of pay. But where popular authority is absolute and unrestrained, the people have an infinitely greater, because a far better founded, confidence in their own power. They are themselves in a great measure their own instruments. They are nearer to their objects. Besides, they are less under responsibility to one of the greatest controlling powers on earth, the sense of fame and estimation. The share of infamy that is likely to fall to the lot of each individual in public acts is small indeed: the operation of opinion being in the inverse ratio to the number of those who abuse power. Their own approbation of their own acts has to them the appearance of a public judgment in their favour. A perfect democracy is therefore the most shameless thing in the world. As it is the most shameless, it is also the most fearless. No man apprehends in his person that he can be made subject to punishment. Certainly the people at large never ought: for, as all punishments are for example towards the conservation of the people at large, the people at large can never become the subject of

---

1. janissaries：亲信，爪牙

punishment by any human hand. It is therefore of infinite importance that they should not be suffered to imagine that their will, any more than that of kings, is the standard of right and wrong. They ought to be persuaded that they are full as little entitled, and far less qualified, with safety to themselves, to use any arbitrary power whatsoever; that therefore they are not, under a false show of liberty, but in truth to exercise an unnatural, inverted domination, tyrannically to exact from those who officiate in the state, not an entire devotion to their interest, which is their right, but an abject submission to their occasional will; extinguishing thereby, in all those who serve them, all moral principle, all sense of dignity, all use of judgment, and all consistency of character; whilst by the very same process they give themselves up a proper, a suitable, but a most contemptible prey to the servile ambition of popular sycophants or courtly flatterers.

When the people have emptied themselves of all the lust of selfish will, which without religion it is utterly impossible they ever should, when they are conscious that they exercise, and exercise perhaps in a higher link of the order of delegation, the power which to be legitimate must be according to that eternal, immutable law in which will and reason are the same, they will be more careful how they place power in base and incapable hands. In their nomination to office, they will not appoint to the exercise of authority as to a pitiful job, but as to a holy function; not according to their sordid, selfish interest, nor to their wanton caprice, nor to their arbitrary will; but they will confer that power (which any man may well tremble to give or to receive) on those only in whom they may discern that predominant proportion of active virtue and wisdom, taken together and fitted to the charge, such as in the great and inevitable mixed mass of human imperfections and infirmities is to be found.

When they are habitually convinced that no evil can be acceptable, either in the act or the permission, to him whose essence is good, they will be better able to extirpate out of the minds of all magistrates, civil, ecclesiastical, or military, anything that bears the least resemblance to a proud and lawless domination.

But one of the first and most leading principles on which the commonwealth and the laws are consecrated is lest the temporary possessors and life-renters in it, unmindful of what they have received from their ancestors, or of what is due to their posterity, should act as if they were the entire masters; that they should not think it amongst their rights to cut off the entail or commit waste on the inheritance, by destroying at their pleasure the whole original fabric of their society; hazarding to leave to those who come after them a ruin instead of an habitation — and teaching these successors as little to respect their contrivances as they had themselves respected the institutions of their forefathers. By this unprincipled facility of changing the state as often and as much and in as many ways as there are floating fancies or fashions, the whole chain and continuity of the commonwealth would be broken; no one generation could link with the other; men would become little better than the flies of a summer.

And first of all, the science of jurisprudence, the pride of the human intellect, which, with all its defects, redundancies, and errors, is the collected reason of ages, combining the principles of original justice with the infinite variety of human concerns, as a heap of old exploded errors, would be no longer studied. Personal self-sufficiency and arrogance (the certain attendants upon all those who have never experienced a wisdom greater than their own) would usurp the tribunal. Of course no certain laws, establishing invariable grounds of hope and fear, would keep the actions of men in a certain course, or direct them to a certain end. Nothing stable in the modes of holding property or exercising function could form a solid ground on which any parent could speculate in the education of his offspring, or in a choice for their future establishment in the world. No principles would be early worked into the habits. As soon as the most able instructor had completed his laborious course of institution, instead of sending forth his pupil accomplished in a virtuous discipline fitted to procure him attention and respect in his place in society, he would find everything altered, and that he had turned out a poor creature to the contempt and derision of the world, ignorant of the true grounds of estimation. Who would insure a tender and delicate sense of honour to beat almost with the first pulses of the heart, when no man could know what would be the test of honour in a nation continually varying the standard of its coin? No part of life would retain its acquisitions. Barbarism with regard to science and literature, unskilfulness with regard to arts and manufactures, would infallibly succeed to the want of a steady education and settled principle; and thus the commonwealth itself would in a few generations crumble away, be disconnected into the dust and powder of individuality, and at length dispersed to all the winds of heaven.

To avoid, therefore, the evils of inconstancy and versatility, ten thousand times worse than those of obstinacy and the blindest prejudice, we have consecrated the state, that no man should approach to look into its defects or corruptions but with due caution; that he should never dream of beginning its reformation by its subversion; that he should approach to the faults of the state as to the wounds of a father, with pious awe and trembling solicitude. By this wise prejudice we are taught to look with horror on those children of their country who are prompt rashly to hack that aged parent in pieces and put him into the kettle of magicians, in hopes that by their poisonous weeds and wild incantations they may regenerate the paternal constitution and renovate their father's life.

Society is indeed a contract. Subordinate contracts for objects of mere occasional interest may be dissolved at pleasure; but the state ought not to be considered as nothing better than a partnership agreement in a trade of pepper and coffee, calico[1] or tobacco, or

---

1. calico: （英）白棉布

some other such low concern, to be taken up for a little temporary interest, and to be dissolved by the fancy of the parties. It is to be looked on with other reverence; because it is not a partnership in things subservient only to the gross animal existence of a temporary and perishable nature. It is a partnership in all science, a partnership in all art, a partnership in every virtue and in all perfection. As the ends of such a partnership cannot be obtained in many generations, it becomes a partnership not only between those who are living, but between those who are living, those who are dead, and those who are to be born. Each contract of each particular state is but a clause in the great primeval contract of eternal society, linking the lower with the higher natures, connecting the visible and invisible world, according to a fixed compact sanctioned by the inviolable oath which holds all physical and all moral natures each in their appointed place. This law is not subject to the will of those who, by an obligation above them, and infinitely superior, are bound to submit their will to that law. The municipal corporations of that universal kingdom are not morally at liberty, at their pleasure, and on their speculations of a contingent improvement, wholly to separate and tear asunder the bands of their subordinate community, and to dissolve it into an unsocial, uncivil, unconnected chaos of elementary principles. It is the first and supreme necessity only, a necessity that is not chosen, but chooses, a necessity paramount to deliberation, that admits no discussion and demands no evidence, which alone can justify a resort to anarchy. This necessity is no exception to the rule; because this necessity itself is a part, too, of that moral and physical disposition of things to which man must be obedient by consent or force; but if that which is only submission to necessity should be made the object of choice, the law is broken, nature is disobeyed, and the rebellious are outlawed, cast forth, and exiled, from this world of reason, and order, and peace, and virtue, and fruitful penitence, into the antagonist world of madness, discord, vice, confusion, and unavailing sorrow.

These, my dear Sir, are, were, and, I think, long will be, the sentiments of not the least learned and reflecting part of this kingdom. They who are included in this description form their opinions on such grounds as such persons ought to form them. The less inquiring receive them from an authority which those whom Providence dooms to live on trust need not be ashamed to rely on. These two sorts of men move in the same direction, though in a different place. They both move with the order of the universe. They all know or feel this great ancient truth: "*Quod illi principi et præpotenti Deo qui omnem hunc mundum regit nihil eorum quæ quidem fiant in terris acceptius quam concilia et coetus hominum jure sociati quæ civitates appellantur.*" [1] They take this tenet of the head and heart, not from the great name which it immediately bears, nor from the greater from whence it is derived, but from that which alone can give true weight and sanction to any learned opinion, the common nature and common relation of men. Persuaded that all things ought to be done with reference, and referring all to the point of reference to which all should be directed, they think themselves bound, not only as individuals in the sanctuary of the heart, or as congregated in that personal capacity, to renew the memory of their high origin and cast, but also in their corporate character to perform their national homage to the institutor and author and protector of civil society, without which civil society man could not by any possibility arrive at the perfection of which his nature is capable, nor even make a remote and faint approach to it. They conceive that He who gave our nature to be perfected by our virtue willed also the necessary means of its perfection — He willed, therefore, the state —

---

1. Quod ... appellantur：〈拉〉引自古罗马雄辩家西塞罗（Cicero，前 106—前 43）的《论共和国》，但与原文稍有出入。英文的大意是："For there is nothing that happens on earth that is more welcome to that supreme God who rules the whole universe than the institutions and congregations of men united by a sense of right which are called states"。

He willed its connection with the source and original archetype of all perfection. They who are convinced of this his will, which is the law of laws and the sovereign of sovereigns, cannot think it reprehensible that this our corporate fealty and homage, that this our recognition of a signiory paramount[1], I had almost said this oblation of the state itself, as a worthy offering on the high altar of universal praise, should be performed, as all public, solemn acts are performed, in buildings, in music, in decoration, in speech, in the dignity of persons, according to the customs of mankind, taught by their nature; that is, with modest splendour, with unassuming state, with mild majesty and sober pomp. For those purposes they think some part of the wealth of the country is as usefully employed as it can be in fomenting the luxury of individuals. It is the public ornament. It is the public consolation. It nourishes the public hope. The poorest man finds his own importance and dignity in it, whilst the wealth and pride of individuals at every moment makes the man of humble rank and fortune sensible of his inferiority, and degrades and vilifies his condition. It is for the man in humble life, and to raise his nature, and to put him in mind of a state in which the privileges of opulence will cease, when he will be equal by nature, and may be more than equal by virtue, that this portion of the general wealth of his country is employed and sanctified.

I assure you I do not aim at singularity. I give you opinions which have been accepted amongst us, from very early times to this moment, with a continued and general approbation, and which, indeed, are so worked into my mind that I am unable to distinguish what I have learned from others from the results of my own meditation.

It is on some such principles that the majority of the people of England, far from thinking a religious national establishment unlawful, hardly think it lawful to be without one. In France you are wholly

---

1. a signiory paramount: 至高无上的君权统治者

mistaken, if you do not believe us above all other things attached to it, and beyond all other nations; and when this people has acted unwisely and unjustifiably in its favour (as in some instances they have done, most certainly) in their very errors you will at least discover their zeal.

This principle runs through the whole system of their polity. They do not consider their church establishment as convenient, but as essential to their state; not as a thing heterogeneous and separable; something added for accommodation; what they may either keep up or lay aside, according to their temporary ideas of convenience. They consider it as the foundation of their whole constitution, with which, and with every part of which, it holds an indissoluble union. Church and state are ideas inseparable in their minds, and scarcely is the one ever mentioned without mentioning the other.

Our education is so formed as to confirm and fix this impression. Our education is in a manner wholly in the hands of ecclesiastics, and in all stages from infancy to manhood. Even when our youth, leaving schools and universities, enter that most important period of life which begins to link experience and study together, and when with that view they visit other countries, instead of old domestics whom we have seen as governors to principal men from other parts, three fourths of those who go abroad with our young nobility and gentlemen are ecclesiastics: not as austere masters, nor as mere followers; but as friends and companions of a graver character, and not seldom persons as well born as themselves. With them, as relations, they most commonly keep up a close connection through life. By this connection we conceive that we attach our gentlemen to the church; and we liberalize the church by an intercourse with the leading characters of the country.

So tenacious are we of the old ecclesiastical modes and fashions of institution, that very little alteration has been made in them since the fourteenth or fifteenth century; adhering in this particular, as in all things else, to our old settled maxim, never entirely nor at once to depart from antiquity. We found these old institutions, on the whole, favourable to morality and discipline; and we thought they were susceptible of amendment, without altering the ground. We thought that they were capable of receiving and meliorating, and above all of preserving, the accessions of science and literature, as the order of Providence should successively produce them. And after all, with this Gothic and monkish education (for such it is in the groundwork) we may put in our claim to as ample and as early a share in all the improvements in science, in arts, and in literature, which have illuminated and adorned the modern world, as any other nation in Europe; we think one main cause of this improvement was our not despising the patrimony of knowledge which was left us by our forefathers.

It is from our attachment to a church establishment, that the English nation did not think it wise to intrust that great fundamental interest of the whole to what they trust no part of their civil or military public service, that is, to the unsteady and precarious contribution of individuals. They go further. They certainly never have suffered, and never will suffer, the fixed estate of the church to be converted into a pension, to depend on the Treasury, and to be delayed, withheld, or perhaps to be extinguished by fiscal difficulties: which difficulties may sometimes be pretended for political purposes, and are in fact often brought on by the extravagance, negligence, and rapacity of politicians. The people of England think that they have constitutional motives, as well as religious, against any project of turning their independent clergy into ecclesiastical pensioners of state. They tremble for their liberty, from the influence of a clergy dependent on the crown; they tremble for the public tranquillity, from the disorders of a factious clergy, if it were made to depend upon any other than the crown. They therefore made their church, like their king and their nobility, independent.

From the united considerations of religion and constitutional policy, from their opinion of a duty to make a sure provision for the consolation of the feeble and the instruction of the ignorant, they have incorporated and identified the estate of the church with the mass of *private property*, of which the state is not the proprietor, either for use or dominion, but the guardian only and the regulator. They have ordained that the provision of this establishment might be as stable as the earth on which it stands, and should not fluctuate with the Euripus[1] of funds and actions.

The men of England, the men, I mean, of light and leading in England, whose wisdom (if they have any) is open and direct, would be ashamed, as of a silly, deceitful trick, to profess any religion in name, which by their proceedings they appear to contemn. If by their conduct (the only language that rarely lies) they seemed to regard the great ruling principle of the moral and the natural world as a mere invention to keep the vulgar in obedience, they apprehend that by such a conduct they would defeat the politic purpose they have in view. They would find it difficult to make others believe in a system to which they manifestly gave no credit themselves. The Christian statesmen of this land would, indeed, first provide for the *multitude*, because it is the *multitude*, and is therefore, as such, the first object in the ecclesiastical institution, and in all institutions. They have been taught that the circumstance of the gospel's being preached to the poor was one of the great tests of its true mission. They think, therefore, that those do not believe it who do not take care it should be preached to the poor. But as they know that charity is not confined to any one description, but ought to apply itself to all men who have wants, they are not deprived of a due and anxious sensation of pity to the distresses of the miserable great. They are not repelled, through a fastidious delicacy, at the stench of their arrogance and presumption, from a medicinal attention to their mental blotches and running sores. They are sensible that religious instruction is of more consequence to them than to any

---

1. Euripus: 位于希腊大陆和埃维厄岛之间的欧利波斯海峡，以水流湍急闻名。

others: from the greatness of the temptation to which they are exposed; from the important consequences that attend their faults; from the contagion of their ill example; from the necessity of bowing down the stubborn neck of their pride and ambition to the yoke of moderation and virtue; from a consideration of the fat stupidity and gross ignorance concerning what imports men most to know, which prevails at courts, and at the head of armies, and in senates, as much as at the loom and in the field.

The English people are satisfied, that to the great the consolations of religion are as necessary as its instructions. They, too, are among the unhappy. They feel personal pain and domestic sorrow. In these they have no privilege, but are subject to pay their full contingent to the contributions levied on mortality. They want this sovereign balm under their gnawing cares and anxieties, which, being less conversant about the limited wants of animal life, range without limit, and are diversified by infinite combinations in the wild and unbounded regions of imagination. Some charitable dole is wanting to these, our often very unhappy brethren[1], to fill the gloomy void that reigns in minds which have nothing on earth to hope or fear; something to relieve in the killing languor and over-laboured lassitude of those who have nothing to do; something to excite an appetite to existence in the palled satiety which attends on all pleasures which may be bought, where Nature is not left to her own process, where even desire is anticipated, and therefore fruition defeated by meditated schemes and contrivances of delight, and no interval, no obstacle, is interposed between the wish and the accomplishment.

The people of England know how little influence the teachers of religion are likely to have with the wealthy and powerful of long standing, and how much less with the newly fortunate, if they appear

---

1. brethren: 〈旧〉同胞，同党

in a manner no way assorted to those with whom they must associate, and over whom they must even exercise, in some cases, something like an authority. What must they think of that body of teachers, if they see it in no part above the establishment of their domestic servants? If the poverty were voluntary, there might be some difference. Strong instances of self-denial operate powerfully on our minds; and a man who has no wants has obtained great freedom and firmness, and even dignity. But as the mass of any description of men are but men, and their poverty cannot be voluntary, that disrespect which attends upon all lay poverty will not depart from the Ecclesiastical. Our provident constitution has therefore taken care that those who are to instruct presumptuous ignorance, those who are to be censors over insolent vice, should neither incur their contempt nor live upon their alms; nor will it tempt the rich to a neglect of the true medicine of their minds. For these reasons, whilst we provide first for the poor, and with a parental solicitude, we have not relegated religion (like something we were ashamed to show) to obscure municipalities or rustic villages. No! we will have her to exalt her mitred front in courts and parliaments. We will have her mixed throughout the whole mass of life, and blended with all the classes of society. The people of England will show to the haughty potentates of the world, and to their talking sophisters, that a free, a generous, an informed nation honours the high magistrates of its church; that it will not suffer the insolence of wealth and titles, or any other species of proud pretension, to look down with scorn upon what they look up to with reverence, nor presume to trample on that acquired personal nobility which they intend always to be, and which often is, the fruit, not the reward, (for what can be the reward?) of learning, piety, and virtue. They can see, without pain or grudging, an archbishop precede a duke. They can see a Bishop of Durham[1] or

---

1. Durham：达拉谟（英格兰一郡及其首府名）

a Bishop of Winchester[1] in possession of ten thousand pounds a year, and cannot conceive why it is in worse hands than estates to the like amount in the hands of this earl or that squire[2]; although it may be true that so many dogs and horses are not kept by the former, and fed with the victuals which ought to nourish the children of the people. It is true, the whole church revenue is not always employed, and to every shilling, in charity; nor perhaps ought it; but something is generally so employed. It is better to cherish virtue and humanity, by leaving much to free will, even with some loss to the object, than to attempt to make men mere machines and instruments of a political benevolence. The world on the whole will gain by a liberty without which virtue cannot exist.

When once the commonwealth has established the estates of the Church as property, it can consistently hear nothing of the more or the less. Too much and too little are treason against property. What evil can arise from the quantity in any hand, whilst the supreme authority has the full, sovereign superintendence over this, as over any property, to prevent every species of abuse; and whenever it notably deviates, to give to it a direction agreeable to the purposes of its institution?

In England most of us conceive that it is envy and malignity towards those who are often the beginners of their own fortune, and not a love of the self-denial and mortification of the ancient church, that makes some look askance at the distinctions and honours and revenues which, taken from no person, are set apart for virtue. The ears of the people of England are distinguishing. They hear these men speak broad. Their tongue betrays them. Their language is in the *patois*[3] of fraud, in the cant and gibberish of hypocrisy. The people of England

---

1. Winchester: 温彻斯特（英格兰南部一城名）
2. in the hands of this earl or that squire: 无论在这个伯爵还是那个乡绅手中
3. *patois*: 方言，土话

must think so, when these praters[1] affect to carry back the clergy to that primitive evangelic poverty which in the spirit ought always to exist in them, (and in us too, however we may like it) but in the thing must be varied, when the relation of that body to the state is altered; when manners, when modes of life, when indeed the whole order of human affairs, has undergone a total revolution. We shall believe those reformers to be then honest enthusiasts, not, as now we think them, cheats and deceivers, when we see them throwing their own goods into common, and submitting their own persons to the austere discipline of the early church.

With these ideas rooted in their minds, the commons of Great Britain, in the national emergencies, will never seek their resource from the confiscation of the estates of the church and poor. Sacrilege and proscription are not among the ways and means of our committee of supply. The Jews in Change Alley[2] have not yet dared to hint their hopes of a mortgage on the revenues belonging to the see of Canterbury[3]. I am not afraid that I shall be disavowed, when I assure you that there is not *one* public man in this kingdom, whom you wish to quote; no, not one, of any party or description, who does not reprobate the dishonest, perfidious, and cruel confiscation which the National Assembly has been compelled to make of that property which it was their first duty to protect.[4]

It is with the exultation of a little national pride I tell you that those amongst us who have wished to pledge the societies of Paris in the cup of their abominations have been disappointed. The robbery of your Church has proved a security to the possessions of ours. It has

---

1. praters: 喋喋不休者
2. Change Alley: 英国伦敦街名，曾设有英国股票交易中心。1720 年引发南海泡沫事件，导致经济危机的南海股票就是在此地交易。
3. the see of Canterbury: 坎特伯雷大主教的辖区
4. dishonest ... protect: 指 1789 年 11 月，法国教会拥有的财产被宣布"听凭国家支配"，财产售后所得被用来偿还国债。

roused the people. They see with horror and alarm that enormous and shameless act of proscription. It has opened, and will more and more open, their eyes upon the selfish enlargement of mind and the narrow liberality of sentiment of insidious men, which, commencing in close hypocrisy and fraud, have ended in open violence and rapine. At home we behold similar beginnings. We are on our guard against similar conclusions.

I hope we shall never be so totally lost to all sense of the duties imposed upon us by the law of social union, as, upon any pretext of public service, to confiscate the goods of a single unoffending citizen. Who but a tyrant (a name expressive of everything which can vitiate and degrade human nature) could think of seizing on the property of men, unaccused, unheard, untried, by whole descriptions, by hundreds and thousands together? Who that had not lost every trace of humanity could think of casting down men of exalted rank and sacred function, some of them of an age to call at once for reverence and compassion, of casting them down from the highest situation in the commonwealth, wherein they were maintained by their own landed property, to a state of indigence, depression, and contempt?

The confiscators truly have made some allowance to their victims from the scraps and fragments of their own tables, from which they have been so harshly driven, and which have been so bountifully spread for a feast to the harpies of usury[1]. But to drive men from independence to live on alms is itself great cruelty. That which might be a tolerable condition to men in one state of life, and not habituated to other things, may, when all these circumstances are altered, be a dreadful revolution, and one to which a virtuous mind would feel pain in condemning any guilt, except that which would demand the life of the offender. But to many minds this punishment of *degradation* and

---

1. harpies of usury: 穷凶极恶的高利贷恶魔

infamy is worse than death. Undoubtedly it is an infinite aggravation of this cruel suffering, that the persons who were taught a double prejudice in favour of religion, by education, and by the place they held in the administration of its functions, are to receive the remnants of their property as alms from the profane and impious hands of those who had plundered them of all the rest; to receive (if they are at all to receive) not from the charitable contributions of the faithful, but from the insolent tenderness of known and avowed atheism, the maintenance of religion, measured out to them on the standard of the contempt in which it is held, and for the purpose of rendering those who receive the allowance vile and of no estimation in the eyes of mankind.

But this act of seizure of property, it seems, is a judgment in law, and not a confiscation. They have, it seems, found out in the academies of the *Palais Royal*[1] and the *Jacobins*[2], that certain men had no right to the possessions which they held under law, usage, the decisions of courts, and the accumulated prescription of a thousand years. They say that ecclesiastics are fictitious persons, creatures of the state, whom at pleasure they may destroy, and of course limit and modify in every particular; that the goods they possess are not properly theirs, but belong to the state which created the fiction; and we are therefore not to trouble ourselves with what they may suffer in their natural feelings and natural persons, on account of what is done towards them in this their constructive character. Of what import is it, under what names you injure men, and deprive them of the just emoluments[3] of a profession in which they were not only permitted, but encouraged by the state to engage, and upon the supposed certainty of which emoluments they had formed the plan of their lives, contracted debts,

---

1. *Palais Royal*: 巴黎王宫
2. *Jacobins*: 雅各宾党人
3. emoluments: （因从事某项工作或担任某种职务而获得的）报酬

and led multitudes to an entire dependence upon them?

You do not imagine, Sir, that I am going to compliment this miserable distinction of persons with any long discussion. The arguments of tyranny are as contemptible as its force is dreadful. Had not your confiscators by their early crimes obtained a power which secures indemnity to all the crimes of which they have since been guilty, or that they can commit, it is not the syllogism of the logician, but the lash of the executioner, that would have refuted a sophistry which becomes an accomplice of theft and murder. The sophistic tyrants of Paris are loud in their declamations against the departed regal tyrants who in former ages have vexed the world. They are thus bold, because they are safe from the dungeons and iron cages of their old masters. Shall we be more tender of the tyrants of our own time, when we see them acting worse tragedies under our eyes? Shall we not use the same liberty that they do, when we can use it with the same safety? when to speak honest truth only requires a contempt of the opinions of those whose actions we abhor?

This outrage on all the rights of property was at first covered with what, on the system of their conduct, was the most astonishing of all pretexts — a regard to national faith. The enemies to property at first pretended a most tender, delicate, and scrupulous anxiety for keeping the king's engagements with the public creditor. These professors of the rights of men are so busy in teaching others, that they have not leisure to learn anything themselves; otherwise they would have known that it is to the property of the citizen, and not to the demands of the creditor of the state, that the first and original faith of civil society is pledged. The claim of the citizen is prior in time, paramount in title, superior in equity. The fortunes of individuals, whether possessed by acquisition, or by descent, or in virtue of a participation in the goods of some community, were no part of the creditor's security, expressed or implied. They never so much as entered into his head, when he made his bargain. He well knew that the public, whether represented by a monarch or by a senate, can pledge nothing but the public estate; and it can have no public estate, except in what it derives from a just and proportioned imposition upon the citizens at large. This was engaged, and nothing else could be engaged, to the public creditor. No man can mortgage his injustice as a pawn for his fidelity.

It is impossible to avoid some observation on the contradictions, caused by the extreme rigor and the extreme laxity of this new public faith, which influenced in this transaction, and which influenced not according to the nature of the obligation, but to the description of the persons to whom it was engaged. No acts of the old government of the kings of France are held valid in the National Assembly, except its pecuniary engagements; acts of all others of the most ambiguous legality. The rest of the acts of that royal government are considered in so odious a light that to have a claim under its authority is looked on as a sort of crime. A pension, given as a reward for service to the state, is surely as good a ground of property as any security for money advanced to the state. It is a better; for money is paid, and well paid, to obtain that service. We have, however, seen multitudes of people under this description in France, who never had been deprived of their allowances by the most arbitrary ministers in the most arbitrary times, by this assembly of the rights of men robbed without mercy. They were told, in answer to their claim to the bread earned with their blood, that their services had not been rendered to the country that now exists.

This laxity of public faith is not confined to those unfortunate persons. The Assembly, with perfect consistency it must be owned, is engaged in a respectable deliberation how far it is bound by the treaties made with other nations under the former government; and their committee is to report which of them they ought to ratify, and which not. By this means they have put the external fidelity of this virgin state on a par with its internal.

It is not easy to conceive upon what rational principle the royal government should not, of the two, rather have possessed the power of rewarding service and making treaties, in virtue of its prerogative, than that of pledging to creditors the revenue of the state, actual and possible. The treasure of the nation, of all things, has been the least allowed to the prerogative of the king of France, or to the prerogative of any king in Europe. To mortgage the public revenue implies the sovereign dominion, in the fullest sense, over the public purse. It goes far beyond the trust even of a temporary and occasional taxation. The acts, however, of that dangerous power (the distinctive mark of a boundless despotism) have been alone held sacred. Whence arose this preference given by a democratic assembly to a body of property deriving its title from the most critical and obnoxious of all the exertions of monarchical authority? Reason can furnish nothing to reconcile inconsistency; nor can partial favour be accounted for upon equitable principles. But the contradiction and partiality which admit no justification are not the less without an adequate cause; and that cause I do not think it difficult to discover.

By the vast debt of France a great moneyed interest has insensibly grown up, and with it a great power. By the ancient usages which prevailed in that kingdom, the general circulation of property, and in particular the mutual convertibility of land into money and of money into land, had always been a matter of difficulty. Family settlements, rather more general and more strict than they are in England, the *jus retractûs*[1], the great mass of landed property held by the crown, and, by a maxim of the French law, held unalienably, the vast estates of the ecclesiastic corporations — all these had kept the landed and moneyed interests more separated in France, less miscible, and the owners of the two distinct species of property not so well disposed to each other as they are in this country.

---

1. *jus retractûs*：〈拉〉收回权，指罗马法中一种收回已让渡的遗产的手段。

The moneyed property was long looked on with rather an evil eye by the people. They saw it connected with their distresses, and aggravating them. It was no less envied by the old landed interests, partly for the same reasons that rendered it obnoxious to the people, but much more so as it eclipsed, by the splendour of an ostentatious luxury, the unendowed pedigrees and naked titles of several among the nobility. Even when the nobility, which represented the more permanent landed interest, united themselves by marriage (which sometimes was the case) with the other description, the wealth which saved the family from ruin was supposed to contaminate and degrade it. Thus the enmities and heart burnings of these parties were increased even by the usual means by which discord is made to cease and quarrels are turned into friendship. In the mean time, the pride of the wealthy men, not noble, or newly noble, increased with its cause. They felt with resentment an inferiority the grounds of which they did not acknowledge. There was no measure to which they were not willing to lend themselves, in order to be revenged of the outrages of this rival pride, and to exalt their wealth to what they considered as its natural rank and estimation. They struck at the nobility through the crown and the church. They attacked them particularly on the side on which they thought them the most vulnerable, that is, the possessions of the church, which, through the patronage of the crown, generally devolved upon the nobility. The bishoprics and the great commendatory abbeys were, with few exceptions, held by that order.

In this state of real, though not always perceived, warfare between the noble ancient landed interest and the new moneyed interest, the greatest, because the most applicable, strength was in the hands of the latter. The moneyed interest is in its nature more ready for any adventure, and its possessors more disposed to new enterprises of any kind. Being of a recent acquisition, it falls in more naturally with any novelties. It is therefore the kind of wealth which will be resorted to by all who wish for change.

Along with the moneyed interest, a new description of men had grown up, with whom that interest soon formed a close and marked union: I mean the political men of letters. Men of letters, fond of distinguishing themselves, are rarely averse to innovation. Since the decline of the life and greatness of Louis XIV, they were not so much cultivated either by him, or by the Regent[1], or the successors to the crown; nor were they engaged to the court by favours and emoluments so systematically as during the splendid period of that ostentatious and not impolitic reign. What they lost in the old court protection they endeavoured to make up by joining in a sort of incorporation of their own; to which the two academies of France, and afterwards the vast undertaking of the Encyclopaedia[2], carried on by a society of these gentlemen, did not a little contribute.

The literary cabal had some years ago formed something like a regular plan for the destruction of the Christian religion. This object they pursued with a degree of zeal which hitherto had been discovered only in the propagators of some system of piety. They were possessed with a spirit of proselytism in the most fanatical degree; and from thence, by an easy progress, with the spirit of persecution according to their means. What was not to be done towards their great end by any direct or immediate act might be wrought by a longer process through the medium of opinion. To command that opinion, the first step is to establish a dominion over those who direct it. They contrived to possess themselves, with great method and perseverance, of all the avenues to literary fame. Many of them, indeed, stood high in

---

1. the Regent: 摄政王，指 1715 年至 1723 年担任法国摄政王的腓力二世奥尔良公爵（1701—1723）。
2. the Encyclopaedia: 百科全书，特指由法国学者德尼·狄德罗率领一批著名学者于 1751 至 1772 年编纂出版的《百科全书，或科学、艺术和手工艺分类字典》。这是近现代世界第一部百科全书。

the ranks of literature and science. The world had done them justice, and in favour of general talents forgave the evil tendency of their peculiar principles. This was true liberality; which they returned by endeavouring to confine the reputation of sense, learning, and taste to themselves or their followers. I will venture to say that this narrow, exclusive spirit has not been less prejudicial to literature and to taste than to morals and true philosophy. These atheistical fathers have a bigotry of their own; and they have learnt to talk against monks with the spirit of a monk. But in some things they are men of the world. The resources of intrigue are called in to supply the defects of argument and wit. To this system of literary monopoly was joined an unremitting industry to blacken and discredit in every way, and by every means, all those who did not hold to their faction. To those who have observed the spirit of their conduct it has long been clear that nothing was wanted but the power of carrying the intolerance of the tongue and of the pen into a persecution which would strike at property, liberty, and life.

The desultory and faint persecution carried on against them, more from compliance with form and decency than with serious resentment, neither weakened their strength nor relaxed their efforts. The issue of the whole was, that what with opposition, and what with success, a violent and malignant zeal, of a kind hitherto unknown in the world, had taken an entire possession of their minds, and rendered their whole conversation, which otherwise would have been pleasing and instructive, perfectly disgusting. A spirit of cabal, intrigue, and proselytism pervaded all their thoughts, words, and actions. And, as controversial zeal soon turns its thoughts on force, they began to insinuate themselves into a correspondence with foreign princes; in hopes, through their authority, which at first they flattered, they might bring about the changes they had in view. To them it was indifferent whether these changes were to be accomplished by the thunderbolt of despotism or by the earthquake of popular commotion. The correspondence between this cabal and the late king of Prussia[1] will throw no small light upon the spirit of all their proceedings. For the same purpose for which they intrigued with princes, they cultivated, in a distinguished manner, the moneyed interest of France; and partly through the means furnished by those whose peculiar offices gave them the most extensive and certain means of communication, they carefully occupied all the avenues to opinion.

Writers, especially when they act in a body and with one direction, have great influence on the public mind; the alliance, therefore, of these writers with the moneyed interest had no small effect in removing the popular odium and envy which attended that species of wealth. These writers, like the propagators of all novelties, pretended to a great zeal for the poor and the lower orders, whilst in their satires they rendered hateful, by every exaggeration, the faults of courts, of nobility, and of priesthood. They became a sort of demagogues. They served as a link to unite, in favour of one object, obnoxious wealth to restless and desperate poverty.

As these two kinds of men appear principal leaders in all the late transactions, their junction and politics will serve to account, not upon any principles of law or of policy, but as a *cause*, for the general fury with which all the landed property of ecclesiastical corporations has been attacked, and the great care which, contrary to their pretended principles, has been taken of a moneyed interest originating from the authority of the crown. All the envy against wealth and power was artificially directed against other descriptions of riches. On what other principle than that which I have stated can we account for an appearance so extraordinary and unnatural as that of the ecclesiastical possessions, which had stood so many successions of ages and shocks of civil violences, and were guarded at once by justice and by

---

1. The correspondence ... Prussia：指普鲁士国王腓特烈二世（1712—1786），他与一些法国作家保持密切的通信联系。

prejudice, being applied to the payment of debts comparatively recent, invidious, and contracted by a decried and subverted government?

Was the public estate a sufficient stake for the public debts? Assume that it was not, and that a loss *must* be incurred somewhere — When the only estate lawfully possessed, and which the contracting parties had in contemplation at the time in which their bargain was made, happens to fail, who, according to the principles of natural and legal equity, ought to be the sufferer? Certainly it ought to be either the party who trusted, or the party who persuaded him to trust, or both; and not third parties who had no concern with the transaction. Upon any insolvency, they ought to suffer who were weak enough to lend upon bad security, or they who fraudulently held out a security that was not valid. Laws are acquainted with no other rules of decision. But by the new institute of the rights of men, the only persons who in equity ought to suffer are the only persons who are to be saved harmless: those are to answer the debt who neither were lenders nor borrowers, mortgagers nor mortgagees.

What had the clergy to do with these transactions? What had they to do with any public engagement further than the extent of their own debt? To that, to be sure, their estates were bound to the last acre. Nothing can lead more to the true spirit of the assembly, which sits for public confiscation with its new equity and its new morality, than an attention to their proceeding with regard to this debt of the clergy. The body of confiscators, true to that moneyed interest for which they were false to every other, have found the clergy competent to incur a legal debt. Of course they declared them legally entitled to the property which their power of incurring the debt and mortgaging the estate implied; recognizing the rights of those persecuted citizens in the very act in which they were thus grossly violated.

If, as I said, any persons are to mate good deficiencies to the public creditor, besides the public at large, they must be those who managed the agreement. Why, therefore, are not the estates of all the comptrollers-general confiscated? Why not those of the long succession of ministers, financiers, and bankers who have been enriched whilst the nation was impoverished by their dealings and their counsels? Why is not the estate of Mr Laborde[1] declared forfeited rather than of the Archbishop of Paris, who has had nothing to do in the creation or in the jobbing of the public funds? Or, if you must confiscate old landed estates in favour of the money-jobbers, why is the penalty confined to one description? I do not know whether the expenses of the Duke de Choiseul have left anything of the infinite sums which he had derived from the bounty of his master, during the transactions of a reign which contributed largely, by every species of prodigality in war and peace, to the present debt of France. If any such remains, why is not this confiscated? I remember to have been in Paris during the time of the old government. I was there just after the Duke d'Aiguillon had been snatched (as it was generally thought) from the block by the hand of a protecting despotism. He was a minister, and had some concern in the affairs of that prodigal period. Why do I not see his estate delivered up to the municipalities in which it is situated? The noble family of Noailles have long been servants (meritorious servants I admit) to the crown of France, and have had of course some share in its bounties. Why do I hear nothing of the application of their estates to the public debt? Why is the estate of the Duke de Rochefoucault more sacred than that of the Cardinal de Rochefoucault? The former is, I doubt not, a worthy person; and (if it were not a sort of profaneness to talk of the use, as affecting the title to property) he makes a good use of his revenues; but it is no disrespect to him to say, what authentic information well warrants me in saying, that the use made of a property equally valid, by his brother, the Cardinal Archbishop of Rouen, was far more laudable and far more public-spirited. Can one

---

1. Mr Laborde：指法国时任主计长、主管财政和经济事务的首相拉博德先生。

hear of the proscription of such persons, and the confiscation of their effects, without indignation, and horror? He is not a man who does not feel such emotions on such occasions. He does not deserve the name of a free man who will not express them.[1]

Few barbarous conquerors have ever made so terrible a revolution in property. None of the heads of the Roman factions, when they established *crudelem illam hastam*[2] in all their auctions of rapine, have ever set up to sale the goods of the conquered citizen to such an enormous amount. It must be allowed in favour of those tyrants of antiquity, that what was done by them could hardly be said to be done in cold blood. Their passions were inflamed, their tempers soured, their understandings confused with the spirit of revenge, with the innumerable reciprocated and recent inflictions and retaliations of blood and rapine. They were driven beyond all bounds of moderation by the apprehension of the return of power with the return of property to the families of those they had injured beyond all hope of forgiveness.

These Roman confiscators, who were yet only in the elements of tyranny, and were not instructed in the rights of men to exercise all sorts of cruelties on each other without provocation, thought it necessary to spread a sort of colour over their injustice. They considered the vanquished party as composed of traitors, who had borne arms, or otherwise had acted with hostility, against the commonwealth. They regarded them as persons who had forfeited their property by their crimes. With you, in your improved state of the human mind, there was no such formality. You seized upon five millions sterling of annual rent, and turned forty or fifty thousand human creatures out of their houses, because "such was your

---

1. 本段文字中所提到一些人均为当时法国贵族，在大革命初期，他们曾对革命持支持态度。
2. *crudelem illam hastam*：〈拉〉那血腥的长矛，引自西塞罗的《论义务》。古罗马拍卖场中央通常设有一支半截埋在地下的长矛。

pleasure." The tyrant, Harry VIII of England, as he was not better enlightened than the Roman Marius's and Sylla's, and had not studied in your new schools, did not know what an effectual instrument of despotism was to be found in that grand magazine of offensive weapons, the rights of men.[1] When he resolved to rob the abbeys, as the club of the Jacobins have robbed all the ecclesiastics, he began by setting on foot a commission to examine into the crimes and abuses which prevailed in those communities. As it might be expected, his commission reported truths, exaggerations, and falsehoods. But truly or falsely, it reported abuses and offences. However, as abuses might be corrected, as every crime of persons does not infer a forfeiture with regard to communities, and as property, in that dark age, was not discovered to be a creature of prejudice, all those abuses (and there were enough of them) were hardly thought sufficient ground for such a confiscation as it was for his purposes to make. He therefore procured the formal surrender of these estates. All these operose[2] proceedings were adopted by one of the most decided tyrants in the rolls of history, as necessary preliminaries, before he could venture, by bribing the members of his two servile houses with a share of the spoil, and holding out to them an eternal immunity from taxation, to demand a confirmation of his iniquitous proceedings by an act of Parliament. Had fate reserved him to our times, four technical terms would have done his business, and saved him all this trouble; he needed nothing more than one short form of incantation — *"Philosophy, Light, Liberality, the Rights of Men."*

I can say nothing in praise of those acts of tyranny, which no voice

---

1. *The tyrant ... the rights of men.*：英格兰国王亨利八世（1509—1547），罗马统帅盖乌斯·马略（前 155—前 86），罗马军队和政治领袖卢修斯·科尼利厄斯·苏拉（前 138—前 78）。作者列举这三个历史人物，称他们是贪恋专制权力的暴君。
2. operose：费力的

has hitherto ever commended under any of their false colours; yet in these false colours an homage was paid by despotism to justice. The power which was above all fear and all remorse was not set above all shame. Whilst shame keeps its watch, virtue is not wholly extinguished in the heart, nor will moderation be utterly exiled from the minds of tyrants.

I believe every honest man sympathizes in his reflections with our political poet on that occasion, and will pray to avert the omen, whenever these acts of rapacious despotism present themselves to his view or his imagination:

— May no such storm
Fall on our times, where rain must reform!
Tell me, my Muse, what monstrous, dire offence,
What crimes could any Christian king incense
To such a rage? Was't luxury, or lust?
Was *he* so temperate, so chaste, so just?
Were these their crimes? They were his own much more;
But wealth is crime enough to him that's poor.[1]

This same wealth, which is at all times treason and *lèze-nation* to indigent and rapacious despotism, under all modes of polity, was your temptation to violate property, law, and religion, united in one object. But was the state of France so wretched and undone, that no other resource but rapine remained to preserve its existence? On this point I wish to receive some information. When the states met, was the condition of the finances of France such, that, after economising on principles of justice and mercy through all departments, no fair repartition of burdens upon all the orders could possibly restore them?

---

1. 引自爱尔兰诗人约翰·丹汉姆（Sir John Denham, 1615—1669）的长诗《库珀山》。

If such an equal imposition would have been sufficient, you well know it might easily have been made. Mr Necker[1], in the budget which he laid before the Orders assembled at Versailles, made a detailed exposition of the state of the French nation.

If we give credit to him, it was not necessary to have recourse to any new impositions whatsoever, to put the receipts of France on a balance with its expenses. He stated the permanent charges of all descriptions, including the interest of a new loan of four hundred millions, at 531,444,000 livres[2]; the fixed revenue at 475,294,000, making the deficiency 56,150,000, or short of 2,200,000 sterling. But to balance it, he brought forward savings and improvements of revenue (considered as entirely certain) to rather more than the amount of that deficiency; and he concludes with these emphatical words (p. 39): — "Quel pays, Messieurs, que celui, où, *sans impôts* et avec de simples objets *inaperçus*, on peut faire disparoître un déficit qui a fait tant de bruit en Europe!" [3] As to the reimbursement, the sinking of debt, and the other great objects of public credit and political arrangement indicated in Monsieur Necker's speech, no doubt could be entertained but that a very moderate and proportioned assessment on the citizens without distinction would have provided for all of them to the fullest extent of their demand.

If this representation of Mons. Necker was false, then the Assembly are in the highest degree culpable for having forced the king to accept as his minister, and, since the king's deposition, for having employed as *their* minister, a man who had been capable of abusing so notoriously the confidence of his master and their own: in a matter,

---

1. Necker：雅克・内克尔（Jacques Necker，1732—1804），法国银行家，路易十六时期的财政总监。
2. livres：里弗赫（法国旧时流通的货币名，当时价值相当于 1 磅白银）
3. Quel pays ... tant de bruit en Europe!：〈法〉英文大意是：What a country, Gentlemen, is that in which, *without taxes* and with simple *unnoticed* objectives, one can make a deficit disappear that created such a stir in Europe!

too, of the highest moment, and directly appertaining to his particular office. But if the representation was exact (as, having always, along with you, conceived a high degree of respect for Mr Necker, I make no doubt it was) then what can be said in favour of those who, instead of moderate, reasonable, and general contribution, have in cold blood, and impelled by no necessity, had recourse to a partial and cruel confiscation?

Was that contribution refused on a pretext of privilege, either on the part of the clergy, or on that of the nobility? No, certainly. As to the clergy, they even ran before the wishes of the third order. Previous to the meeting of the states, they had in all their instructions expressly directed their deputies to renounce every immunity, which put them upon a footing distinct from the condition of their fellow-subjects. In this renunciation the clergy were even more explicit than the nobility.

But let us suppose that the deficiency had remained at the fifty-six millions, (or £ 2,200,000 sterling[1]) as at first stated by Mr Necker. Let us allow that all the resources he opposed to that deficiency were impudent and groundless fictions, and that the Assembly (or their lords of articles[2] at the Jacobins) were from thence justified in laying the whole burden of that deficiency on the clergy, — yet allowing all this, a necessity of £ 2,200,000 sterling will not support a confiscation to the amount of five millions. The imposition of £ 2,200,000 on the clergy, as partial, would have been oppressive and unjust, but it would not have been altogether ruinous to those on whom it was imposed; and therefore it would not have answered the real purpose of the managers.

---

1. sterling：英镑（英国货币）
2. lords of articles：议会立法委员会。斯图亚特王朝时期，苏格兰宪法规定议会中设立一个专门委员会来起草、制定各种法案。任何法案不经该委员会的批准，不能获得议会通过。此处指国民议会也有类似的、同等权利的委员会。

Perhaps persons unacquainted with the state of France, on hearing the clergy and the noblesse were privileged in point of taxation, may be led to imagine, that, previous to the revolution, these bodies had contributed nothing to the state. This is a great mistake. They certainly did not contribute equally with each other, nor either of them equally with the commons. They both, however, contributed largely. Neither nobility nor clergy enjoyed any exemption from the excise on consumable commodities, from duties of custom, or from any of the other numerous *indirect* impositions, which in France, as well as here, make so very large a proportion of all payments to the public. The noblesse paid the capitation[1]. They paid also a land-tax, called the twentieth penny, to the height sometimes of three, sometimes of four shillings in the pound: both of them *direct* impositions, of no light nature, and no trivial produce. The clergy of the provinces annexed by conquest to France (which in extent make about an eighth part of the whole, but in wealth a much larger proportion) paid likewise to the capitation and the twentieth penny, at the rate paid by the nobility. The clergy in the old provinces did not pay the capitation; but they had redeemed themselves at the expense of about twenty-four millions, or a little more than a million sterling. They were exempted from the twentieths: but then they made free gifts; they contracted debts for the state; and they were subject to some other charges, the whole computed at about a thirteenth part of their clear income. They ought to have paid annually about forty thousand pounds more, to put them on a par with the contribution of the nobility.

When the terrors of this tremendous proscription hung over the clergy, they made an offer of a contribution, through the Archbishop of Aix, which, for its extravagance, ought not to have been accepted. But it was evidently and obviously more advantageous to the public

---

1. capitation: 人头税

creditor than anything which could rationally be promised by the confiscation. Why was it not accepted? The reason is plain: There was no desire that the church should be brought to serve the state. The service of the state was made a pretext to destroy the church. In their way to the destruction of the church they would not scruple to destroy their country: and they have destroyed it. One great end in the project would have been defeated, if the plan of extortion had been adopted in lieu of the scheme of confiscation. The new landed interest connected with the new republic, and connected with it for its very being, could not have been created. This was among the reasons why that extravagant ransom was not accepted.

The madness of the project of confiscation, on the plan that was first pretended, soon became apparent. To bring this unwieldy mass of landed property, enlarged by the confiscation of all the vast landed domain of the crown, at once into market was obviously to defeat the profits proposed by the confiscation, by depreciating the value of those lands, and indeed of all the landed estates throughout France. Such a sudden diversion of all its circulating money from trade to land must be an additional mischief. What step was taken? Did the Assembly, on becoming sensible of the inevitable ill effects of their projected sale, revert to the offers of the clergy? No distress could oblige them to travel in a course which was disgraced by any appearance of justice. Giving over all hopes from a general immediate sale, another project seems to have succeeded. They proposed to take stock in exchange for the church lands. In that project great difficulties arose in equalizing the objects to be exchanged. Other obstacles also presented themselves, which threw them back again upon some project of sale. The municipalities had taken an alarm. They would not hear of transferring the whole plunder of the kingdom to the stockholders in Paris. Many of those municipalities had been (upon system) reduced to the most deplorable indigence. Money was nowhere to be seen. They were therefore led to the point that was so ardently desired. They panted for a currency of any kind which might revive their perishing industry. The municipalities were, then, to be admitted to a share in the spoil, which evidently rendered the first scheme (if ever it had been seriously entertained) altogether impracticable. Public exigencies pressed upon all sides. The Minister of Finance reiterated his call for supply with, a most urgent, anxious, and boding voice. Thus pressed on all sides, instead of the first plan of converting their bankers into bishops and abbots, instead of paying the old debt, they contracted a new debt, at three per cent, creating a new paper currency, founded on an eventual sale of the church lands.[1] They issued this paper currency to satisfy in the first instance chiefly the demands made upon them by the *bank of discount*, the great machine or paper-mill of their fictitious wealth.

The spoil of the church was now become the only resource of all their operations in finance, the vital principle of all their politics, the sole security for the existence of their power. It was necessary, by all, even the most violent means, to put every individual on the same bottom, and to bind the nation in one guilty interest to uphold this act, and the authority of those by whom it was done. In order to force the most reluctant into a participation of their pillage, they rendered their paper circulation compulsory in all payments. Those who consider the general tendency of their schemes to this one object as a centre, and a centre from which afterwards all their measures radiate, will not think that I dwell too long upon this part of the proceedings of the National Assembly.

To cut off all appearance of connection between the crown and public justice, and to bring the whole under implicit obedience to the

---

1. a new paper currency ... the church lands：法国革命时期新的流通纸币叫 "指券 (assignat)"。如作者所说，由于新货币的币值是由出售教会的资产来支撑的，因此其价值是随着革命形势起伏而波动的。详见"术语汇编与简释"。

dictators in Paris, the old independent judicature of the parliaments[1], with all its merits and all its faults, was wholly abolished. Whilst the parliaments existed, it was evident that the people might some time or other come to resort to them, and rally under the standard of their ancient laws. It became, however, a matter of consideration, that the magistrates and officers in the courts now abolished *had purchased their places* at a very high rate, for which, as well as for the duty they performed, they received but a very low return of interest. Simple confiscation is a boon only for the clergy: to the lawyers some appearances of equity are to be observed; and they are to receive compensation to an immense amount. Their compensation becomes part of the national debt, for the liquidation of which there is the one exhaustless fund. The lawyers are to obtain their compensation in the new church paper, which is to march with the new principles of judicature and legislature. The dismissed magistrates are to take their share of martyrdom with the ecclesiastics, or to receive their own property from such a fund and in such a manner as all those who have been seasoned with the ancient principles of jurisprudence, and had been the sworn guardians of property, must look upon with horror. Even the clergy are to receive their miserable allowance out of the depreciated paper, which is stamped with the indelible character of sacrilege, and with the symbols of their own ruin, or they must starve. So violent an outrage upon credit, property, and liberty, as this compulsory paper currency, has seldom been exhibited by the alliance of bankruptcy and tyranny, at any time, or in any nation.

In the course of all these operations, at length comes out the grand *arcanum;* [2] — that in reality, and in a fair sense, the lands of the church (so far as anything certain can be gathered from their proceedings) are

---

1. the parliaments：最高法院，即 parlements。详见"术语汇编与简释"。
2. *arcanum*：〈拉〉奥秘。在炼金术中常用来指灵丹妙药，此处也采用这一词义。

not to be sold at all. By the late resolutions of the National Assembly, they are indeed to be delivered to the highest bidder. But it is to be observed, that *a certain portion only of the purchase-money is to be laid down.* A period of twelve years is to be given for the payment of the rest. The philosophic purchasers are therefore, on payment of a sort of fine, to be put instantly into possession of the estate. It becomes in some respects a sort of gift to them; to be held on the feudal tenure of zeal to the new establishment. This project is evidently to let in a body of purchasers without money. The consequence will be, that these purchasers, or rather grantees, will pay, not only from the rents as they accrue, which might as well be received by the state, but from the spoil of the materials of buildings, from waste in woods, and from whatever money, by hands habituated to the gripings of usury, they can wring from the miserable peasant. He is to be delivered over to the mercenary and arbitrary discretion of men who will be stimulated to every species of extortion by the growing demands on the growing profits of an estate held under the precarious settlement of a new political system.

When all the frauds, impostures, violences, rapines, burnings, murders, confiscations, compulsory paper currencies, and every description of tyranny and cruelty employed to bring about and to uphold this revolution have their natural effect, that is, to shock the moral sentiments of all virtuous and sober minds, the abettors of this philosophic system immediately strain their throats in a declamation against the old monarchical government of France. When they have rendered that deposed power sufficiently black, they then proceed in argument, as if all those who disapprove of their new abuses must of course be partisans of the old; that those who reprobate their crude and violent schemes of liberty ought to be treated as advocates for servitude. I admit that their necessities do compel them to this base and contemptible fraud. Nothing can reconcile men to their proceedings and projects but the supposition that there is no third option between them and some tyranny as odious as can be furnished by the records of history or by the invention of poets. This prattling of theirs hardly deserves the name of sophistry. It is nothing but plain impudence. Have these gentlemen never heard, in the whole circle of the worlds of theory and practice, of anything between the despotism of the monarch and the despotism of the multitude? Have they never heard of a monarchy directed by laws, controlled and balanced by the great hereditary wealth and hereditary dignity of a nation, and both again controlled by a judicious check from the reason and feeling of the people at large, acting by a suitable and permanent organ? Is it, then, impossible that a man may be found who, without criminal ill intention or pitiable absurdity, shall prefer such a mixed and tempered government to either of the extremes; and who may repute that nation to be destitute of all wisdom and of all virtue, which, having in its choice to obtain such a government with ease, *or rather to confirm it when actually possessed*, thought proper to commit a thousand crimes, and to subject their country to a thousand evils, in order to avoid it? Is it, then, a truth so universally acknowledged, that a pure democracy is the only tolerable form into which human society can be thrown, that a man is not permitted to hesitate about its merits, without the suspicion of being a friend to tyranny, that is, of being a foe to mankind?

I do not know under what description to class the present ruling authority in France. It affects to be a pure democracy, though I think it in a direct train of becoming shortly a mischievous and ignoble oligarchy. But for the present I admit it to be a contrivance of the nature and effect of what it pretends to. I reprobate no form of government merely upon abstract principles. There may be situations in which the purely democratic form will become necessary. There may be some (very few, and very particularly circumstanced) where it would be clearly desirable. This I do not take to be the case of France, or of any other great country. Until now, we have seen no examples of considerable democracies. The ancients were better acquainted with them. Not being wholly unread in the authors who had seen the most of those constitutions, and who best understood them, I cannot help concurring with their opinion, that an absolute democracy no more than absolute monarchy is to be reckoned among the legitimate forms of government. They think it rather the corruption and degeneracy than the sound constitution of a republic. If I recollect rightly, Aristotle observes, that a democracy has many striking points of resemblance with a tyranny. Of this I am certain, that in a democracy the majority of the citizens is capable of exercising the most cruel oppressions upon the minority, whenever strong divisions prevail in that kind of polity, as they often must; and that oppression of the minority will extend to far greater numbers, and will be carried on with much greater fury, than can almost ever be apprehended from the dominion of a single sceptre[1]. In such a popular persecution, individual sufferers are in a much more deplorable condition than in any other. Under a cruel prince they have the balmy compassion of mankind to assuage the smart of their wounds, they have the plaudits of the people to animate their generous constancy under their sufferings: but those who are subjected to wrong under multitudes are deprived of all external consolation; they seem deserted by mankind, overpowered by a conspiracy of their whole species.

But admitting democracy not to have that inevitable tendency to party tyranny which I suppose it to have, and admitting it to possess as much good in it when unmixed as I am sure it possesses when compounded with other forms; does monarchy, on its part, contain nothing at all to recommend it? I do not often quote Bolingbroke, nor have his works in general left any permanent impression on my mind. He is a presumptuous and a superficial writer. But he has one observation which in my opinion is not without depth and solidity.

---

1. sceptre: 权杖，王权

He says that he prefers a monarchy to other governments, because you can better ingraft[1] any description of republic on a monarchy than anything of monarchy upon the republican forms. I think him perfectly in the right. The fact is so historically, and it agrees well with the speculation.

I know how easy a topic it is to dwell on the faults of departed greatness. By a revolution in the state, the fawning sycophant of yesterday is converted into the austere critic of the present hour. But steady, independent minds, when they have an object of so serious a concern to mankind as government under their contemplation, will disdain to assume the part of satirists and declaimers. They will judge of human institutions as they do of human characters. They will sort out the good from the evil, which is mixed in mortal institutions as it is in mortal men.

Your government in France, though usually, and I think justly, reputed the best of the unqualified or ill-qualified monarchies, was still full of abuses. These abuses accumulated in a length of time, as they must accumulate in every monarchy not under the constant inspection of a popular representative. I am no stranger to the faults and defects of the subverted government of France; and I think I am not inclined by nature or policy to make a panegyric[2] upon anything which is a just and natural object of censure. But the question is not now of the vices of that monarchy, but of its existence. Is it, then, true, that the French government was such as to be incapable or undeserving of reform, so that it was of absolute necessity the whole fabric should be at once pulled down, and the area cleared for the erection of a theoretic, experimental edifice in its place? All France was of a different opinion in the beginning of the year 1789. The instructions to the representatives to the States-General, from every district in

---

1. ingraft: 讨好，迎合
2. panegyric: 赞颂

that kingdom, were filled with projects for the reformation of that government, without the remotest suggestion of a design to destroy it. Had such a design been then even insinuated, I believe there would have been but one voice, and that voice for rejecting it with scorn and horror. Men have been sometimes led by degrees, sometimes hurried, into things of which, if they could have seen the whole together, they never would have permitted the most remote approach. When those instructions were given, there was no question but that abuses existed, and that they demanded a reform; nor is there now. In the interval between the instructions and the revolution, things changed their shape; and in consequence of that change, the true question at present is, whether those who would have reformed, or those who have destroyed, are in the right.

To hear some men speak of the late monarchy of France, you would imagine that they were talking of Persia bleeding under the ferocious sword of Thamas Kouli Khân[1], — or at least describing the barbarous anarchic despotism of Turkey, where the finest countries in the most genial climates in the world are wasted by peace more than any countries have been worried by war, where arts are unknown, where manufactures languish, where science is extinguished, where agriculture decays, where the human race itself melts away and perishes under the eye of the observer. Was this the case of France? I have no way of determining the question but by a reference to facts. Facts do not support this resemblance. Along with much evil, there is some good in monarchy itself; and some corrective to its evil from religion, from laws, from manners, from opinions, the French monarchy must have received, which rendered it (though by no means a free, and therefore by no means a good constitution) a despotism rather in appearance than in reality.

---

1. Thamas Kouli Khân: 指波斯统治者纳迪尔·沙阿·阿夫沙尔 (Nadir Shah Afshar, 1736—1747 年在位)。

Among the standards upon which the effects of government on any country are to be estimated, I must consider the state of its population as not the least certain. No country in which population flourishes, and is in progressive improvement, can be under a *very* mischievous government. About sixty years ago, the Intendants of the Generalities of France[1] made, with other matters, a report of the population of their several districts. I have not the books, which are very voluminous, by me, nor do I know where to procure them (I am obliged to speak by memory, and therefore the less positively) but I think the population of France was by them, even at that period, estimated at twenty-two millions of souls. At the end of the last century it had been generally calculated at eighteen. On either of these estimations, France was not ill-peopled. Mr Necker, who is an authority for his own time at least equal to the Intendants for theirs, reckons, and upon apparently sure principles, the people of France, in the year 1780, at twenty-four millions six hundred and seventy thousand. But was this the probable ultimate term under the old establishment? Dr Price is of opinion that the growth of population in France was by no means at its *acmé*[2] in that year. I certainly defer to Dr Price's authority a good deal more in these speculations than I do in his general politics. This gentleman, taking ground on Mr Necker's data, is very confident that since the period of that minister's calculation the French population has increased rapidly, so rapidly that in the year 1789 he will not consent to rate the people of that kingdom at a lower number than thirty millions. After abating much (and much I think ought to be abated) from the sanguine calculation of Dr Price, I have no doubt that the population of France did increase considerably during this

---

1. Intendants of the Generalities of France：法国总务部。路易十六时期，法国政府的主要行政部门称为 *generality*，负责监督、管理这些部门的总督叫 *intendant*。
2. *acmé*：〈法〉顶点

latter period: but supposing that it increased to nothing more than will be sufficient to complete the twenty-four millions six hundred and seventy thousand to twenty-five millions, still a population of twenty-five millions, and that in an increasing progress, on a space of about twenty-seven thousand square leagues[1], is immense. It is, for instance, a good deal more than the proportionable population of this island, or even than that of England, the best peopled part of the United Kingdom.

It is not universally true that France is a fertile country. Considerable tracts of it are barren, and labour under other natural disadvantages. In the portions of that territory where things are more favourable, as far as I am able to discover, the numbers of the people correspond to the indulgence of nature. The Generality of Lisle[2] (this I admit is the strongest example) upon an extent of 404 1/4 leagues, about ten years ago contained 734,600 souls, which is 1,772 inhabitants to each square league. The middle term for the rest of France is about 900 inhabitants to the same admeasurement.

I do not attribute this population to the deposed government; because I do not like to compliment the contrivances of men with what is due in a great degree to the bounty of Providence. But that decried government could not have obstructed, most probably it favored, the operation of those causes (whatever they were) whether of nature in the soil, or habits of industry among the people, which has produced so large a number of the species throughout that whole kingdom, and exhibited in some particular places such prodigies of population. I never will suppose that fabric of a state to be the worst of all political institutions which by experience is found to contain a principle favourable (however latent it may be) to the increase of mankind.

---

1. leagues：里格（旧时长度单位）。1 里格约为 3 英里、5 公里或 3 海里。
2. Lisle：里尔县（Lisle Commune），现属于法国西南部新阿基坦地区的多尔多涅省。在法国历史上，里尔一直是个人口稠密地区。

The wealth of a country is another, and no contemptible standard, by which we may judge whether, on the whole, a government be protecting or destructive. France far exceeds England in the multitude of her people; but I apprehend that her comparative wealth is much inferior to ours; that it is not so equal in the distribution, nor so ready in the circulation. I believe the difference in the form of the two governments to be amongst the causes of this advantage on the side of England: I speak of England, not of the whole British dominions, which, if compared with those of France, will in some degree weaken the comparative rate of wealth upon our side. But that wealth, which will not endure a comparison with the riches of England, may constitute a very respectable degree of opulence. Mr Necker's book, published in 1785, contains an accurate and interesting collection of facts relative to public economy and to political arithmetic; and his speculations on the subject are in general wise and liberal. In that work he gives an idea of the state of France, very remote from the portrait of a country whose government was a perfect grievance, an absolute evil, admitting no cure but through the violent and uncertain remedy of a total revolution. He affirms, that from the year 1726 to the year 1784 there was coined at the mint of France, in the species of gold and silver, to the amount of about one hundred millions of pounds sterling.

It is impossible that Mr Necker should be mistaken in the amount of the bullion which has been coined in the mint. It is a matter of official record. The reasonings of this able financier concerning the quantity of gold and silver which remained for circulation, when he wrote in 1785 that is, about four years before the deposition and imprisonment of the French king, are not of equal certainty; but they are laid on grounds so apparently solid, that it is not easy to refuse a considerable degree of assent to his calculation. He calculates the *numéraire*[1], or what

---

1. *numéraire*: 〈法〉法定货币; 硬币

we call *specie*[1], then actually existing in France, at about eighty-eight millions of the same English money. A great accumulation of wealth for one country, large as that country is! Mr Necker was so far from considering this influx of wealth as likely to cease, when he wrote in 1785, that he presumes upon a future annual increase of two per cent upon the money brought into France during the periods from which he computed.

Some adequate cause must have originally introduced all the money coined at its mint into that kingdom; and some cause as operative must have kept at home, or returned into its bosom, such a vast flood of treasure as Mr Necker calculates to remain for domestic circulation. Suppose any reasonable deductions from Mr Necker's computation, the remainder must still amount to an immense sum. Causes thus powerful to acquire and to retain cannot be found in discouraged industry, insecure property, and a positively destructive government. Indeed, when I consider the face of the kingdom of France, the multitude and opulence of her cities, the useful magnificence of her spacious high-roads and bridges, the opportunity of her artificial canals and navigations opening the conveniences of maritime communication through a solid continent of so immense an extent; when I turn my eyes to the stupendous works of her ports and harbours, and to her whole naval apparatus, whether for war or trade; when I bring before my view the number of her fortifications, constructed with so bold and masterly a skill, and made and maintained at so prodigious a charge, presenting an armed front and impenetrable barrier to her enemies upon every side; when I recollect how very small a part of that extensive region is without cultivation, and to what complete perfection the culture of many of the best productions of the earth have been brought in France; when I reflect

---

1. *specie*: 硬币

on the excellence of her manufactures and fabrics, second to none but ours, and in some particulars not second; when I contemplate the grand foundations of charity, public and private; when I survey the state of all the arts that beautify and polish life; when I reckon the men she has bled for extending her fame in war, her able statesmen, the multitude of her profound lawyers and theologians, her philosophers, her critics, her historians and antiquaries, her poets and her orators, sacred and profane, I behold in all this something which awes and commands the imagination, which checks the mind on the brink of precipitate and indiscriminate censure, and which demands that we should very seriously examine what and how great are the latent vices that could authorize us at once to level so spacious a fabric with the ground. I do not recognize in this view of things the despotism of Turkey. Nor do I discern the character of a government that has been on the whole so oppressive, or so corrupt, or so negligent, as to be utterly unfit *for all reformation*[1]. I must think such a government well deserved to have its excellences heightened, its faults corrected, and its capacities improved into a British constitution.

Whoever has examined into the proceedings of that deposed government for several years back cannot fail to have observed, amidst the inconstancy and fluctuation natural to courts, an earnest endeavour towards the prosperity and improvement of the country; he must admit that it had long been employed, in some instances wholly to remove, in many considerably to correct, the abusive practices and usages that had prevailed in the state; and that even the unlimited power of the sovereign over the persons of his subjects, inconsistent, as undoubtedly it was, with law and liberty, had yet been every day growing more mitigated in the exercise. So far from refusing itself to reformation, that government was open, with a censurable degree of

---

1. *for all reformation*：所有的宗教改革

facility, to all sorts of projects and projectors on the subject. Rather too much countenance was given to the spirit of innovation, which soon was turned against those who fostered it, and ended in their ruin. It is but cold, and no very flattering justice to that fallen monarchy, to say, that, for many years, it trespassed more by levity and want of judgment in several of its schemes than from any defect in diligence or in public spirit. To compare the government of France for the last fifteen or sixteen years with wise and well-constituted establishments during that, or during any period, is not to act with fairness. But if in point of prodigality in the expenditure of money, or in point of rigor in the exercise of power, it be compared with any of the former reigns, I believe candid judges will give little credit to the good intentions of those who dwell perpetually on the donations to favourites, or on the expenses of the court, or on the horrors of the Bastille, in the reign of Louis XVI.

Whether the system, if it deserves such a name, now built on the ruins of that ancient monarchy, will be able to give a better account of the population and wealth of the country, which it has taken under its care, is a matter very doubtful. Instead of improving by the change, I apprehend that a long series of years must be told, before it can recover in any degree the effects of this philosophic revolution, and before the nation can be replaced on its former footing. If Dr Price should think fit, a few years hence, to favour us with an estimate of the population of France, he will hardly be able to make up his tale of thirty millions of souls, as computed in 1789, or the Assembly's computation of twenty-six millions of that year, or even Mr Necker's twenty-five millions in 1780. I hear that there are considerable emigrations from France; and that many, quitting that voluptuous climate, and that seductive *Circean*[1] liberty, have taken refuge in the frozen regions and

---

1. *Circean*：喀尔刻（荷马史诗《奥德塞》中会巫术的美丽仙女）；使人着迷的

under the British despotism of Canada.

In the present disappearance of coin, no person could think it the same country in which the present minister of the finances has been able to discover fourscore millions sterling in specie. From its general aspect one would conclude that it had been for some time past under the special direction of the learned academicians of Laputa and Balnibarbi[1]. Already the population of Paris has so declined, that Mr Necker stated to the National Assembly the provision to be made for its subsistence at a fifth less than what had formerly been found requisite. It is said (and I have never heard it contradicted) that a hundred thousand people are out of employment in that city, though it is become the seat of the imprisoned court and National Assembly. Nothing, I am credibly informed, can exceed the shocking and disgusting spectacle of mendicancy displayed in that capital. Indeed, the votes of the National Assembly leave no doubt of the fact. They have lately appointed a standing committee of mendicancy. They are contriving at once a vigorous police on this subject, and, for the first time, the imposition of a tax to maintain the poor, for whose present relief great sums appear on the face of the public accounts of the year. In the mean time the leaders of the legislative clubs and coffee-houses are intoxicated with admiration at their own wisdom and ability. They speak with the most sovereign contempt of the rest of the world. They toll the people, to comfort them in the rags with which they have clothed them, that they are a nation of philosophers; and sometimes, by all the arts of quackish parade, by show, tumult, and bustle, sometimes by the alarms of plots and invasions, they attempt to drown the cries of indigence, and to divert the eyes of the observer from the ruin and wretchedness of the state. A brave people will certainly

---

1. Laputa and Balnibarbi：拉普塔和巴尔尼巴比国，指英国作家乔纳森·斯威夫特的小说《格列佛游记》中虚构的两个被哲学家们所迷惑的国家。

prefer liberty, accompanied with a virtuous poverty, to a depraved and wealthy servitude. But before the price of comfort and opulence is paid, one ought to be pretty sure it is real liberty which is purchased, and that she is to be purchased at no other price. I shall always, however, consider that liberty as very equivocal in her appearance, which has not wisdom and justice for her companions, and does not lead prosperity and plenty in her train.

The advocates for this revolution, not satisfied with exaggerating the vices of their ancient government, strike at the fame of their country itself, by painting almost all that could have attracted the attention of strangers, I mean their nobility and their clergy, as objects of horror. If this were only a libel, there had not been much in it. But it has practical consequences. Had your nobility and gentry, who formed the great body of your landed men and the whole of your military officers, resembled those of Germany, at the period when the Hanse-towns[1] were necessitated to confederate against the nobles in defence of their property — had they been like the *Orsini and Vitelli*[2] in Italy, who used to sally from their fortified dens to rob the trader and traveller — had they been such as the *Mamelukes* in Egypt, or the *Nayres* on the coast of Malabar[3], I do admit that too critical an inquiry might not be advisable into the means of freeing the world from such a nuisance. The statues of Equity and Mercy might be veiled for a moment. The tenderest minds, confounded with the dreadful exigence in which morality submits to the suspension of its own rules in favour

---

1. Hanse-towns：（中世纪）汉萨同盟城，即德意志北部城市之间形成的商业、政治联盟。
2. *Orsini and Vitelli*：奥尔西尼家族是自中世纪以来一个很有影响力的意大利贵族家族，出过三位教皇、至少 34 位天主教枢机、为数甚多的重要政治人物；维特里家族自 15 世纪以来出过不少富可敌国的商贾。
3. the *Mamelukes* ... Malabar：作者用马穆鲁克族人泛指统治埃及和叙利亚的苏丹；而内瑞斯民族则居住在印度南部马拉巴尔海岸附近，以好战著称。

of its own principles, might turn aside whilst fraud and violence were accomplishing the destruction of a pretended nobility, which disgraced, whilst it persecuted, human nature. The persons most abhorrent from blood and treason and arbitrary confiscation might remain silent spectators of this civil war between the vices.

But did the privileged nobility who met under the king's precept at Versailles in 1789, or their constituents, deserve to be looked on as the *Nayres* or *Mamelukes* of this age, or as the *Orsini* and *Vitelli* of ancient times? If I had then asked the question, I should have passed for a madman. What have they since done, that they were to be driven into exile, that their persons should be hunted about, mangled, and tortured, their families dispersed, their houses laid in ashes, and that their order should be abolished, and the memory of it, if possible, extinguished, by ordaining them to change the very names by which they were usually known?[1] Read their instructions to their representatives. They breathe the spirit of liberty as warmly, and they recommend reformation as strongly, as any other order. Their privileges relative to contribution were voluntarily surrendered; as the king, from the beginning, surrendered all pretence to a right of taxation. Upon a free constitution there was but one opinion in France. The absolute monarchy was at an end. It breathed its last without a groan, without struggle, without convulsion. All the struggle, all the dissension, arose afterwards, upon the preference of a despotic democracy to a government of reciprocal control. The triumph of the victorious party was over the principles of a British constitution.

I have observed the affectation which for many years past has prevailed in Paris, even to a degree perfectly childish, of idolizing the memory of your Henry IV. If anything could put any one out of humour with that ornament to the kingly character, it would be this

---

1. by ordaining ... usually known: 指国民会议于 1790 年 6 月 19 日发布法令，取消贵族拥有的所有头衔和徽章。

overdone style of insidious panegyric. The persons who have worked this engine the most busily are those who have ended their panegyrics in dethroning his successor and descendant: a man as good-natured, at the least, as Henry IV; altogether as fond of his people; and who has done infinitely more to correct the ancient vices of the state than that great monarch did, or we are sure he ever meant to do. Well it is for his panegyrists that they have not him to deal with! For Henry of Navarre[1] was a resolute, active, and politic prince. He possessed, indeed, great humanity and mildness, but an humanity and mildness that never stood in the way of his interests. He never sought to be loved without putting himself first in a condition to be feared. He used soft language with determined conduct. He asserted and maintained his authority in the gross, and distributed his acts of concession only in the detail. He spent the income of his prerogative nobly, but he took care not to break in upon the capital; never abandoning for a moment any of the claims which he made under the fundamental laws, nor sparing to shed the blood of those who opposed him, often in the field, sometimes upon the scaffold. Because he knew how to make his virtues respected by the ungrateful, he has merited the praises of those whom, if they had lived in his time, he would have shut up in the Bastille, and brought to punishment along with the regicides whom he hanged after he had famished Paris into a surrender.

If these panegyrists are in earnest in their admiration of Henry IV, they must remember that they cannot think more highly of him than he did of the noblesse of France, whose virtue, honour, courage, patriotism, and loyalty were his constant theme.

But the nobility of France are degenerated since the days of Henry IV. — This is possible. But it is more than I can believe to be true in

---

1. Henry of Navarre: 法兰西国王亨利四世（1553—1610）。整个法国革命期间，亨利四世被捧为治理有方、宗教宽容的好国王。巴黎首座大桥"新桥"上亨利四世的塑像是革命期间极少数没有被破坏的塑像之一。

any great degree. I do not pretend to know France as correctly as some others; but I have endeavoured through my whole life to make myself acquainted with human nature: otherwise I should be unfit to take even my humble part in the service of mankind. In that study I could not pass by a vast portion of our nature as it appeared modified in a country but twenty-four miles from the shore of this island. On my best observation, compared with my best inquiries, I found your nobility for the greater part composed of men of a high spirit, and of a delicate sense of honour, both with regard to themselves individually, and with regard to their whole corps, over whom they kept, beyond what is common in other countries, a censorial eye. They were tolerably well bred; very officious, humane, and hospitable; in their conversation frank and open; with a good military tone; and reasonably tinctured with literature, particularly of the authors in their own language. Many had pretensions far above this description. I speak of those who were generally met with.

As to their behaviour to the inferior classes, they appeared to me to comport themselves towards them with good-nature, and with something more nearly approaching to familiarity than is generally practised with us in the intercourse between the higher and lower ranks of life. To strike any person, even in the most abject condition, was a thing in a manner unknown, and would be highly disgraceful. Instances of other ill-treatment of the humble part of the community were rare; and as to attacks made upon the property or the personal liberty of the commons, I never heard of any whatsoever from *them*; nor, whilst the laws were in vigour under the ancient government, would such tyranny in subjects have been permitted. As men of landed estates, I had no fault to find with their conduct, though much to reprehend, and much to wish changed, in many of the old tenures. Where the letting of their land was by rent, I could not discover that their agreements with their farmers were oppressive; nor when they were in partnership with the farmer, as often was the case, have I heard that they had taken the lion's share. The proportions seemed not inequitable. There might be exceptions; but certainly they were exceptions only. I have no reason to believe that in these respects the landed noblesse of France were worse than the landed gentry of this country; certainly in no respect more vexatious than the landholders, not noble, of their own nation. In cities the nobility had no manner of power; in the country very little. You know, Sir, that much of the civil government, and the police in the most essential parts, was not in the hands of that nobility which presents itself first to our consideration. The revenue, the system and collection of which were the most grievous parts of the French government, was not administered by the men of the sword; nor were they answerable for the vices of its principle, or the vexations, where any such existed, in its management.

Denying, as I am well warranted to do, that the nobility had any considerable share in the oppression of the people, in cases in which real oppression existed, I am ready to admit that they were not without considerable faults and errors. A foolish imitation of the worst part of the manners of England, which impaired their natural character, without substituting in its place what perhaps they meant to copy, has certainly rendered them worse than formerly they were. Habitual dissoluteness of manners, continued beyond the pardonable period of life, was more common amongst them than it is with us; and it reigned with the less hope of remedy, though possibly with something of less mischief, by being covered with more exterior decorum. They countenanced too much that licentious philosophy which has helped to bring on their ruin. There was another error amongst them more fatal. Those of the commons who approached to or exceeded many of the nobility in point of wealth were not fully admitted to the rank and estimation which wealth, in reason and good policy, ought to bestow in every country, though I think not equally with that of other nobility. The two kinds of aristocracy were too punctiliously kept asunder: less so, however, than in Germany and some other nations.

This separation, as I have already taken the liberty of suggesting to you, I conceive to be one principal cause of the destruction of the old nobility. The military, particularly, was too exclusively reserved for men of family.[1] But, after all, this was an error of opinion, which a conflicting opinion would have rectified. A permanent Assembly, in which the commons had their share of power, would soon abolish whatever was too invidious and insulting in these distinctions; and even the faults in the morals of the nobility would have been probably corrected, by the greater varieties of occupation and pursuit to which a constitution by orders would have given rise.

All this violent cry against the nobility I take to be a mere work of art. To be honoured and even privileged by the laws, opinions, and inveterate usages of our country, growing out of the prejudice of ages, has nothing to provoke horror and indignation in any man. Even to be too tenacious of those privileges is not absolutely a crime. The strong struggle in every individual to preserve possession of what he has found to belong to him, and to distinguish him, is one of the securities against injustice and despotism implanted in our nature. It operates as an instinct to secure property, and to preserve communities in a settled state. What is there to shock in this? Nobility is a graceful ornament to the civil order. It is the Corinthian[2] capital of polished society. "*Omnes boni nobilitati semper favemus*[3]," was the saying of a wise and good man. It is, indeed, one sign of a liberal and benevolent mind to incline to it with some sort of partial propensity. He feels no ennobling principle in his own heart, who wishes to level all the artificial institutions which have been adopted for giving a body to opinion and permanence to

---

1. The military ... for men of family.：指 1781 年路易十六批准的一项法令，法国军官候选人必须提供至少四代贵族血统的证明。
2. Corinthian：科林斯式的（古希腊建筑风格，采用顶部雕刻叶饰的细圆柱）
3. *Omnes ... semper favemus*：〈拉〉引自西塞罗的《为色斯提乌斯辩护》。译成英文的大意是：All good people always favour the highborn。

fugitive esteem. It is a sour, malignant, envious disposition, without taste for the reality, or for any image or representation of virtue, that sees with joy the unmerited fall of what had long nourished in splendour and in honour. I do not like to see anything destroyed, any void produced in society, any ruin on the face of the land. It was therefore with no disappointment or dissatisfaction that my inquiries and observations did not present to me any incorrigible vices in the noblesse of France, or any abuse which could not be removed by a reform very short of abolition. Your noblesse did not deserve punishment; but to degrade is to punish.

It was with the same satisfaction I found that the result of my inquiry concerning your clergy was not dissimilar. It is no soothing news to my ears, that great bodies of men are incurably corrupt. It is not with much credulity I listen to any, when they speak evil of those whom they are going to plunder. I rather suspect that vices are feigned or exaggerated, when profit is looked for in their punishment. An enemy is a bad witness; a robber is a worse. Vices and abuses there were undoubtedly in that order, and must be. It was an old establishment, and not frequently revised. But I saw no crimes in the individuals that merited confiscation of their substance, nor those cruel insults and degradations, and that unnatural persecution, which have been substituted in the place of meliorating regulation.

If there had been any just cause for this new religions persecution, the atheistic libellers, who act as trumpeters to animate the populace to plunder, do not love anybody so much as not to dwell with complacence on the vices of the existing clergy. This they have not done. They find themselves obliged to rake into the histories of former ages (which they have ransacked with a malignant and profligate industry) for every instance of oppression and persecution which has been made by that body or in its favour, in order to justify, upon very iniquitous because very illogical principles of retaliation, their own persecutions and their own cruelties. After destroying all other genealogies and family distinctions, they invent a sort of pedigree of crimes. It is not very just to chastise men for the offences of their natural ancestors; but to take the fiction of ancestry in a corporate succession, as a ground for punishing men who have no relation to guilty acts, except in names and general descriptions, is a sort of refinement in injustice belonging to the philosophy of this enlightened age. The Assembly punishes men, many, if not most, of whom abhor the violent conduct of ecclesiastics in former times as much as their present persecutors can do, and who would be as loud and as strong in the expression of that sense, if they were not well aware of the purposes for which all this declamation is employed.

Corporate bodies are immortal for the good of the members, but not for their punishment. Nations themselves are such corporations. As well might we in England think of waging inexpiable war upon all Frenchmen for the evils which they have brought upon us in the several periods of our mutual hostilities. You might, on your part, think yourselves justified in falling upon all Englishmen on account of the unparalleled calamities brought upon the people of France by the unjust invasions of our Henrys and our Edwards. Indeed, we should be mutually justified in this exterminatory war upon each other, full as much as you are in the unprovoked persecution of your present countrymen, on account of the conduct of men of the same name in other times.

We do not draw the moral lessons we might from history. On the contrary, without care it may be used to vitiate our minds and to destroy our happiness. In history a great volume is unrolled for our instruction, drawing the materials of future wisdom from the past errors and infirmities of mankind. It may, in the perversion, serve for a magazine, furnishing offensive and defensive weapons for parties in church and state, and supplying the means of keeping alive, or reviving dissensions and animosities, and adding fuel to civil fury. History consists, for the greater part, of the miseries brought upon the world by pride, ambition, avarice, revenge, lust, sedition, hypocrisy, ungoverned zeal, and all the train of disorderly appetites, which shake the public with the same

— troublous storms that toss
The private state, and render life unsweet.[1]

These vices are the *causes* of those storms. Religion, morals, laws, prerogatives, privileges, liberties, rights of men, are the *pretexts*. The pretexts are always found in some specious appearance of a real good. You would not secure men from tyranny and sedition by rooting out of the mind the principles to which these fraudulent pretexts apply? If you did, you would root out everything that is valuable in the human breast. As these are the pretexts, so the ordinary actors and instruments in great public evils are kings, priests, magistrates, senates, parliaments, national assemblies, judges, and captains. You would not cure the evil by resolving that there should be no more monarchs, nor ministers of state, nor of the gospel; no interpreters of law, no general officers, no public councils. You might change the names. The things in some shape must remain. A certain *quantum* of power must always exist in the community, in some hands, and under some appellation. Wise men will apply their remedies to vices, not to names; to the causes of evil, which are permanent, not to the occasional organs by which they act, and the transitory modes in which they appear. Otherwise you will be wise historically, a fool in practice. Seldom have two ages the same fashion in their pretexts, and the same modes of mischief. Wickedness is a little more inventive. Whilst you are discussing fashion, the fashion is gone by. The very

---

1. troublous ... life unsweet：引自英国诗人埃德蒙·斯宾塞的史诗《仙后》。 这节诗的全句是：Long were to tell the troublous stormes, that tosse | The private state, and make the life unsweet。

same vice assumes a new body. The spirit transmigrates; and, far from losing its principle of life by the change of its appearance, it is renovated in its new organs with the fresh vigour of a juvenile activity. It walks abroad, it continues its ravages, whilst you are gibbeting the carcass or demolishing the tomb. You are terrifying yourselves with ghosts and apparitions, whilst your house is the haunt of robbers. It is thus with all those who, attending only to the shell and husk of history, think they are waging war with intolerance, pride, and cruelty, whilst, under colour of abhorring the ill principles of antiquated parties, they are authorizing and feeding the same odious vices in different factions, and perhaps in worse.

Your citizens of Paris formerly had lent themselves as the ready instruments to slaughter the followers of Calvin, at the infamous massacre of St. Bartholomew[1]. What should we say to those who could think of retaliating on the Parisians of this day the abominations and horrors of that time? They are, indeed, brought to abhor *that* massacre. Ferocious as they are, it is not difficult to make them dislike it, because the politicians and fashionable teachers have no interest in giving their passions exactly the same direction. Still, however, they find it their interest to keep the same savage dispositions alive. It was but the other day that they caused this very massacre to be acted on the stage for the diversion of the descendants of those who committed it. In this tragic farce they produced the Cardinal of Lorraine[2] in his robes of function, ordering general slaughter. Was this spectacle intended to make the Parisians abhor persecution and loathe the effusion of

---

1. massacre of St. Bartholomew: 圣巴托洛谬大屠杀，指 1572 年 8 月 24 日至 25 日，2 000 多名法国胡格诺派（新教徒）在巴黎遭到杀害。此次大屠杀由当时法国国王的母亲凯瑟琳·德·美第奇策划，以吉斯家族为主导的罗马天主教贵族实施。这是 16 世纪晚期法国天主教徒和胡格诺派教徒之间一系列内战中又一次重大流血事件。
2. the Cardinal of Lorraine: 指洛林红衣主教查尔斯（1524—1574），属于最有权势的天主教吉斯（Guise）家族。

blood? No, it was to teach them to persecute their own pastors; it was to excite them, by raising a disgust and horror of their clergy, to an alacrity in hunting down to destruction an order which, if it ought to exist at all, ought to exist not only in safety, but in reverence. It was to stimulate their cannibal appetites (which one would think had been gorged sufficiently) by variety and seasoning; and to quicken them to an alertness in new murders and massacres, if it should suit the purpose of the Guises of the day. An Assembly in which sat a multitude of priests and prelates was obliged to suffer this indignity at its door. The author was not sent to the galleys, nor the players to the house of correction. Not long after this exhibition, those players came forward to the Assembly to claim the rites of that very religion which they had dared to expose, and to show their prostituted faces in the senate, whilst the Archbishop of Paris, whose function was known to his people only by his prayers and benedictions, and his wealth only by alms, is forced to abandon his house, and to fly from his flock, (as from ravenous wolves,) because, truly, in the sixteenth century, the Cardinal of Lorraine was a rebel and a murderer.

Such is the effect of the perversion of history by those who, for the same nefarious[1] purposes, have perverted every other part of learning. But those who will stand upon that elevation of reason which places centuries under our eye and brings things to the true point of comparison, which obscures little names and effaces the colours of little parties, and to which nothing can ascend but the spirit and moral quality of human actions, will say to the teachers of the Palais Royal, — The Cardinal of Lorraine was the murderer of the sixteenth century; you have the glory of being the murderers in the eighteenth; and this is the only difference between you. But history in the nineteenth century, better understood and better employed,

---

1. nefarious: 邪恶的

will, I trust, teach a civilized posterity to abhor the misdeeds of both these barbarous ages. It will teach future priests and magistrates not to retaliate upon the speculative and inactive atheists of future times the enormities committed by the present practical zealots and furious fanatics of that wretched error, which, in its quiescent state, is more than punished, whenever it is embraced. It will teach posterity not to make war upon either religion or philosophy for the abuse which the hypocrites of both have made of the two most valuable blessings conferred upon us by the bounty of the universal Patron, who in all things eminently favours and protects the race of man.

If your clergy, or any clergy, should show themselves vicious beyond the fair bounds allowed to human infirmity, and to those professional faults which can hardly be separated from professional virtues, though their vices never can countenance the exercise of oppression, I do admit that they would naturally have the effect of abating very much of our indignation against the tyrants who exceed measure and justice in their punishment. I can allow in clergymen, through all their divisions, some tenaciousness of their own opinion, some overflowings of zeal for its propagation, some predilection to their own state and office, some attachment to the interest of their own corps, some preference to those who listen with docility to their doctrines, beyond those who scorn and deride them. I allow all this, because I am a man who have to deal with men, and who would not, through a violence of toleration, run into the greatest of all intolerance. I must bear with infirmities until they fester into crimes.

Undoubtedly, the natural progress of the passions, from frailty to vice, ought to be prevented by a watchful eye and a firm hand. But is it true that the body of your clergy had passed those limits of a just allowance? From the general style of your late publications of all sorts, one would be led to believe that your clergy in France were a sort of monsters: an horrible composition of superstition, ignorance, sloth, fraud, avarice, and tyranny. But is this true? Is it true that the lapse of time, the cessation of conflicting interests, the woeful experience of the evils resulting from party rage, have had no sort of influence gradually to meliorate their minds? Is it true that they were daily renewing invasions on the civil power, troubling the domestic quiet of their country, and rendering the operations of its government feeble and precarious? Is it true that the clergy of our times have pressed down the laity with an iron hand, and were in all places lighting up the fires of a savage persecution? Did they by every fraud endeavour to increase their estates? Did they use to exceed the due demands on estates that were their own? Or, rigidly screwing up right into wrong, did they convert a legal claim into a vexatious extortion? When not possessed of power, were they filled with the vices of those who envy it? Were they inflamed with a violent, litigious spirit of controversy? Goaded on with the ambition of intellectual sovereignty, were they ready to fly in the face of all magistracy, to fire churches, to massacre the priests of other descriptions, to pull down altars, and to make their way over the ruins of subverted governments to an empire of doctrine, sometimes flattering, sometimes forcing, the consciences of men from the jurisdiction of public institutions into a submission to their personal authority, beginning with a claim of liberty and ending with an abuse of power?

These, or some of these, were the vices objected, and not wholly without foundation, to several of the churchmen of former times, who belonged to the two great parties which then divided and distracted Europe.

If there was in France, as in other countries there visibly is, a great abatement, rather than any increase of these vices, instead of loading the present clergy with the crimes of other men and the odious character of other times, in common equity they ought to be praised, encouraged, and supported, in their departure from a spirit which disgraced their predecessors, and for having assumed a temper of mind and manners more suitable to their sacred function.

When my occasions took me into France, towards the close of the late reign, the clergy, under all their forms, engaged a considerable part of my curiosity. So far from finding (except from one set of men, not then very numerous, though very active) the complaints and discontents against that body which some publications had given me reason to expect, I perceived little or no public or private uneasiness on their account. On further examination, I found the clergy, in general, persons of moderate minds and decorous manners: I include the seculars, and the regulars of both sexes. I had not the good fortune to know a great many of the parochial clergy, but in general I received a perfectly good account of their morals, and of their attention to their duties. With some of the higher clergy I had a personal acquaintance, and of the rest in that class a very good means of information. They were almost all of them persons of noble birth. They resembled others of their own rank; and where there was any difference, it was in their favour. They were more fully educated than the military noblesse, so as by no means to disgrace their profession by ignorance, or by want of fitness for the exercise of their authority. They seemed to me, beyond the clerical character, liberal and open, with the hearts of gentlemen and men of honour, neither insolent nor servile in their manners and conduct. They seemed to me rather a superior class, a set of men amongst whom you would not be surprised to find a Fénelon[1]. I saw among the clergy in Paris (many of the description are not to be met with anywhere) men of great learning and candour; and I had reason to believe that this description was not confined to Paris. What I found in other places I know was accidental, and therefore to be presumed a fair sample. I spent a few days in a provincial town, where, in the absence of the bishop, I passed my evenings with three clergymen, his vicars-general, persons who would have done honour

---

1. Fénelon: 指坎布雷大主教费内隆 (François Fénelon, 1651—1715), 法国神学家、诗人和作家。

to any church. They were all well-informed; two of them of deep, general, and extensive erudition, ancient and modern, Oriental and Western, particularly in their own profession. They had a more extensive knowledge of our English divines than I expected; and they entered into the genius of those writers with a critical accuracy. One of these gentlemen is since dead, the Abbé Morangis. I pay this tribute without reluctance to the memory of that noble, reverend, learned, and excellent person; and I should do the same with equal cheerfulness to the merits of the others, who I believe are still living, if I did not fear to hurt those whom I am unable to serve.

Some of these ecclesiastics of rank are, by all titles, persons deserving of general respect. They are deserving of gratitude from me, and from many English. If this letter should ever come into their hands, I hope they will believe there are those of our nation who feel for their unmerited fall, and for the cruel confiscation of their fortunes, with no common sensibility. What I say of them is a testimony, as far as one feeble voice can go, which I owe to truth. Whenever the question of this unnatural persecution is concerned, I will pay it. No one shall prevent me from being just and grateful. The time is fitted for the duty; and it is particularly becoming to show our justice and gratitude, when those who have deserved well of us and of mankind are labouring under popular obloquy and the persecutions of oppressive power.

You had before your revolution about a hundred and twenty bishops. A few of them were men of eminent sanctity, and charity without limit. When we talk of the heroic, of course we talk of rare virtue. I believe the instances of eminent depravity may be as rare amongst them as those of transcendent goodness. Examples of avarice and of licentiousness may be picked out, I do not question it, by those who delight in the investigation which leads to such discoveries. A man as old as I am will not be astonished that several, in every description, do not lead that perfect life of self-denial, with regard to wealth or to pleasure, which is wished for by all, by some expected, but by none exacted with more rigor than by those who are the most attentive to their own interests or the most indulgent to their own passions. When I was in France, I am certain that the number of vicious prelates was not great. Certain individuals among them, not distinguishable for the regularity of their lives, made some amends for their want of the severe virtues in their possession of the liberal, and wore endowed with qualities which made them useful in the church and state. I am told, that, with few exceptions, Louis XVI had been more attentive to character, in his promotions to that rank, than his immediate predecessor; and I believe (as some spirit of reform has prevailed through the whole reign) that it may be true. But the present ruling power has shown a disposition only to plunder the church. It has punished *all* prelates: which is to favour the vicious, at least in point of reputation. It has made a degrading pensionary establishment, to which no man of liberal ideas or liberal condition will destine his children. It must settle into the lowest classes of the people. As with you the inferior clergy are not numerous enough for their duties, as these duties are beyond measure minute and toilsome, as you have left no middle classes of clergy at their ease, in future nothing of science or erudition can exist in the Gallican church. To complete the project, without the least attention to the rights of patrons, the Assembly has provided in future an elective clergy: an arrangement which will drive out of the clerical profession all men of sobriety, all who can pretend to independence in their function or their conduct; and which will throw the whole direction of the public mind into the hands of a set of licentious, bold, crafty, factious, flattering wretches, of such condition and such habits of life as will make their contemptible pensions (in comparison of which the stipend of an exciseman is lucrative and honourable) an object of low and illiberal intrigue. Those officers whom they still call bishops are to be elected to a provision comparatively mean, through the same arts, (that is, electioneering arts) by men of all religious tenets that are known or can be invented. The new lawgivers have not ascertained anything whatsoever concerning their qualifications, relative either to doctrine or to morals, no more than they have done with regard to the subordinate clergy; nor does it appear but that both the higher and the lower may, at their discretion, practise or preach any mode of religion or irreligion that they please. I do not yet see what the jurisdiction of bishops over their subordinates is to be, or whether they are to have any jurisdiction at all.

In short, Sir, it seems to me that this new ecclesiastical establishment is intended only to be temporary, and preparatory to the utter abolition, under any of its forms, of the Christian religion, whenever the minds of men are prepared for this last stroke against it by the accomplishment of the plan for bringing its ministers into universal contempt. They who will not believe that the philosophical fanatics who guide in these matters have long entertained such a design are utterly ignorant of their character and proceedings. These enthusiasts do not scruple to avow their opinion, that a state can subsist without any religion better than with one, and that they are able to supply the place of any good which may be in it by a project of their own — namely, by a sort of education they have imagined, founded in a knowledge of the physical wants of men, progressively carried to an enlightened self-interest, which, when well understood, they tell us, will identify with an interest more enlarged and public. The scheme of this education has been long known. Of late they distinguish it (as they have got an entirely new nomenclature of technical terms) by the name of a *Civic Education*[1].

I hope their partisans in England (to whom I rather attribute very

---

1. *Civic Education*：即世俗教育制度。法国 18 世纪启蒙运动代表人物，让·雅克·卢梭（Jean-Jacques Rousseau, 1712—1778）和孔多塞侯爵（the Marquis de Condorcet, 1743—1794）是法国世俗教育制度的积极倡导者，也因此为作者所不容。

inconsiderate conduct than the ultimate object in this detestable design) will succeed neither in the pillage of the ecclesiastics nor in the introduction of a principle of popular election to our bishoprics and parochial cures. This, in the present condition of the world, would be the last corruption of the church; the utter ruin of the clerical character, the most dangerous shock that the state ever received through a misunderstood arrangement of religion. I know well enough that the bishoprics and cures, under kingly and seigniorial patronage, as now they are in England, and as they have been lately in France, are sometimes acquired by unworthy methods; but the other mode of ecclesiastical canvass subjects them infinitely more surely and more generally to all the evil arts of low ambition, which, operating on and through greater numbers, will produce mischief in proportion.

Those of you who have robbed the clergy think that they shall easily reconcile their conduct to all Protestant nations, because the clergy whom they have thus plundered, degraded, and given over to mockery and scorn, are of the Roman Catholic, that is, of *their own* pretended persuasion. I have no doubt that some miserable bigots will be found here as well as elsewhere, who hate sects and parties different from their own more than they love the substance of religion, and who are more angry with those who differ from them in their particular plans and systems than displeased with those who attack the foundation of our common hope. These men will write and speak on the subject in the manner that is to be expected from their temper and character. Burnet[1] says, that, when he was in France, in the year 1683, "the method which carried over the men of the finest parts to Popery was this: they brought themselves to doubt of the whole Christian religion: when that was once done, it seemed a more indifferent thing of what side or form they continued outwardly." If this was then the

---

1. Burnet: 吉尔伯特·伯内特 (Gilbert Burnet, 1643—1715), 英国国教的主教和历史学家, 强烈反对天主教, 政治上倾向辉格党。

ecclesiastic policy of France, it is what they have since but too much reason to repent of. They preferred atheism to a form of religion not agreeable to their ideas. They succeeded in destroying that form; and atheism has succeeded in destroying them. I can readily give credit to Burnet's story; because I have observed too much of a similar spirit (for a little of it is "much too much") amongst ourselves. The humour, however, is not general.

The teachers who reformed our religion in England bore no sort of resemblance to your present reforming doctors in Paris. Perhaps they were (like those whom they opposed) rather more than could be wished under the influence of a party spirit; but they were most sincere believers; men of the most fervent and exalted piety; ready to die (as some of them did die) like true heroes in defence of their particular ideas of Christianity; as they would with equal fortitude, and more cheerfully, for that stock of general truth for the branches of which they contended with their blood. These men would have disavowed with horror those wretches who claimed a fellowship with them upon no other titles than those of their having pillaged the persons with whom they maintained controversies, and their having despised the common religion, for the purity of which they exerted themselves with a zeal which unequivocally bespoke their highest reverence for the substance of that system which they wished to reform. Many of their descendants have retained the same zeal, but (as less engaged in conflict) with more moderation. They do not forget that justice and mercy are substantial parts of religion. Impious men do not recommend themselves to their communion by iniquity and cruelty towards any description of their fellow-creatures.

We hear these new teachers continually boasting of their spirit of toleration[1]. That those persons should tolerate all opinions, who think

---

1. spirit of toleration: 1789 年 12 月 24 日，国民议会颁布法令，赋予法国犹太人和新教徒完全的公民权利。

none to be of estimation, is a matter of small merit. Equal neglect is not impartial kindness. The species of benevolence which arises from contempt is no true charity. There are in England abundance of men who tolerate in the true spirit of toleration. They think the dogmas of religion, though in different degrees, are all of moment, and that amongst them there is, as amongst all things of value, a just ground of preference. They favour, therefore, and they tolerate. They tolerate, not because they despise opinions, but because they respect justice. They would reverently and affectionately protect all religions, because they love and venerate the great principle upon which they all agree, and the great object to which they are all directed. They begin more and more plainly to discern that we have all a common cause, as against a common enemy. They will not be so misled by the spirit of faction as not to distinguish what is done in favour of their subdivision from those acts of hostility which, through some particular description, are aimed at the whole corps in which they themselves, under another denomination, are included. It is impossible for me to say what may be the character of every description of men amongst us. But I speak for the greater part; and for them, I must tell you, that sacrilege is no part of their doctrine of good works; that, so far from calling you into their fellowship on such title, if your professors are admitted to their communion, they must carefully conceal their doctrine of the lawfulness of the proscription of innocent men, and that they must make restitution of all stolen goods whatsoever. Till then they are none of ours.

You may suppose that we do not approve your confiscation of the revenues of bishops, and deans, and chapters, and parochial clergy possessing independent estates arising from land, because we have the same sort of establishment in England. That objection, you will say, cannot hold as to the confiscation of the goods of monks and nuns, and the abolition of their order. It is true that this particular part of your general confiscation does not affect England, as a precedent in point; but the reason applies, and it goes a great way. The Long Parliament[1] confiscated the lands of deans and chapters in England on the same ideas upon which your Assembly set to sale the lands of the monastic orders. But it is in the principle of injustice that the danger lies, and not in the description of persons on whom it is first exercised. I see, in a country very near us, a course of policy pursued, which sets justice, the common concern of mankind, at defiance. With the National Assembly of France possession is nothing; law and usage are nothing. I see the National Assembly openly reprobate the doctrine of prescription, which one of the greatest of their own lawyers tells us, with great truth, is a part of the law of nature. He tells us that the positive ascertainment of its limits, and its security from invasion, were among the causes for which civil society itself has been instituted. If prescription be once shaken, no species of property is secure, when it once becomes an object large enough to tempt the cupidity of indigent power. I see a practice perfectly correspondent to their contempt of this great fundamental part of natural law. I see the confiscators begin with bishops, and chapters, and monasteries; but I do not see them end there. I see the princes of the blood, who, by the oldest usages of that kingdom, held large landed estates, (hardly with the compliment of a debate) deprived of their possessions, and in lieu of their stable, independent property, reduced to the hope of some precarious charitable pension at the pleasure of an assembly, which of course will pay little regard to the rights of pensioners at pleasure, when it despises those of legal proprietors. Flushed with the insolence of their first inglorious victories, and pressed by the distresses caused by their lust of unhallowed lucre, disappointed, but not discouraged, they have at length ventured completely to subvert all property of all descriptions throughout the extent of a great kingdom. They have

---

1. Long Parliament：长期议会，指英国查理一世在 1640 年召集的议会，1653 年被克伦威尔废除，1660 年被最终解散。

compelled all men, in all transactions of commerce, in the disposal of lands, in civil dealing, and through the whole communion of life, to accept, as perfect payment and good and lawful tender, the symbols of their speculations on a projected sale of their plunder. What vestiges of liberty or property have they left? The tenant-right of a cabbage-garden, a year's interest in a hovel, the good-will of an ale-house or a baker's shop, the very shadow of a constructive property, are more ceremoniously treated in our Parliament than with you the oldest and most valuable landed possessions, in the hands of the most respectable personages, or than the whole body of the moneyed and commercial interest of your country. We entertain a high opinion of the legislative authority; but we have never dreamt that Parliaments had any right whatever to violate property, to overrule prescription, or to force a currency of their own fiction in the place of that which is real, and recognized by the law of nations. But you, who began with refusing to submit to the most moderate restraints, have ended by establishing an unheard-of despotism. I find the ground upon which your confiscators go is this: that, indeed, their proceedings could not be supported in a court of justice, but that the rules of prescription cannot bind a legislative assembly. So that this legislative assembly of a free nation sits, not for the security, but for the destruction of property, and not of property only, but of every rule and maxim which can give it stability, and of those instruments which can alone give it circulation.

When the Anabaptists of Munster[1], in the sixteenth century, had filled Germany with confusion, by their system of levelling, and their wild opinions concerning property, to what country in Europe did not the progress of their fury furnish just cause of alarm? Of all things, wisdom is the most terrified with epidemical fanaticism, because of

---

1. Anabaptists of Munster: 明斯特再洗礼教派，指 16 世纪欧洲宗教改革时期在德国西北部城市明斯特产生的一个激进的基督教教派，一度统治整个城市，建立自己的宗教公社。

all enemies it is that against which she is the least able to furnish any kind of resource. We cannot be ignorant of the spirit of atheistical fanaticism, that is inspired by a multitude of writings dispersed with incredible assiduity and expense, and by sermons delivered in all the streets and places of public resort in Paris. These writings and sermons have filled the populace with a black and savage atrocity of mind, which supersedes in them the common feelings of nature, as well as all sentiments of morality and religion; insomuch that these wretches are induced to bear with a sullen patience the intolerable distresses brought upon them by the violent convulsions and permutations that have been made in property. The spirit of proselytism attends this spirit of fanaticism. They have societies to cabal and correspond at home and abroad for the propagation of their tenets. The republic of Berne[1], one of the happiest, the most prosperous, and the best-governed countries upon earth, is one of the great objects at the destruction of which they aim. I am told they have in some measure succeeded in sowing there the seeds of discontent. They are busy throughout Germany. Spain and Italy have not been untried. England is not left out of the comprehensive scheme of their malignant charity; and in England we find those who stretch out their arms to them, who recommend their example from more than one pulpit, and who choose, in more than one periodical meeting, publicly to correspond with them, to applaud them, and to hold them up as objects for imitation; who receive from them tokens of confraternity, and standards consecrated amidst their rites and mysteries; who suggest to them leagues of perpetual amity, at the very time when the power to which our constitution has exclusively delegated the federative

---

1. republic of Berne：伯尔尼共和国，指 1790 年一个以巴黎为基地的组织（Club Helvetique）派人去伯尔尼宣讲，伯尔尼政府向法国提出正式抗议。18 世纪 90 年代前的瑞士是一个松散的城邦联合体，伯尔尼只是十三个城邦中的一个。

capacity of this kingdom may find it expedient to make war upon them.

It is not the confiscation of our church property from this example in France that I dread, though I think this would be no trifling evil. The great source of my solicitude is, lest it should ever be considered in England as the policy of a state to seek a resource in confiscations of any kind, or that any one description of citizens should be brought to regard any of the others as their proper prey. Nations are wading deeper and deeper into an ocean of boundless debt. Public debts, which at first were a security to governments, by interesting many in the public tranquillity, are likely in their excess to become the means of their subversion. If governments provide for these debts by heavy impositions, they perish by becoming odious to the people. If they do not provide for them, they will be undone by the efforts of the most dangerous of all parties; I mean an extensive, discontented moneyed interest, injured and not destroyed. The men who compose this interest look for their security, in the first instance, to the fidelity of government; in the second, to its power. If they find the old governments effete, worn out, and with their springs relaxed, so as not to be of sufficient vigour for their purposes, they may seek new ones that shall be possessed of more energy; and this energy will be derived, not from an acquisition of resources, but from a contempt of justice. Revolutions are favourable to confiscation; and it is impossible to know under what obnoxious names the next confiscations will be authorized. I am sure that the principles predominant in France extend to very many persons, and descriptions of persons, in all countries, who think their innoxious indolence their security. This kind of innocence in proprietors may be argued into inutility; and inutility into an unfitness for their estates. Many parts of Europe are in open disorder. In many others there is a hollow murmuring under ground; a confused movement is felt, that threatens a general earthquake in the political world. Already confederacies and correspondences of the most extraordinary nature are forming in several countries. In such a state of things we ought to hold ourselves upon our guard. In all mutations (if mutations must be) the circumstance which will serve most to blunt the edge of their mischief, and to promote what good may be in them, is, that they should find us with our minds tenacious of justice and tender of property.

But it will be argued, that this confiscation in France ought not to alarm other nations. They say it is not made from wanton rapacity; that it is a great measure of national policy, adopted to remove an extensive, inveterate[1], superstitious mischief. It is with the greatest difficulty that I am able to separate policy from justice. Justice is itself the great standing policy of civil society; and any eminent departure from it, under any circumstances, lies under the suspicion of being no policy at all.

When men are encouraged to go into a certain mode of life by the existing laws, and protected in that mode as in a lawful occupation — when they have accommodated all their ideas and all their habits to it — when the law had long made their adherence to its rules a ground of reputation, and their departure from them a ground of disgrace and even of penalty — I am sure it is unjust in legislature, by an arbitrary act, to offer a sudden violence to their minds and their feelings, forcibly to degrade them from their state and condition, and to stigmatize with shame and infamy that character and those customs which before had been made the measure of their happiness and honour. If to this be added an expulsion from their habitations and a confiscation of all their goods, I am not sagacious enough to discover how this despotic sport made of the feelings, consciences, prejudices, and properties of men can be discriminated from the rankest tyranny.

If the injustice of the course pursued in France be clear, the policy

---

1. inveterate: 根深蒂固的

of the measure, that is, the public benefit to be expected from it, ought to be at least as evident, and at least as important. To a man who acts under the influence of no passion, who has nothing in view in his projects but the public good, a great difference will immediately strike him, between what policy would dictate on the original introduction of such institutions, and on a question of their total abolition, where they have cast their roots wide and deep, and where, by long habit, things more valuable than themselves are so adapted to them, and in a manner interwoven with them, that the one cannot be destroyed without notably impairing the other. He might be embarrassed, if the case were really such as sophisters represent it in their paltry style of debating. But in this, as in most questions of state, there is a middle. There is something else than the mere alternative of absolute destruction or unreformed existence. *Spartam nactus es; hanc exorna*[1]. This is, in my opinion, a rule of profound sense, and ought never to depart from the mind of an honest reformer. I cannot conceive how any man can have brought himself to that pitch of presumption, to consider his country as nothing but *carte blanche*[2], upon which he may scribble whatever he pleases. A man full of warm, speculative benevolence may wish his society otherwise constituted than he finds it; but a good patriot, and a true politician, always considers how he shall make the most of the existing materials of his country. A disposition to preserve, and an ability to improve, taken together, would be my standard of a statesman. Everything else is vulgar in the conception, perilous in the execution.

There are moments in the fortune of states, when particular men are called to make improvements by great mental exertion. In those moments, even when they seem to enjoy the confidence of their prince

---

1. *Spartam nactus es; hanc exorna*：〈拉〉引自西塞罗的《致阿特提库斯书》。英文的大意是：Now that Sparta has fallen to your lot, adorn it.
2. *carte blanche*：〈法〉签好字的空白纸，全权委托

and country, and to be invested with full authority, they have not always apt instruments. A politician, to do great things, looks for a *power*, what our workmen call a *purchase*; and if he finds that power, in politics as in mechanics, he cannot be at a loss to apply it. In the monastic institutions, in my opinion, was found a great *power* for the mechanism of politic benevolence. There were revenues with a public direction; there were men wholly set apart and dedicated to public purposes, without any other than public ties and public principles; men without the possibility of converting the estate of the community into a private fortune; men denied to self-interests, whose avarice is for some community; men to whom personal poverty is honour, and implicit obedience stands in the place of freedom. In vain shall a man look to the possibility of making such things when he wants them. The winds blow as they list. These institutions are the products of enthusiasm; they are the instruments of wisdom. Wisdom cannot create materials; they are the gifts of nature or of chance; her pride is in the use. The perennial existence of bodies corporate and their fortunes are things particularly suited to a man who has long views; who meditates designs that require time in fashioning, and which propose duration when they are accomplished. He is not deserving to rank high, or even to be mentioned in the order of great statesmen, who, having obtained the command and direction of such a power as existed in the wealth, the discipline, and the habits of such corporations as those which you have rashly destroyed, cannot find any way of converting it to the great and lasting benefit of his country. On the view of this subject, a thousand uses suggest themselves to a contriving mind. To destroy any power growing wild from the rank productive force of the human mind is almost tantamount[1], in the moral world, to the destruction of the apparently active properties of bodies in the material. It would be

---

1. tantamount: 相当于……的

like the attempt to destroy (if it were in our competence to destroy) the expansive force of fixed air in nitre, or the power of steam, or of electricity, or of magnetism. These energies always existed in nature, and they were always discernible. They seemed, some of them unserviceable, some noxious, some no better than a sport to children, until contemplative ability, combining with practic skill, tamed their wild nature, subdued them to use, and rendered them at once the most powerful and the most tractable agents, in subservience to the great views and designs of men. Did fifty thousand persons, whose mental and whose bodily labour you might direct, and so many hundred thousand a year of a revenue, which was neither lazy nor superstitious, appear too big for your abilities to wield? Had you no way of using the men, but by converting monks into pensioners? Had you no way of turning the revenue to account, but through the improvident resource of a spendthrift sale? If you were thus destitute of mental funds, the proceeding is in its natural course. Your politicians do not understand their trade; and therefore they sell their tools.

But the institutions savour of superstition in their very principle; and they nourish it by a permanent and standing influence. This I do not mean to dispute; but this ought not to hinder you from deriving from superstition itself any resources which may thence be furnished for the public advantage. You derive benefits from many dispositions and many passions of the human mind which are of as doubtful a colour, in the moral eye, as superstition itself. It was your business to correct and mitigate everything which was noxious in this passion, as in all the passions. But is superstition the greatest of all possible vices? In its possible excess I think it becomes a very great evil. It is, however, a moral subject, and of course admits of all degrees and all modifications. Superstition is the religion of feeble minds; and they must be tolerated in an intermixture of it, in some trifling or some enthusiastic shape or other, else you will deprive weak minds of a resource found necessary to the strongest. The body of all true religion consists, to be sure, in obedience to the will of the sovereign of the world, in a confidence in his declarations, and in imitation of his perfections. The rest is our own. It may be prejudicial to the great end; it may be auxiliary. Wise men, who, as such, are not *admirers* (not admirers at least of the *Munera Terræ*[1]) are not violently attached to these things, nor do they violently hate them. Wisdom is not the most severe corrector of folly. They are the rival follies which mutually wage so unrelenting a war, and which make so cruel a use of their advantages, as they can happen to engage the immoderate vulgar, on the one side or the other, in their quarrels. Prudence would be neuter; but if, in the contention between fond attachment and fierce antipathy concerning things in their nature not made to produce such heats, a prudent man were obliged to make a choice of what errors and excesses of enthusiasm he would condemn or bear, perhaps he would think the superstition which builds to be more tolerable than that which demolishes — that which adorns a country, than that which deforms it — that which endows, than that which plunders — that which disposes to mistaken beneficence, than that which stimulates to real injustice — that which leads a man to refuse to himself lawful pleasures, than that which snatches from others the scanty subsistence of their self-denial. Such, I think, is very nearly the state of the question between the ancient founders of monkish superstition and the superstition of the pretended philosophers of the hour.

For the present I postpone all consideration of the supposed public profit of the sale, which, however, I conceive to be perfectly delusive. I shall here only consider it as a transfer of property. On the policy of that transfer I shall trouble you with a few thoughts.

In every prosperous community something more is produced than goes to the immediate support of the producer. This surplus forms the

---

1. *Munera Terræ*:〈拉〉引自贺拉斯的《颂歌集》。英文的大意是：Gifts of the Earth。

income of the landed capitalist. It will be spent by a proprietor who does not labour. But this idleness is itself the spring of labour, this repose the spur to industry. The only concern for the state is, that the capital taken in rent from the land should be returned again to the industry from whence it came, and that its expenditure should be with the least possible detriment to the morals of those who expend it and to those of the people to whom it is returned.

In all the views of receipt, expenditure, and personal employment, a sober legislator would carefully compare the possessor whom he was recommended to expel with the stranger who was proposed to fill his place. Before the inconveniences are incurred which *must* attend all violent revolutions in property through extensive confiscation, we ought to have some rational assurance that the purchasers of the confiscated property will be in a considerable degree more laborious, more virtuous, more sober, less disposed to extort an unreasonable proportion of the gains of the labourer, or to consume on themselves a larger share than is fit for the measure of an individual, or that they should be qualified to dispense the surplus in a more steady and equal mode, so as to answer the purposes of a politic expenditure, than the old possessors, call those possessors bishops, or canons, or commendatory abbots, or monks, or what you please. The monks are lazy. Be it so. Suppose them no otherwise employed than by singing in the choir. They are as usefully employed as those who neither sing nor say, as usefully even as those who sing upon the stage. They are as usefully employed as if they worked from dawn to dark in the innumerable servile, degrading, unseemly, unmanly, and often most unwholesome and pestiferous occupations to which by the social economy so many wretches are inevitably doomed. If it were not generally pernicious to disturb the natural course of things, and to impede in any degree the great wheel of circulation which is turned by the strangely directed labour of these unhappy people, I should be infinitely more inclined forcibly to rescue them from their miserable industry than violently to disturb the tranquil repose of monastic quietude. Humanity, and perhaps policy, might better justify me in the one than in the other. It is a subject on which I have often reflected, and never reflected without feeling from it. I am sure that no consideration, except the necessity of submitting to the yoke of luxury and the despotism of fancy, who in their own imperious way will distribute the surplus product of the soil, can justify the toleration of such trades and employments in a well-regulated state. But for this purpose of distribution, it seems to me that the idle expenses of monks are quite as well directed as the idle expenses of us lay loiterers[1].

When the advantages of the possession and of the project are on a par, there is no motive for a change. But in the present case, perhaps, they are not upon a par, and the difference is in favour of the possession. It does not appear to me that the expenses of those whom you are going to expel do in fact take a course so directly and so generally leading to vitiate and degrade and render miserable those through whom they pass as the expenses of those favourites whom you are intruding into their houses. Why should the expenditure of a great landed property, which is a dispersion of the surplus product of the soil, appear intolerable to you or to me, when it takes its course through the accumulation of vast libraries, which are the history of the force and weakness of the human mind; through great collections of ancient records, medals, and coins, which attest and explain laws and customs; through paintings and statues, that, by imitating nature, seem to extend the limits of creation; through grand monuments of the dead, which continue the regards and connections of life beyond the grave; through collections of the specimens of nature, which become a representative assembly of all the classes and families of the world, that by disposition facilitate, and by exciting curiosity open,

---

1. loiterers: 混日子的人，闲荡的人

the avenues to science? If by great permanent establishments all these objects of expense are better secured from the inconstant sport of personal caprice and personal extravagance, are they worse than if the same tastes prevailed in scattered individuals? Does not the sweat of the mason and carpenter, who toil in order to partake the sweat of the peasant, flow as pleasantly and as salubriously in the construction and repair of the majestic edifices of religion as in the painted booths and sordid sties of vice and luxury? as honourably and as profitably in repairing those sacred works which grow hoary with innumerable years as on the momentary receptacles of transient voluptuousness, in opera-houses, and brothels, and gaming-houses, and club-houses, and obelisks in the Champ de Mars[1]? Is the surplus product of the olive and the vine worse employed in the frugal sustenance of persons whom the fictions of a pious imagination raise to dignity by construing in the service of God than in pampering the innumerable multitude of those who are degraded by being made useless domestics, subservient to the pride of man? Are the decorations of temples an expenditure less worthy a wise man than ribbons, and laces, and national cockades, and petites maisons[2], and petit soupers[3], and all the innumerable fopperies and follies in which opulence sports away the burden of its superfluity?

We tolerate even these, not from love of them, but for fear of worse. We tolerate them, because property and liberty, to a degree, require that toleration. But why proscribe the other, and surely, in every point of view, the more laudable use of estates? Why, through the violation of all property, through an outrage upon every principle of liberty, forcibly carry them from the better to the worse?

---

1. Champ de Mars：指 1790 年 7 月 14 日为实现法国全民和解之目的在巴黎火星竞技场举办的一项联欢活动。
2. petites maisons：〈法〉小屋，也可能指包养情妇的住处。
3. petit soupers：〈法〉晚餐小聚

This comparison between the new individuals and the old corps is made upon a supposition that no reform could be made in the latter. But, in a question of reformation, I always consider corporate bodies, whether sole or consisting of many, to be much more susceptible of a public direction, by the power of the state, in the use of their property, and in the regulation of modes and habits of life in their members, than private citizens ever can be, or perhaps ought to be; and this seems to me a very material consideration for those who undertake anything which merits the name of a politic enterprise. — So far as to the estates of monasteries.

With regard to the estates possessed by bishops and canons and commendatory abbots, I cannot find out for what reason some landed estates may not be held otherwise than by inheritance. Can any philosophic spoiler undertake to demonstrate the positive or the comparative evil of having a certain, and that, too, a large, portion of landed property passing in succession through persons whose title to it is, always in theory and often in fact, an eminent degree of piety, morals, and learning; a property which by its destination, in their turn, and on the score of merit, gives to the noblest families renovation and support, to the lowest the means of dignity and elevation; a property, the tenure of which is the performance of some duty (whatever value you may choose to set upon that duty) and the character of whose proprietors demands at least an exterior decorum and gravity of manners; who are to exercise a generous, but temperate hospitality; part of whose income they are to consider as a trust for charity; and who, even when they fail in their trust, when they slide from their character, and degenerate into a mere common secular nobleman or gentleman, are in no respect worse than those who may succeed them in their forfeited possessions? Is it better that estates should be held by those who have no duty than by those who have one? by those whose character and destination point to virtues, than by those who have no rule and direction in the expenditure of their estates but their own will and appetite? Nor are these estates held altogether in the character or with the evils supposed inherent in mortmain. They pass from hand to hand with a more rapid circulation than any other. No excess is good, and therefore too great a proportion of landed property may be held officially for life; but it does not seem to me of material injury to any common wealth that there should exist some estates that have a chance of being acquired by other means than the previous acquisition of money.

* * * * *

This letter is grown to a great length, though it is, indeed, short with regard to the infinite extent of the subject. Various avocations have from time to time called my mind from the subject. I was not sorry to give myself leisure to observe whether in the proceedings of the National Assembly I might not find reasons to change or to qualify some of my first sentiments. Everything has confirmed me more strongly in my first opinions. It was my original purpose to take a view of the principles of the National Assembly with regard to the great and fundamental establishments, and to compare the whole of what you have substituted in the place of what you have destroyed with the several members of our British constitution. But this plan is of greater extent than at first I computed, and I find that you have little desire to take the advantage of any examples. At present I must content myself with some remarks upon your establishments, reserving for another time what I proposed to say concerning the spirit of our British monarchy, aristocracy, and democracy, as practically they exist.

I have taken a view of what has been done by the governing power in France. I have certainly spoken of it with freedom. Those whose principle it is to despise the ancient, permanent sense of mankind, and to set up a scheme of society on new principles, must naturally expect that such of us who think better of the judgment of the human race than, of theirs should consider both them and their devices as men and schemes upon their trial. They must take it for granted that we attend much to their reason, but not at all to their authority. They have not one of the great influencing prejudices of mankind in their favor. They avow their hostility to opinion. Of course they must expect no support from that influence, which, with every other authority, they have deposed from the seat of its jurisdiction.

I can never consider this assembly as anything else than a voluntary association of men who have availed themselves of circumstances to seize upon the power of the state. They have not the sanction and authority of the character under which they first met. They have assumed another of a very different nature, and have completely altered and inverted all the relations in which they originally stood. They do not hold the authority they exercise under any constitutional law of the state. They have departed from the instructions of the people by whom they were sent; which instructions, as the assembly did not act in virtue of any ancient usage or settled law, were the sole source of their authority. The most considerable of their acts have not been done by great majorities; and in this sort of near divisions, which carry only the constructive authority of the whole, strangers will consider reasons as well as resolutions.

If they had set up this new, experimental government as a necessary substitute for an expelled tyranny, mankind would anticipate the time of prescription, which through long usage mellows into legality governments that were violent in their commencement. All those who have affections which lead them to the conservation of civil order would recognize, even in its cradle, the child as legitimate, which has been produced from those principles of cogent expediency to which all just governments owe their birth, and on which they justify their continuance. But they will be late and reluctant in giving any sort of countenance to the operations of a power which has derived its birth from no law and no necessity, but which, on the contrary, has had its origin in those vices and sinister practices by which the social union is often disturbed and sometimes destroyed. This assembly has hardly a year's prescription. We have their own word for it that they have made a revolution. To make a revolution is a measure which, *primâ fronte*[1], requires an apology. To make a revolution is to subvert the ancient state of our country; and no common reasons are called for to justify so violent a proceeding. The sense of mankind authorizes us to examine into the mode of acquiring new power, and to criticize on the use that is made of it, with less awe and reverence than that which is usually conceded to a settled and recognized authority.

In obtaining and securing their power, the assembly proceeds upon principles the most opposite from those which appear to direct them in the use of it. An observation on this difference will let us into the true spirit of their conduct. Everything which they have done, or continue to do, in order to obtain and keep their power, is by the most common arts. They proceed exactly as their ancestors of ambition have done before them. Trace them through all their artifices, frauds, and violences, you can find nothing at all that is new. They follow precedents and examples with the punctilious exactness of a pleader. They never depart an iota[2] from the authentic formulas of tyranny and usurpation. But in all the regulations relative to the public good the spirit has been the very reverse of this. There they commit the whole to the mercy of untried speculations; they abandon the dearest interests of the public to those loose theories to which none of them would choose to trust the slightest of his private concerns. They make this difference, because in their desire of obtaining and securing power they are thoroughly in earnest; there they travel in the beaten road. The public interests, because about them they have no real solicitude, they abandon wholly to chance; I say to chance, because their schemes

---

1. *primâ fronte*：〈拉〉首当其冲，最重要的
2. iota：极少量，些微

have nothing in experience to prove their tendency beneficial.

We must always see with a pity not unmixed with respect the errors of those who are timid and doubtful of themselves with regard to points wherein the happiness of mankind is concerned. But in these gentlemen there is nothing of the tender parental solicitude which fears to cut up the infant for the sake of an experiment. In the vastness of their promises and the confidence of their predictions they far outdo all the boasting of empirics[1]. The arrogance of their pretensions in a manner provokes and challenges us to an inquiry into their foundation.

I am convinced that there are men of considerable parts among the popular leaders in the National Assembly. Some of them display eloquence in their speeches and their writings. This cannot be without powerful and cultivated talents. But eloquence may exist without a proportionable degree of wisdom. When I speak of ability, I am obliged to distinguish. What they have done towards the support of their system bespeaks no ordinary men. In the system itself, taken as the scheme of a republic constructed for procuring the prosperity and security of the citizen, and for promoting the strength and grandeur of the state, I confess myself unable to find out anything which displays, in a single instance, the work of a comprehensive and disposing mind, or even the provisions of a vulgar prudence. Their purpose everywhere seems to have been to evade and slip aside from *difficulty*. This it has been the glory of the great masters in all the arts to confront, and to overcome; and when they had overcome the first difficulty, to turn it into an instrument for new conquests over new difficulties; thus to enable them to extend the empire of their science, and even to push forward, beyond the reach of their original thoughts, the landmarks of the human understanding itself. Difficulty is a severe instructor, set over us by the supreme ordinance of a parental guardian and

---

1. empirics：经验主义

legislator, who knows us better than we know ourselves, as He loves us better too. *Pater ipse colendi haud facilem esse viam voluit.*[1] He that wrestles with us strengthens our nerves and sharpens our skill. Our antagonist is our helper. This amicable conflict with difficulty obliges us to an intimate acquaintance with our object, and compels us to consider it in all its relations. It will not suffer us to be superficial. It is the want of nerves of understanding for such a task, it is the degenerate fondness for tricking short-outs and little fallacious facilities, that has in so many parts of the world created governments with arbitrary powers. They have created the late arbitrary monarchy of France. They have created the arbitrary republic of Paris. With them defects in wisdom are to be supplied by the plenitude of force. They get nothing by it. Commencing their labours on a principle of sloth, they have the common fortune of slothful men. The difficulties, which they rather had eluded than escaped, meet them again in their course; they multiply and thicken on them; they are involved, through a labyrinth of confused detail, in an industry without limit and without direction; and in conclusion, the whole of their work becomes feeble, vicious, and insecure.

It is this inability to wrestle with difficulty which has obliged the arbitrary Assembly of France to commence their schemes of reform with abolition and total destruction. But is it in destroying and pulling down that skill is displayed? Your mob can do this as well at least as your assemblies. The shallowest understanding, the rudest hand, is more than equal to that task. Rage and frenzy will pull down more in half an hour than prudence, deliberation, and foresight can build up in a hundred years. The errors and defects of old establishments are visible and palpable. It calls for little ability to point them out; and where absolute power is given, it requires but a word wholly to abolish

---

1. *Pater ipse ... viam voluit*：〈拉〉引自维吉尔的《农事诗》。英文的大意是：God himself wished that the farmer's life should not be an easy one。

the vice and the establishment together. The same lazy, but restless disposition, which loves sloth and hates quiet, directs these politicians, when they come to work for supplying the place of what they have destroyed. To make everything the reverse of what they have seen is quite as easy as to destroy. No difficulties occur in what has never been tried. Criticism is almost baffled in discovering the defects of what has not existed; and eager enthusiasm and cheating hope have all the wide field of imagination, in which they may expatiate with little or no opposition.

At once to preserve and to reform is quite another thing. When the useful parts of an old establishment are kept, and what is superadded is to be fitted to what is retained, a vigorous mind, steady, persevering attention, various powers of comparison and combination, and the resources of an understanding fruitful in expedients are to be

exercised; they are to be exercised in a continued conflict with the combined force of opposite vices, with the obstinacy that rejects all improvement, and the levity that is fatigued and disgusted with everything of which it is in possession. But you may object — "A process of this kind is slow. It is not fit for an assembly which glories in performing in a few months the work of ages. Such a mode of reforming, possibly, might take up many years." Without question it might; and it ought. It is one of the excellences of a method in which time is amongst the assistants, that its operation is slow, and in some cases almost imperceptible. If circumspection and caution are a part of wisdom, when we work only upon inanimate matter, surely they become a part of duty too, when the subject of our demolition and construction is not brick and timber, but sentient beings, by the sudden alteration of whose state, condition, and habits, multitudes may be rendered miserable. But it seems as if it were the prevalent opinion in Paris, that an unfeeling heart and an undoubting confidence are the sole qualifications for a perfect legislator. Far different are my ideas of that high office. The true lawgiver ought to have a heart full of sensibility. He ought to love and respect his kind, and to fear himself. It may be allowed to his temperament to catch his ultimate object with an intuitive glance; but his movements towards it ought to be deliberate. Political arrangement, as it is a work for social ends, is to be only wrought by social means. There mind must conspire with mind. Time is required to produce that union of minds which alone can produce all the good we aim at. Our patience will achieve more than our force. If I might venture to appeal to what is so much out of fashion in Paris, I mean to experience, I should tell you, that in my course I have known, and, according to my measure, have co-operated with great men; and I have never yet seen any plan which has not been mended by the observations of those who were much inferior in understanding to the person who took the lead in the business. By a slow, but well-sustained progress, the effect of each step is watched; the good or ill success of the first gives light to us in the second; and so, from light to light, we are conducted with safety through the whole series. We see that the parts of the system do not clash. The evils latent in the most promising contrivances are provided for as they arise. One advantage is as little as possible sacrificed to another. We compensate, we reconcile, we balance. We are enabled to unite into a consistent whole the various anomalies and contending principles that are found in the minds and affairs of men. From hence arises, not an excellence in simplicity, but one far superior, an excellence in composition. Where the great interests of mankind are concerned through a long succession of generations, that succession ought to be admitted into some share in the councils which are so deeply to affect them. If justice requires this, the work itself requires the aid of more minds than one age can furnish. It is from this view of things that the best legislators have been often satisfied with the establishment of some sure, solid, and ruling principle in government, a power like that which some of the philosophers have called a plastic nature; and having fixed the principle, they have left it afterwards to its own operation.

To proceed in this manner, that is, to proceed with a presiding principle and a prolific energy, is with me the criterion of profound wisdom. What your politicians think the marks of a bold, hardy genius are only proofs of a deplorable want of ability. By their violent haste, and their defiance of the process of nature, they are delivered over blindly to every projector and adventurer, to every alchemist and empiric. They despair of turning to account anything that is common. Diet is nothing in their system of remedy. The worst of it is, that this their despair of curing common distempers by regular methods arises not only from defect of comprehension, but, I fear, from some malignity of disposition. Your legislators seem to have taken their opinions of all professions, ranks, and offices from the declamations and buffooneries of satirists, who would themselves be astonished, if they were held to the letter of their own descriptions. By listening only to these, your leaders regard all things only on the side of their vices and faults, and view those vices and faults under every colour of exaggeration. It is undoubtedly true, though it may seem paradoxical, but in general, those who are habitually employed in finding and displaying faults are unqualified for the work of reformation; because their minds are not only unfurnished with patterns of the fair and good, but by habit they come to take no delight in the contemplation of those things. By hating vices too much, they come to love men too little. It is therefore not wonderful that they should be indisposed and unable to serve them. From hence arises the complexional disposition of some of your guides to pull everything in pieces. At this malicious game they display the whole of their *quadrimanous*[1] activity. As to the rest, the paradoxes of eloquent writers, brought forth purely as a sport of fancy, to try their talents, to rouse attention, and excite surprise, are taken up by these gentlemen, not in the spirit of the original

---

1. *quadrimanous*：〈法〉四肢并用，意指他们四处出击。

authors, as means of cultivating their taste and improving their style: these paradoxes become with them serious grounds of action, upon which they proceed in regulating the most important concerns of the state. Cicero ludicrously describes Cato as endeavouring to act in the commonwealth upon the school paradoxes which exercised the wits of the junior students in the Stoic philosophy.[1] If this was true of Cato, these gentlemen copy after him in the manner of some persons who lived about his time — *pede nudo Catonem*.[2] Mr. Hume[3] told me that he had from Rousseau himself the secret of his principles of composition. That acute, though eccentric observer, had perceived, that, to strike and interest the public, the marvellous must be produced; that the marvellous of the heathen mythology had long since lost its effects; that giants, magicians, fairies, and heroes of romance, which succeeded, had exhausted the portion of credulity which belonged to their age; that now nothing was left to a writer but that species of the marvellous, which might still be produced, and with as great an effect as ever, though in another way; that is, the marvellous in life, in manners, in characters, and in extraordinary situations, giving rise to new and unlooked-for strokes in politics and morals. I believe, that were Rousseau alive, and in one of his lucid intervals, he would be shocked at the practical frenzy of his scholars, who in their paradoxes are servile imitators, and even in their incredulity discover an implicit faith.

Men who undertake considerable things, even in a regular way,

---

1. Cicero ... describes Cato ... Stoic philosophy：指西塞罗在《为穆热纳辩护》中所引述的案例。
2. *pede nudo Catonem*：〈拉〉赤裸的卡图之问，常用来表示美德往往会被假象所掩盖。贺拉斯在《书信集》中对谁是真正的卡图有这样的论述：If anyone imitates Cato, stern of face, barefooted and wearing mean clothes, does he also exemplify the morals and virtue of Cato?
3. Hume：戴维·休谟（David Hume，1711—1776），苏格兰哲学家，苏格兰启蒙运动以及西方哲学史中最重要的人物之一。

ought to give us ground to presume ability. But the physician of the state, who, not satisfied with the cure of distempers, undertakes to regenerate constitutions, ought to show uncommon powers. Some very unusual appearances of wisdom ought to display themselves on the face of the designs of those who appeal to no practice and who copy after no model. Has any such been manifested? I shall take a view (it shall for the subject be a very short one) of what the Assembly has done, with regard, first, to the constitution of the legislature; in the next place, to that of the executive power; then to that of the judicature; afterwards to the model of the army; and conclude with the system of finance: to see whether we can discover in any part of their schemes the portentous ability which may justify these bold undertakers in the superiority which they assume over mankind.

It is in the model of the sovereign and presiding part of this new republic that we should expect their grand display. Here they were to prove their title to their proud demands. For the plan itself at large, and for the reasons on which it is grounded, I refer to the journals of the Assembly of the 29th of September, 1789, and to the subsequent proceedings which have made any alterations in the plan. So far as in a matter somewhat confused I can see light, the system remains substantially as it has been originally framed. My few remarks will be such as regard its spirit, its tendency, and its fitness for framing a popular commonwealth, which they profess theirs to be, suited to the ends for which any commonwealth, and particularly such a commonwealth, is made. At the same time I mean to consider its consistency with itself and its own principles.

Old establishments are tried by their effects. If the people are happy, united, wealthy, and powerful, we presume the rest. We conclude that to be good from whence good is derived. In old establishments various correctives have been found for their aberrations from theory. Indeed, they are the results of various necessities and expediences. They are not often constructed after any theory: theories are rather drawn from them. In them we often see the end best obtained, where the means seem not perfectly reconcilable to what we may fancy was the original scheme. The means taught by experience may be better suited to political ends than those contrived in the original project. They again react upon the primitive constitution, and sometimes improve the design itself, from which they seem to have departed. I think all this might be curiously exemplified in the British constitution. At worst, the errors and deviations of every kind in reckoning are found and computed, and the ship proceeds in her course. This is the case of old establishments; but in a new and merely theoretic system, it is expected that every contrivance shall appear, on the face of it, to answer its ends, especially where the projectors are no way embarrassed with an endeavour to accommodate the new building to an old one, either in the walls or on the foundations.

The French builders, clearing away as mere rubbish whatever they found, and, like their ornamental gardeners, forming everything into an exact level, propose to rest the whole local and general legislature on three bases of three different kinds: one geometrical, one arithmetical, and the third financial; the first of which they call *the basis of territory*; the second, *the basis of population*; and the third, *the basis of contribution*. For the accomplishment of the first of these purposes, they divide the area of their country into eighty-three pieces, regularly square, of eighteen leagues by eighteen. These large divisions are called *Departments*. These they portion, proceeding by square measurement, into seventeen hundred and twenty districts, called *Communes*. These again they subdivide, still proceeding by square measurement, into smaller districts, called *Cantons*, making in all 6,400.

At first view this geometrical basis of theirs presents not much to admire or to blame. It calls for no great legislative talents. Nothing more than an accurate land-surveyor, with his chain, sight, and theodolite, is requisite for such a plan as this. In the old divisions of the country, various accidents at times, and the ebb and flow of various properties and jurisdictions, settled their bounds. These bounds were not made upon any fixed system, undoubtedly. They were subject to some inconveniences; but they were inconveniences for which use had found remedies, and habit had supplied accommodation and patience. In this new pavement of square within square, and this organization and semi-organization, made on the system of Empedocles[1] and Buffon[2], and not upon any politic principle, it is impossible that innumerable local inconveniences, to which men are not habituated, must not arise. But these I pass over, because it requires an accurate knowledge of the country, which I do not possess, to specify them.

When these state surveyors came to take a view of their work of measurement, they soon found that in politics the most fallacious of all things was geometrical demonstration. They had then recourse to another basis (or rather buttress) to support the building, which tottered on that false foundation. It was evident that the goodness of the soil, the number of the people, their wealth, and the largeness of their contribution, made such infinite variations between square and square as to render mensuration a ridiculous standard of power in the commonwealth, and equality in geometry the most unequal of all measures in the distribution of men. However, they could not give it up. But dividing their political and civil representation into three parts, they allotted one of those parts to the square measurement, without a single fact or calculation to ascertain whether this territorial proportion of representation was fairly assigned, and ought upon any principle really to be a third. Having, however, given to geometry this

---

1. Empedocles: 恩培多克勒（前 495—前 435），古希腊哲学家。他认为世上万物皆由土、气、火与水四种基本元素组成。
2. Buffon: 布冯伯爵（Georges-Louis Leclerc, comte de Buffon, 1707—1788），法国贵族、博物学家，著有 36 卷自然知识百科全书《自然史，一般和特殊》。

portion (of a third for her dower) out of compliment, I suppose, to that sublime science, they left the other two to be scuffled for between the other parts, population and contribution.

When they came to provide for population, they were not able to proceed quite so smoothly as they had done in the field of their geometry. Here their arithmetic came to bear upon their juridical metaphysics. Had they stuck to their metaphysic principles, the arithmetical process would be simple indeed. Men, with them, are strictly equal, and are entitled to equal rights in their own government. Each head, on this system, would have its vote, and every man would vote directly for the person who was to represent him in the legislature. "But soft — by regular degrees, not yet." [1] This metaphysic principle, to which law, custom, usage, policy, reason, were to yield, is to yield itself to their pleasure. There must be many degrees, and some stages, before the representative can come in contact with his constituent. Indeed, as we shall soon see, these two persons are to have no sort of communion with each other. First, the voters in the *Canton*, who compose what they call *primary assemblies*, are to have a *qualification*[2]. What! a qualification on the indefeasible rights of men? Yes; but it shall be a very small qualification. Our injustice shall be very little oppressive: only the local valuation of three days' labour paid to the public. Why, this is not much, I readily admit, for anything but the utter subversion of your equalizing principle. As a qualification it might as well be let alone; for it answers no one purpose for which qualifications are established; and, on your ideas, it excludes from a

---

1. "But soft ... not yet.": 引自英国诗人亚历山大·蒲柏《致伯灵顿伯爵理查德·博伊尔的书信》。原句为：But soft — by regular approach — not yet。
2. *qualification*: 指公民资格。法国大革命时期，公民被划分为"积极 (active)"和"消极 (passive)"两大类。所有公民都依法享有法律面前人人平等、宗教宽容等"公民权利 (civic rights)"，而投票、担任审判员等这些"政治权利 (political rights)"，只有"积极"公民才可享受。一个人是否有资格成为积极公民取决于是否缴纳了一定数量的税款。

vote the man of all others whose natural equality stands the most in need of protection and defence; I mean the man who has nothing else but his natural equality to guard him. You order him to buy the right which you before told him nature had given to him gratuitously at his birth, and of which no authority on earth could lawfully deprive him. With regard to the person who cannot come up to your market, a tyrannous aristocracy, as against him, is established at the very outset, by you who pretend to be its sworn foe.

The gradation proceeds. These primary assemblies of the *Canton* elect deputies to the *Commune*; one for every two hundred qualified inhabitants. Here is the first medium put between the primary elector and the representative legislator; and here a new turnpike is fixed for taxing the rights of men with a second qualification: for none can be elected into the *Commune* who does not pay the amount of ten days' labour. Nor have we yet done. There is still to be another gradation. These *Communes*, chosen by the *Canton*, choose to the *Department*; and the deputies of the *Department* choose their deputies to the *National Assembly*. Here is a third barrier of a senseless qualification. Every deputy to the National Assembly must pay, in direct contribution, to the value of a *mark of silver*. Of all these qualifying barriers we must think alike: that they are impotent to secure independence, strong only to destroy the rights of men.[1]

In all this process, which in its fundamental elements affects to consider only *population* upon a principle of natural right, there is a manifest attention to *property;* which, however just and reasonable on other schemes, is on theirs perfectly unsupportable.

When they come to their third basis, that of *Contribution*, we find that they have more completely lost sight of the rights of men. This last

1. These primary assemblies ... destroy the rights of men.：作者此处对选举人团产生的描述并不确切。一些批评家指出，作者把选举人团制度与地方政府体制搞混了。

basis rests *entirely* on property. A principle totally different from the equality of men, and utterly irreconcilable to it, is thereby admitted: but no sooner is this principle admitted than (as usual) it is subverted; and it is not subverted (as we shall presently see) to approximate the inequality of riches to the level of nature. The additional share in the third portion of representation (a portion reserved exclusively for the higher contribution) is made to regard the *district* only, and not the individuals in it who pay. It is easy to perceive, by the course of their reasonings, how much they were embarrassed by their contradictory ideas of the rights of men and the privileges of riches. The committee of constitution do as good as admit that they are wholly irreconcilable. "The relation, with regard to the contributions, is without doubt *null* (say they) when the question is on the balance of the political rights as between individual and individual; without which *personal equality would be destroyed*, and *an aristocracy of the rich* would be established. But this inconvenience entirely disappears, when the proportional relation of the contribution is only considered in the *great masses*, and is solely between province and province; it serves in that case only to form a just reciprocal proportion between the cities, without affecting the personal rights of the citizens."

Here the principle of *contribution*, as taken between man and man, is reprobated as *null*, and destructive to equality; and as pernicious, too, because it leads to the establishment of an *aristocracy of the rich*. However, it must not be abandoned. And the way of getting rid of the difficulty is to establish the inequality as between department and department, leaving all the individuals in each department upon an exact par. Observe, that this parity between individuals had been before destroyed, when the qualifications within the departments were settled; nor does it seem a matter of great importance whether the equality of men be injured by masses or individually. An individual is not of the same importance in a mass represented by a few as in a mass represented by many. It would be too much to tell a man jealous of his equality, that the elector has the same franchise who votes for three members as he who votes for ten.

Now take it in the other point of view, and let us suppose their principle of representation according to contribution, that is according to riches, to be well imagined, and to be a necessary basis for their republic. In this their third basis they assume that riches ought to be respected, and that justice and policy require that they should entitle men, in some mode or other, to a larger share in the administration of public affairs; it is now to be seen how the Assembly provides for the pre-eminence, or even for the security of the rich, by conferring, in virtue of their opulence, that larger measure of power to their district which is denied to them personally. I readily admit (indeed, I should lay it down as a fundamental principle) that in a republican government, which has a democratic basis, the rich do require an additional security above what is necessary to them in monarchies. They are subject to envy, and through envy to oppression. On the present scheme it is impossible to divine what advantage they derive from the aristocratic preference upon which the unequal representation of the masses is founded. The rich cannot feel it, either as a support to dignity or as security to fortune: for the aristocratic mass is generated from purely democratic principles; and the prevalence given to it in the general representation has no sort of reference to or connection with the persons upon account of whose property this superiority of the mass is established. If the contrivers of this scheme meant any sort of favour to the rich, in consequence of their contribution, they ought to have conferred the privilege either on the individual rich, or on some class formed of rich persons (as historians represent Servius Tullius[1]

---

1. Servius Tullius: 塞尔维乌斯·图利乌斯（约前 578—前 535），古代罗马王政时代第六位国王，据说罗马实行的各项制度和民权法都是由他撰写的。在其统治期间，罗马经历了一系列改革，其中最突出的措施就是把治下的臣民按地域不同和财产多寡，以百人一组进行划分。

to have done in the early constitution of Rome); because the contest between the rich and the poor is not a struggle between corporation and corporation, but a contest between men and men; a competition, not between districts, but between descriptions. It would answer its purpose better, if the scheme were inverted: that the votes of the masses were rendered equal, and that the votes within each mass were proportioned to property.

Let us suppose one man in a district (it is an easy supposition) to contribute as much as a hundred of his neighbours. Against these he has but one vote. If there were but one representative for the mass, his poor neighbours would outvote him by an hundred to one for that single representative. Bad enough! But amends are to be made him. How? The district, in virtue of his wealth, is to choose, say ten members instead of one: that is to say, by paying a very large contribution he has the happiness of being outvoted, an hundred to one, by the poor, for ten representatives, instead of being outvoted exactly in the same proportion for a single member. In truth, instead of benefiting by this superior quantity of representation, the rich man is subjected to an additional hardship. The increase of representation within his province sets up nine persons more, and as many more than nine as there may be democratic candidates, to cabal and intrigue and to flatter the people at his expense and to his oppression. An interest is by this means held out to multitudes of the inferior sort, in obtaining a salary of eighteen livres a day (to them a vast object) besides the pleasure of a residence in Paris, and their share in the government of the kingdom. The more the objects of ambition are multiplied and become democratic, just in that proportion the rich are endangered.

Thus it must fare between the poor and the rich in the province deemed aristocratic, which in its internal relation is the very reverse of that character. In its external relation, that is, in its relation to the other provinces, I cannot see how the unequal representation which is given to masses on account of wealth becomes the means of preserving the equipoise and the tranquillity of the commonwealth. For, if it be one of the objects to secure the weak from being crushed by the strong (as in all society undoubtedly it is), how are the smaller and poorer of these masses to be saved from the tyranny of the more wealthy? Is it by adding to the wealthy further and more systematical means of oppressing them? When we come to a balance of representation between corporate bodies, provincial interests, emulations, and jealousies are full as likely to arise among them as among individuals; and their divisions are likely to produce a much hotter spirit of dissension, and something leading much more nearly to a war.

I see that these aristocratic masses are made upon what is called the principle of direct contribution. Nothing can be a more unequal standard than this. The indirect contribution, that which arises from duties on consumption, is in truth a better standard, and follows and discovers wealth more naturally than this of direct contribution. It is difficult, indeed, to fix a standard of local preference on account of the one, or of the other, or of both, because some provinces may pay the more of either or of both on account of causes not intrinsic, but originating from those very districts over whom they have obtained a preference in consequence of their ostensible contribution. If the masses were independent, sovereign bodies, who were to provide for a federative treasury by distinct contingents, and that the revenue had not (as it has) many impositions running through the whole, which affect men individually, and not corporately, and which, by their nature, confound all territorial limits, something might be said for the basis of contribution as founded on masses. But, of all things, this representation, to be measured by contribution, is the most difficult to settle upon principles of equity in a country which considers its districts as members of a whole. For a great city, such as Bordeaux[1] or

_____

1. Bordeaux：波尔多（法国西南部城市），被诩为世界葡萄酒中心。

Paris, appears to pay a vast body of duties, almost out of all assignable proportion to other places, and its mass is considered accordingly. But are these cities the true contributors in that proportion? No. The consumers of the commodities imported into Bordeaux, who are scattered through all France, pay the import duties of Bordeaux. The produce of the vintage in Guienne[1] and Languedoc[2] give to that city the means of its contribution growing out of an export commerce. The landholders who spend their estates in Paris, and are thereby the creators of that city, contribute for Paris from the provinces out of which their revenues arise. Very nearly the same arguments will apply to the representative share given on account of *direct* contribution: because the direct contribution must be assessed on wealth, real or presumed; and that local wealth will itself arise from causes not local, and which therefore in equity ought not to produce a local preference.

It is very remarkable, that in this fundamental regulation which settles the representation of the mass upon the direct contribution, they have not yet settled how that direct contribution shall be laid, and how apportioned. Perhaps there is some latent policy towards the continuance of the present Assembly in this strange procedure. However, until they do this, they can have no certain constitution. It must depend at last upon the system of taxation, and must vary with every variation in that system. As they have contrived matters, their taxation does not so much depend on their constitution as their constitution on their taxation. This must introduce great confusion among the masses; as the variable qualification for votes within the district must, if ever real contested elections take place, cause infinite internal controversies.

To compare together the three bases, not on their political reason, but on the ideas on which the Assembly works, and to try its

---

1. Guienne：吉耶纳（法国西南部旧省名）
2. Languedoc：朗格多克（法国南部一地区名）

consistency with itself, we cannot avoid observing that the principle which the committee call the basis of *population* does not begin to operate from the same point with the two other principles, called the bases of *territory* and of *contribution*, which are both of an aristocratic nature. The consequence is, that where all three begin to operate together, there is the most absurd inequality produced by the operation of the former on the two latter principles. Every canton contains four square leagues, and is estimated to contain, on the average, 4,000 inhabitants, or 680 voters in the *primary assemblies*, which vary in numbers with the population of the canton, and send *one deputy* to the *commune* for every 200 voters. *Nine cantons* make a *commune*.

Now let us take *a canton* containing *a seaport town of trade*, or *a great manufacturing town*. Let us suppose the population of this canton to be 12,700 inhabitants, or 2,193 voters, forming *three primary assemblies*, and sending *ten deputies* to the *commune*.

Oppose to this *one* canton *two* others of the remaining eight in the same commune. These we may suppose to have their fair population, of 4,000 inhabitants, and 680 voters each, or 8,000 inhabitants and 1,360 voters, both together. These will form only *two primary assemblies*, and send only *six* deputies to the *commune*.

When the assembly of the *commune* comes to vote on the *basis of territory*, which principle is first admitted to operate in that assembly, the *single canton*, which has *half* the territory of the *other two*, will have *ten* voices to *six* in the election of *three deputies* to the assembly of the department, chosen on the express ground of a representation of territory.

This inequality, striking as it is, will be yet highly aggravated, if we suppose, as we fairly may, the *several* other cantons of the *commune* to fall proportionally short of the average population, as much as the *principal canton* exceeds it. Now as to *the basis of contribution*, which also is a principle admitted first to operate in the assembly of the *commune*. Let us again take *one* canton, such as is stated above. If the whole of the direct contributions paid by a great trading or manufacturing town be divided equally among the inhabitants, each individual will be found to pay much more than an individual living in the country according to the same average. The whole paid by the inhabitants of the former will be more than the whole paid by the inhabitants of the latter — we may fairly assume one third more. Then the 12,700 inhabitants, or 2,193 voters of the canton, will pay as much as 19,050 inhabitants, or 3,289 voters of the *other cantons*, which are nearly the estimated proportion of inhabitants and voters of *five* other cantons. Now the 2,193 voters will, as I before said, send only *ten* deputies to the assembly; the 3,289 voters will send *sixteen*. Thus, for an *equal* share in the contribution of the whole *commune*, there will be a difference of *sixteen* voices to *ten* in voting for deputies to be chosen on the principle of representing the general contribution of the whole *commune*.

By the same mode of computation, we shall find 15,875 inhabitants, or 2,741 voters of the *other* cantons, who pay *one-sixth LESS* to the contribution of the whole *commune*, will have *three voices MORE* than the 12,700 inhabitants, or 2,193 voters of the *one* canton.

Such is the fantastical and unjust inequality between mass and mass, in this curious repartition of the rights of representation arising out of *territory* and *contribution*. The qualifications which these confer are in truth negative qualifications, that give a right in an inverse proportion to the possession of them.

In this whole contrivance of the three bases, consider it in any light you please, I do not see a variety of objects reconciled in one consistent whole, but several contradictory principles reluctantly and irreconcilably brought and held together by your philosophers, like wild beasts shut up in a cage, to claw and bite each other to their mutual destruction.

I am afraid I have gone too far into their way of considering the formation of a Constitution. They have much, but bad, metaphysics; much, but bad, geometry; — much, but false, proportionate arithmetic;

but if it were all as exact as metaphysics, geometry, and arithmetic ought to be, and if their schemes were perfectly consistent in all their parts, it would make only a more fair and sightly vision. It is remarkable, that, in a great arrangement of mankind, not one reference whatsoever is to be found to anything moral or anything politic; nothing that relates to the concerns, the actions, the passions, the interests of men. *Hominem non sapiunt.*[1]

You see I only consider this constitution as electoral, and leading by steps to the National Assembly. I do not enter into the internal government of the departments, and their genealogy through the communes and cantons. These local governments are, in the original plan, to be as nearly as possible composed in the same manner and on the same principles with the elective assemblies. They are each of them bodies perfectly compact and rounded in themselves.

You cannot but perceive in this scheme, that it has a direct and immediate tendency to sever France into a variety of republics, and to render them totally independent of each other, without any direct constitutional means of coherence, connection, or subordination, except what may be derived from their acquiescence in the determinations of the general congress of the ambassadors from each independent republic. Such in reality is the National Assembly; and such governments, I admit, do exist in the world, though, in forms infinitely more suitable to the local and habitual circumstances of their people. But such associations, rather than bodies politic, have generally been the effect of necessity, not choice; and I believe the present French power is the very first body of citizens who, having obtained full authority to do with their country what they pleased, have chosen to dissever it in this barbarous manner.

It is impossible not to observe, that, in the spirit of this geometrical

---

1. *Hominem non sapiunt*: 〈拉〉他们不在乎。

distribution and arithmetical arrangement, these pretended citizens treat France exactly like a country of conquest. Acting as conquerors, they have imitated the policy of the harshest of that harsh race. The policy of such barbarous victors, who contemn a subdued people, and insult their feelings, has ever been, as much as in them lay, to destroy all vestiges of the ancient country, in religion, in polity, in laws, and in manners; to confound all territorial limits; to produce a general poverty; to put up their properties to auction; to crush their princes, nobles, and pontiffs; to lay low everything which had lifted its head above the level, or which could serve to combine or rally, in their distresses, the disbanded people, under the standard of old opinion. They have made France free in the manner in which those sincere friends to the rights of mankind, the Romans, freed Greece, Macedon, and other nations. They destroyed the bonds of their union, under colour of providing for the independence of each of their cities.

When the members who compose these new bodies of cantons, communes, and departments — arrangements purposely produced through the medium of confusion — begin to act, they will find themselves, in a great measure, strangers to one another. The electors and elected throughout, especially in the rural *cantons*, will be frequently without any civil habitudes or connections, or any of that natural discipline which is the soul of a true republic. Magistrates and collectors of revenue are now no longer acquainted with their districts, bishops with their dioceses[1], or curates with their parishes. These new colonies of the rights of men bear a strong resemblance to that sort of military colonies which Tacitus[2] has observed upon in the declining policy of Rome. In better and wiser days (whatever course they took with foreign nations) they were careful to make the elements of a

---

1. dioceses：（天主教）主教辖区
2. Tacitus：塔西佗（Publius Cornelius Tacitus, 55—120），古罗马杰出的历史学家。

methodical subordination and settlement to be coeval, and even to lay
the foundations of discipline in the military. But when all the good
arts had fallen into ruin, they proceeded, as your Assembly does, upon
the equality of men, and with as little judgment, and as little care for
those things which make a republic tolerable or durable. But in this,
as well as almost every instance, your new commonwealth is born and
bred and fed in those corruptions which mark degenerated and worn-
out republics. Your child comes into the world with the symptoms of
death; the *facies Hippocratica*[1] forms the character of its physiognomy
and the prognostic of its fate.

The legislators who framed the ancient republics knew that their
business was too arduous to be accomplished with no better apparatus
than the metaphysics of an under-graduate and the mathematics
and arithmetic of an exciseman. They had to do with men, and they
were obliged to study human nature. They had to do with citizens,
and they were obliged to study the effects of those habits which are
communicated by the circumstances of civil life. They were sensible
that the operation of this second nature on the first produced a
new combination; and thence arose many diversities amongst men,
according to their birth, their education, their professions, the periods
of their lives, their residence in towns or in the country, their several
ways of acquiring and of fixing property, and according to the quality
of the property itself, all which rendered them, as it were, so many
different species of animals. From hence they thought themselves
obliged to dispose their citizens into such classes, and to place them
in such situations in the state, as their peculiar habits might qualify
them to fill, and to allot to them such appropriated privileges as might
secure to them what their specific occasions required, and which
might furnish to each description such force as might protect it in

---

1. *facies Hippocratica*：【医】希波克拉底氏面容，指死者临终前瞬间呈现的相貌。

the conflict caused by the diversity of interests that must exist, and must contend, in all complex society: for the legislator would have been ashamed that the coarse husbandman should well know how to assort and to use his sheep, horses, and oxen, and should have enough of common sense not to abstract and equalize them all into animals, without providing for each kind an appropriate food, care, and employment; whilst he, the economist, disposer, and shepherd of his own kindred, subliming himself into an airy metaphysician, was resolved to know nothing of his flocks but as men in general. It is for this reason that Montesquieu[1] observed, very justly, that, in their classification of the citizens, the great legislators of antiquity made the greatest display of their powers, and even soared above themselves. It is here that your modern legislators have gone deep into the negative series, and sunk even below their own nothing. As the first sort of legislators attended to the different kinds of citizens, and combined them into one commonwealth, the others, the metaphysical and alchemistical legislators, have taken the directly contrary course. They have attempted to confound all sorts of citizens, as well as they could, into one homogeneous mass; and then they divided this their amalgama[2] into a number of incoherent republics. They reduce men to loose counters, merely for the sake of simple telling, and not to figures, whose power is to arise from their place in the table. The elements of their own metaphysics might have taught them better lessons. The troll[3] of their categorical table might have informed them that there was something else in the intellectual world besides *substance* and *quantity*. They might learn from the catechism of metaphysics that

---

1. Montesquieu：孟德斯鸠（1689—1755），法国启蒙思想家、法学家，《论法的精神》是其代表作。
2. amalgama：混合物，大杂烩
3. troll：圆形的物品。有学者怀疑这段文字不是伯克本人写的。

there were eight heads more[1], in every complex deliberation, which they have never thought of; though these, of all the ten, are the subject on which the skill of man can operate anything at all.

So far from this able disposition of some of the old republican legislators, which follows with a solicitous accuracy the moral conditions and propensities of men, they have levelled and crushed together all the orders which they found, even under the coarse, unartificial arrangement of the monarchy, in which mode of government the classing of the citizens is not of so much importance as in a republic. It is true, however, that every such classification, if properly ordered, is good in all forms of government, and composes a strong barrier against the excesses of despotism, as well as it is the necessary means of giving effect and permanence to a republic. For want of something of this kind, if the present project of a republic should fail, all securities to a moderated freedom fail along with it, all the indirect restraints which mitigate despotism are removed; insomuch that, if monarchy should ever again obtain an entire ascendency in France, under this or any other dynasty, it will probably be, if not voluntarily tempered, at setting out, by the wise and virtuous counsels of the prince, the most completely arbitrary power that has ever appeared on earth. This is to play a most desperate game.

The confusion which attends on all such proceedings they even declare to be one of their objects, and they hope to secure their constitution by a terror of a return of those evils which attended their making it. "By this," say they, "its destruction will become difficult to authority, which cannot break it up without the entire disorganization of the whole state." They presume, that if this

---

1. besides *substance* and *quantity* ... that there were eight heads more：指古希腊著名思想家、哲学家亚里士多德（Aristotle，前 384—前 322）在其著作《范畴篇》中把基本概念划分成十大范畴，它们是：实体、数量、性质、关系、行动、承受、场所、时间、姿态、状态。

authority should ever come to the same degree of power that they have acquired, it would make a more moderate and chastised use of it, and would piously tremble entirely to disorganize the state in the savage manner that they have done. They expect from the virtues of returning despotism the security which is to be enjoyed by the offspring of their popular vices.

I wish, Sir, that you and my readers would give an attentive perusal to the work of M. de Calonne[1] on this subject. It is, indeed, not only an eloquent, but an able and instructive performance. I confine myself to what he says relative to the Constitution of the new state, and to the condition of the revenue. As to the disputes of this minister with his rivals, I do not wish to pronounce upon them. As little do I mean to hazard any opinion concerning his ways and means, financial or political, for taking his country out of its present disgraceful and deplorable situation of servitude, anarchy, bankruptcy, and beggary. I cannot speculate quite so sanguinely as he does, but he is a Frenchman, and has a closer duty relative to those objects, and better means of judging of them, than I can have. I wish that the formal avowal which he refers to, made by one of the principal leaders in the Assembly, concerning the tendency of their scheme to bring France not only from a monarchy to a republic, but from a republic to a mere confederacy, may be very particularly attended to. It adds new force to my observations: and, indeed, M. de Calonne's work supplies my deficiencies by many new and striking arguments on most of the subjects of this letter.

It is this resolution to break their country into separate republics which has driven them into the greatest number of their difficulties

---

1. M. de Calonne：德·卡洛讷子爵 (Charles Alexandre, vicomte de Calonne, 1734—1802)，路易十六时期的财政总监，因主导财政改革失利，被路易十六革职，出走英国。在英期间发表一系列有关法国政府财政状况的文章，为旧政权辩护。

and contradictions. If it were not for this, all the questions of exact equality, and these balances, never to be settled, of individual rights, population, and contribution, would be wholly useless. The representation, though derived from parts, would be a duty which equally regarded the whole. Each deputy to the Assembly would be the representative of France, and of all its descriptions, of the many and of the few, of the rich and of the poor, of the great districts and of the small. All these districts would themselves be subordinate to some standing authority, existing independently of them — an authority in which their representation, and everything that belongs to it, originated, and to which it was pointed. This standing, unalterable, fundamental government would make, and it is the only thing which could make, that territory truly and properly a whole. With us, when we elect popular representatives, we send them to a council in which each man individually is a subject, and submitted to a government complete in all its ordinary functions. With you the elective Assembly is the sovereign, and the sole sovereign; all the members are therefore integral parts of this sole sovereignty. But with us it is totally different. With us the representative, separated from the other parts, can have no action and no existence. The government is the point of reference of the several members and districts of our representation. This is the centre of our unity. This government of reference is a trustee for the *whole*, and not for the parts. So is the other branch of our public council: I mean the House of Lords. With us the King and the Lords are several and joint securities for the equality of each district, each province, each city. When did you hear in Great Britain of any province suffering from the inequality of its representation? what district from having no representation at all? Not only our monarchy and our peerage secure the equality on which our unity depends, but it is the spirit of the House of Commons itself. The very inequality of representation, which is so foolishly complained of, is perhaps the very thing which prevents us from thinking or acting as members for districts. Cornwall[1] elects as many members as all Scotland. But is Cornwall better taken care of than Scotland? Few trouble their heads about any of your bases, out of some giddy clubs. Most of those who wish for any change, upon any plausible grounds, desire it on different ideas.

Your new constitution is the very reverse of ours in its principle; and I am astonished how any persons could dream of holding out anything done in it as an example for Great Britain. With you there is little, or rather no, connection between the last representative and the first constituent. The member who goes to the National Assembly is not chosen by the people, nor accountable to them. There are three elections before he is chosen; two sets of magistracy intervene between him and the primary assembly, so as to render him, as I have said, an ambassador of a state, and not the representative of the people within a state. By this the whole spirit of the election is changed; nor can any corrective your constitution-mongers have devised render him anything else than what he is. The very attempt to do it would inevitably introduce a confusion, if possible, more horrid than the present. There is no way to make a connection between the original constituent and the representative, but by the circuitous means which may lead the candidate to apply in the first instance to the primary electors, in order that by their authoritative instructions (and something more perhaps) these primary electors may force the two succeeding bodies of electors to make a choice agreeable to their wishes. But this would plainly subvert the whole scheme. It would be to plunge them back into that tumult and confusion of popular election, which, by their interposed gradation of elections, they mean to avoid, and at length to risk the whole fortune of the state with those who have the least knowledge of it and the least interest in it. This is a perpetual

---

1. Cornwall: 康沃尔郡（英格兰西南部一郡名）

dilemma, into which they are thrown by the vicious, weak, and contradictory principles they have chosen. Unless the people break up and level this gradation, it is plain that they do not at all substantially elect to the Assembly; indeed, they elect as little in appearance as reality.

What is it we all seek for in an election? To answer its real purposes, you must first possess the means of knowing the fitness of your man; and then you must retain some hold upon him by personal obligation or dependence. For what end are these primary electors complimented, or rather mocked, with a choice? They can never know anything of the qualities of him that is to serve them, nor has he any obligation whatsoever to them. Of all the powers unfit to be delegated by those who have any real means of judging, that most peculiarly unfit is what relates to a *personal* choice. In case of abuse, that body of primary electors never can call the representative to an account for his conduct. He is too far removed from them in the chain of representation. If he acts improperly at the end of his two years' lease, it does not concern him for two years more. By the new French Constitution the best and the wisest representatives go equally with the worst into this *Limbus Patrum*[1]. Their bottoms are supposed foul, and they must go into dock to be refitted. Every man who has served in an assembly is ineligible for two years after. Just as these magistrates begin to learn their trade, like chimney-sweepers, they are disqualified for exercising it. Superficial, new, petulant acquisition, and interrupted, dronish, broken, ill recollection, is to be the destined character of all your future governors. Your constitution has too much of jealousy to have much of sense in it. You consider the breach of trust in the representative so principally that you do not at all regard the question of his fitness to execute it.

---

1. *Limbus Patrum*：〈拉〉义人居所，亦称 Limbo。按照天主教神学的说法，义人居所是介于天堂和地狱之间义人等待耶稣复活时所居住的地方。

This purgatory interval is not unfavourable to a faithless representative, who may be as good a canvasser as he was a bad governor. In this time he may cabal himself into a superiority over the wisest and most virtuous. As, in the end, all the members of this elective constitution are equally fugitive, and exist only for the election, they may be no longer the same persons who had chosen him, to whom he is to be responsible when he solicits for a renewal of his trust. To call all the secondary electors of the *Commune* to account is ridiculous, impracticable, and unjust: they may themselves have been deceived in their choice, as the third set of electors, those of the *Department*, may be in theirs. In your elections responsibility cannot exist.

Finding no sort of principle of coherence with each other in the nature and constitution of the several new republics of France, I considered what cement the legislators had provided for them from any extraneous materials. Their confederations, their *spectacles*, their civic feasts, and their enthusiasm I take no notice of; they are nothing but mere tricks; but tracing their policy through their actions, I think I can distinguish the arrangements by which they propose to hold these republics together. The first is the *confiscation*, with the compulsory paper currency annexed to it; the second is the supreme power of the city of Paris; the third is the general army of the state. Of this last I shall reserve what I have to say, until I come to consider the army as a head by itself.

As to the operation of the first (the confiscation and paper currency) merely as a cement, I cannot deny that these, the one depending on the other, may for some time compose some sort of cement, if their madness and folly in the management, and in the tempering of the parts together, does not produce a repulsion in the very outset. But allowing to the scheme some coherence and some duration, it appears to me that if, after a while, the confiscation should not be found sufficient to support the paper coinage (as I am morally certain it will not) then, instead of cementing, it will add infinitely to the dissociation, distraction, and confusion of these confederate republics, both with relation to each other and to the several parts within themselves. But if the confiscation should so far succeed as to sink the paper currency, the cement is gone with the circulation. In the mean time its binding force will be very uncertain, and it will straiten or relax with every variation in the credit of the paper.

One thing only is certain in this scheme, which is an effect seemingly collateral, but direct, I have no doubt, in the minds of those who conduct this business; that is, its effect in producing an *oligarchy* in every one of the republics. A paper circulation, not founded on any real money deposited or engaged for, amounting already to four-and-forty millions of English money, and this currency by force substituted in the place of the coin of the kingdom, becoming thereby the substance of its revenue, as well as the medium of all its commercial and civil intercourse, must put the whole of what power, authority, and influence is left, in any form whatsoever it may assume, into the hands of the managers and conductors of this circulation.

In England we feel the influence of the Bank, though it is only the centre of a voluntary dealing. He knows little, indeed, of the influence of money upon mankind, who does not see the force of the management of a moneyed concern which is so much more extensive, and in its nature so much more depending on the managers, than any of ours. But this is not merely a money concern. There is another member in the system inseparably connected with this money management. It consists in the means of drawing out at discretion portions of the confiscated lands for sale, and carrying on a process of continual transmutation of paper into land and land into paper. When we follow this process in its effects, we may conceive something of the intensity of the force with which this system must operate. By this means the spirit of money-jobbing and speculation goes into the mass of land itself, and incorporates with it. By this kind of operation, that species of property becomes, as it were, volatilized; it assumes an unnatural and monstrous activity, and thereby throws into the hands of the several managers, principal and subordinate, Parisian and provincial, all the representative of money, and perhaps a full tenth part of all the land in France, which has now acquired the worst and most pernicious part of the evil of a paper circulation, the greatest possible uncertainty in its value. They have reversed the Latonian kindness to the landed property of Delos[1]. They have sent theirs to be blown about, like the light fragments of a wreck, *oras et littora circum*[2].

The new dealers, being all habitually adventurers, and without any fixed habits or local predilections, will purchase to job out again, as the market of paper or of money or of land shall present an advantage. For though a holy bishop thinks that agriculture will derive great advantages from the "*enlightened*" usurers who are to purchase the church confiscations, I, who am not a good, but an old farmer, with great humility beg leave to tell his late Lordship that usury is not a tutor of agriculture; and if the word "enlightened" be understood according to the new dictionary, as it always is in your new schools, I cannot conceive how a man's not believing in God can teach him to cultivate the earth with the least of any additional skill or encouragement. "*Diis immortalibus sero*," said an old Roman, when he held one handle of the plough, whilst Death held the other[3]. Though you were to join in the commission all the directors of the

---

1. They have ... Delos：据古希腊神话，亚耳特弥斯和阿波罗的母亲莱托（Latona）临盆待产，为了让自己未来的孩子有一个安稳的出生地，就用四个锚链把浮岛德洛斯锁定在爱琴海的底部，以确保浮岛的稳定。
2. *oras et littora circum*：〈拉〉引自维吉尔的诗歌《埃涅阿斯纪》。英文的大意是：around the shores and coasts。
3. "*Diis immortalibus* ... the other：〈拉〉此段论述是作者对西塞罗《论老年》中的一段话的意译。西塞罗原话的英文大意是这样的：A farmer, however old, will not hesitate to reply to one who asks for whom he sows："for the immortal gods, who willed it that I should not only receive these things from my forebears but should also produce for posterity"。

two Academies to the directors of the *Caisse d'Escompte*[1], one old experienced peasant is worth them all. I have got more information upon a curious and interesting branch of husbandry, in one short conversation with an old Carthusian monk[2], than I have derived from all the bank directors that I have ever conversed with. However, there is no cause for apprehension from the meddling of money-dealers with rural economy. These gentlemen are too wise in their generation. At first, perhaps, their tender and susceptible imaginations may be captivated with the innocent and unprofitable delights of a pastoral life; but in a little time they will find that agriculture is a trade much more laborious and much less lucrative than that which they had left. After making its panegyric, they will turn their backs on it, like their great precursor and prototype. — They may, like him, begin by singing "*Beatus ille*"[3] — but what will be the end?

> *Hæc ubi locutus fœnerator Alphius,*
> *Jam jam futurus rusticus*
> *Omnem relegit Idibus pecuniam,*
> *Quærit calendis ponere.*[4]

They will cultivate the *Caisse d'Église*[5], under the sacred auspices of this prelate, with much more profit than its vineyards and its corn-fields. They will employ their talents according to their habits and their interests. They will not follow the plough, whilst they can direct

---

1. *Caisse d'Escompte*：〈法〉贴现银行 (discount bank)
2. Carthusian monk：卡尔特会僧侣
3. "*Beatus ille*"：〈拉〉引自贺拉斯的《长短句集 II》的开场白。英文的大意是：Happy is the man ....。
4. *Hæc ubi ... ponere*：〈拉〉引自贺拉斯的《长短句集 II》。英文的大意是：With these words, the moneylender Alfius, who was always thinking of becoming a farmer, has called in all his money in the middle of the month and seeks to lend it out again at the beginning of the month。
5. *Caisse d'Église*：〈法〉教堂的奉献箱

treasuries and govern provinces.

Your legislators, in everything new, are the very first who have founded a commonwealth upon gaming, and infused this spirit into it as its vital breath. The great object in these politics is to metamorphose France from a great kingdom into one great play-table; to turn its inhabitants into a nation of gamesters; to make speculation as extensive as life; to mix it with all its concerns; and to divert the whole of the hopes and fears of the people from their usual channels into the impulses, passions, and superstitions of those who live on chances. They loudly proclaim their opinion, that this their present system of a republic cannot possibly exist without this kind of gaming fund, and that the very thread of its life is spun out of the staple of these speculations. The old gaming in funds was mischievous enough, undoubtedly; but it was so only to individuals. Even when it had its greatest extent, in the Mississippi and South Sea[1], it affected but few, comparatively; where it extends further, as in lotteries, the spirit has but a single object. But where the law, which in most circumstances forbids, and in none countenances gaming, is itself debauched, so as to reverse its nature and policy, and expressly to force the subject to this destructive table, by bringing the spirit and symbols of gaming into the minutest matters, and engaging everybody in it, and in everything, a more dreadful epidemic distemper of that kind is spread than yet has appeared in the world. With you a man can neither earn nor buy his dinner without a speculation. What he receives in the morning will not have the same value at night. What he is compelled to take as pay for an old debt will not be received as the same, when he comes to pay a debt contracted by himself; nor will it be the same, when by prompt payment he would avoid contracting any debt at all. Industry must wither away. Economy must be driven from your country. Careful

---

1. Mississippi and South Sea: 指法英两国的两家股份公司，因深陷丑闻而先后于 1720 年代倒闭。

provision will have no existence. Who will labour without knowing the amount of his pay? Who will study to increase what none can estimate? Who will accumulate, when he does not know the value of what he saves? If you abstract it from its uses in gaming, to accumulate your paper wealth would be, not the providence of a man, but the distempered instinct of a jackdaw.

The truly melancholy part of the policy of systematically making a nation of gamesters is this; that though all are forced to play, few can understand the game, and fewer still are in a condition to avail themselves of that knowledge. The many must be the dupes of the few who conduct the machine of these speculations. What effect it must have on the country-people is visible. The townsman can calculate from day to day; not so the inhabitant of the country. When the peasant first brings his corn to market, the magistrate in the towns obliges him to take the assignat at par; when he goes to the shop with this money, he finds it seven per cent the worse for crossing the way. This market he will not readily resort to again. The towns-people will be inflamed! They will force the country-people to bring their corn. Resistance will begin, and the murders of Paris and St Dennis[1] may be renewed through all France.

What signifies the empty compliment paid to the country, by giving it, perhaps, more than its share in the theory of your representation? Where have you placed the real power over moneyed and landed circulation? Where have you placed the means of raising and falling the value of every man's freehold? Those whose operations can take from or add ten per cent to the possessions of every man in France must be the masters of every man in France. The whole of the power obtained by this Revolution will settle in the towns among the burghers, and the moneyed directors who lead them. The landed

---

1. St Dennis：圣丹尼斯（巴黎一郊区名）

gentleman, the yeoman, and the peasant have, none of them, habits or inclinations or experience which can lead them to any share in this the sole source of power and influence now left in France. The very nature of a country life, the very nature of landed property, in all the occupations and all the pleasures they afford, render combination and arrangement (the sole way of procuring and exerting influence) in a manner impossible amongst country-people. Combine them by all the art you can, and all the industry, they are always dissolving into individuality. Anything in the nature of incorporation is almost impracticable amongst them. Hope, fear, alarm, jealousy, the ephemerous tale that does its business and dies in a day, all these things, which are the reins and spurs by which leaders check or urge the minds of followers, are not easily employed, or hardly at all, amongst scattered people. They assemble, they arm, they act, with the utmost difficulty, and at the greatest charge. Their efforts, if ever they can be commenced, cannot be sustained. They cannot proceed systematically. If the country-gentlemen attempt an influence through the mere income of their property, what is it to that of those who have ten times their income to sell, and who can ruin their property by bringing their plunder to meet it at market? If the landed man wishes to mortgage, he falls the value of his land and raises the value of assignats. He augments the power of his enemy by the very means he must take to contend with him. The country-gentleman, therefore, the officer by sea and land, the man of liberal views and habits, attached to no profession, will be as completely excluded from the government of his country as if he were legislatively proscribed. It is obvious, that, in the towns, all the things which conspire against the country-gentleman combine in favour of the money manager and director. In towns combination is natural. The habits of burghers, their occupations, their diversion, their business, their idleness, continually bring them into mutual contact. Their virtues and their vices are sociable; they are always in garrison; and they come embodied and half-disciplined into the hands of those who mean to form them for civil or military action.

All these considerations leave no doubt on my mind, that, if this monster of a constitution can continue, France will be wholly governed by the agitators in corporations, by societies in the towns, formed of directors in assignats, and trustees for the sale of church lands, attorneys, agents, money-jobbers, speculators, and adventurers, composing an ignoble oligarchy, founded on the destruction of the crown, the church, the nobility, and the people. Here end all the deceitful dreams and visions of the equality and rights of men. In "the Serbonian bog"[1] of this base oligarchy they are all absorbed, sunk, and lost forever.

Though human eyes cannot trace them, one would be tempted to think some great offences in France must cry to Heaven, which has thought fit to punish it with a subjection to a vile and inglorious domination, in which no comfort or compensation is to be found in any even of those false splendours which, playing about other tyrannies, prevent mankind from feeling themselves dishonoured even whilst they are oppressed. I must confess I am touched with a sorrow mixed with some indignation, at the conduct of a few men, once of great rank, and still of great character, who, deluded with specious names, have engaged in a business too deep for the line of their understanding to fathom, who have lent their fair reputation, and the authority of their high-sounding names to the designs of men with whom they could not be acquainted, and have thereby made their very virtues operate to the ruin of their country.

So far as to the first cementing principle.

---

1. "the Serbonian bog"：引自英国诗人约翰·弥尔顿（John Milton, 1608—1674）的《失乐园》。原句是这样的：A gulf profound as that Serbonian Bog | Betwixt Damiata and Mount Casius old, | Where armies whole have sunk。

The second material of cement for their new republic is the superiority of the city of Paris; and this, I admit, is strongly connected with the other cementing principle of paper circulation and confiscation. It is in this part of the project we must look for the cause of the destruction of all the old bounds of provinces and jurisdictions, ecclesiastical and secular, and the dissolution of all ancient combinations of things, as well as the formation of so many small unconnected republics. The power of the city of Paris is evidently one great spring of all their politics. It is through the power of Paris, now become the centre and focus of jobbing, that the leaders of this faction direct, or rather command, the whole legislative and the whole executive government. Everything, therefore, must be done which can confirm the authority of that city over the other republics. Paris is compact; she has an enormous strength, wholly disproportioned to the force of any of the square republics; and this strength is collected and condensed within a narrow compass. Paris has a natural and easy connection of its parts, which will not be affected by any scheme of a geometrical constitution; nor does it much signify whether its proportion of representation be more or less, since it has the whole draught of fishes in its drag-net. The other divisions of the kingdom, being hackled and torn to pieces, and separated from all their habitual means and even principles of union, cannot, for some time at least, confederate against her.[1] Nothing was to be left in all the subordinate members, but weakness, disconnection, and confusion. To confirm this part of the plan, the Assembly has lately come to a resolution that no two of their republics shall have the same commander-in-chief.

To a person who takes a view of the whole, the strength of Paris, thus formed, will appear a system of general weakness. It is boasted that

---

1. The other divisions ... against her: 作者此番论述似乎颇有预见性。1793 年春夏之交的法国，许多地方的确发生了一些反革命的运动，但是这些 运动相互之间并没有合作与串联。

the geometrical policy has been adopted, that all local ideas should be sunk, and that the people should be no longer Gascons, Picards, Bretons, Normans[1], but Frenchmen, with one country, one heart, and one Assembly. But, instead of being all Frenchmen, the greater likelihood is that the inhabitants of that region will shortly have no country. No man ever was attached by a sense of pride, partiality, or real affection, to a description of square measurement. He never will glory in belonging to the Chequer No. 71, or to any other badge-ticket[2]. We begin our public affections in our families. No cold relation is a zealous citizen. We pass on to our neighbourhoods, and our habitual provincial connections. These are inns and resting-places. Such divisions of our country as have been formed by habit, and not by a sudden jerk of authority, were so many little images of the great country, in which the heart found something which it could fill. The love to the whole is not extinguished by this subordinate partiality. Perhaps it is a sort of elemental training to those higher and more large regards by which alone men come to be affected, as with their own concern, in the prosperity of a kingdom so extensive as that of France. In that general territory itself, as in the old name of provinces, the citizens are interested from old prejudices and unreasoned habits, and not on account of the geometric properties of its figure. The power and pre-eminence of Paris does certainly press down and hold these republics together as long as it lasts. But, for the reasons I have already given you, I think it can not last very long.

Passing from the civil creating and the civil cementing principles of this Constitution to the National Assembly, which is to appear and act as sovereign, we see a body in its constitution with every possible power and no possible external control. We see a body without fundamental laws, without established maxims, without respected

---

1. Gascons, Picards, Bretons, Normans: 这些都是法国人常用的人名。
2. badge-ticket: (简明扼要的) 行动纲领

rules of proceeding, which nothing can keep firm to any system whatsoever. Their idea of their powers is always taken at the utmost stretch of legislative competency, and their examples for common cases from the exceptions of the most urgent necessity. The future is to be in most respects like the present assembly; but, by the mode of the new elections and the tendency of the new circulations, it will be purged of the small degree of internal control existing in a minority chosen originally from various interests, and preserving something of their spirit. If possible, the next assembly must be worse than the present. The present, by destroying and altering everything, will leave to their successors apparently nothing popular to do. They will be roused by emulation and example to enterprises the boldest and the most absurd. To suppose such an assembly sitting in perfect quietude is ridiculous.

Your all-sufficient legislators, in their hurry to do everything at once, have forgotten one thing that seems essential, and which, I believe, never has been before, in the theory or the practice, omitted by any projector of a republic. They have forgotten to constitute a *Senate*[1], or something of that nature and character. Never, before this time, was heard of a body politic composed of one legislative and active assembly, and its executive officers, without such a council: without something to which foreign states might connect themselves; something to which, in the ordinary detail of government, the people could look up; something which might give a bias and steadiness, and preserve something like consistency in the proceedings of state. Such a body kings generally have as a council. A monarchy may exist without it; but it seems to be in the very essence of a republican government. It holds a sort of middle place between the supreme power exercised by the people, or immediately delegated from them, and the mere

---

1. They have forgotten to constitute a *Senate*: 意指立法机构没有设元老院，没有实行两院制。

executive. Of this there are no traces in your Constitution; and in providing nothing of this kind, your Solons[1] and Numas[2] have, as much as in anything else, discovered a sovereign incapacity.

Let us now turn our eyes to what they have done towards the formation of an executive power. For this they have chosen a degraded king. This their first executive officer is to be a machine, without any sort of deliberative discretion in any one act of his function. At best, he is but a channel to convey to the National Assembly such matter as may import that body to know. If he had been made the exclusive channel, the power would not have been without its importance, though infinitely perilous to those who would choose to exercise it. But public intelligence and statement of facts may pass to the Assembly with equal authenticity through any other conveyance. As to the means, therefore, of giving a direction to measures by the statement of an authorized reporter, this office of intelligence is as nothing.

To consider the French scheme of an executive officer, in its two natural divisions of civil and political. — In the first it must be observed, that, according to the new constitution, the higher parts of judicature, in either of its lines, are not in the king. The king of France is not the fountain of justice. The judges, neither the original nor the appellate, are of his nomination. He neither proposes the candidates nor has a negative on the choice. He is not even the public prosecutor. He serves only as a notary, to authenticate the choice made of the judges in the several districts. By his officers he is to execute their sentence. When we look into the true nature of his authority, he appears to be nothing more than a chief of bumbailiffs[3], sergeants-

---

1. Solon：梭伦（Solon，约前 640—前 558），古希腊杰出政治家，出任雅典执行官时实行立法改革，史称"梭伦改革"。
2. Numa：努马（Numa Pompilius，前 753—前 673），罗马王政时期第二任国王，曾改革罗马历法，确立了一年十二个月的新罗马日历。
3. bumbailiffs：〈贬〉（旧时专司查封无力偿还债务者之财产的）法警

at-mace[1], catchpoles[2], jailers, and hangmen. It is impossible to place anything called royalty in a more degrading point of view. A thousand times better it had been for the dignity of this unhappy prince, that he had nothing at all to do with the administration of justice, deprived as he is of all that is venerable and all that is consolatory in that function, without power of originating any process, without a power of suspension, mitigation, or pardon. Everything in justice that is vile and odious is thrown upon him. It was not for nothing that the Assembly has been at such pains to remove the stigma from certain offices, when they were resolved to place the person who had lately been their king in a situation but one degree above the executioner, and in an office nearly of the same quality. It is not in nature that, situated as the king of the French now is, he can respect himself or can be respected by others.

View this new executive officer on the side of his political capacity, as he acts under the orders of the National Assembly. To execute laws is a royal office; to execute orders is not to be a king. However, a political executive magistracy, though merely such, is a great trust. It is a trust, indeed, that has much depending upon its faithful and diligent performance, both in the person presiding in it and in all its subordinates. Means of performing this duty ought to be given by regulation; and dispositions towards it ought to be infused by the circumstances attendant on the trust. It ought to be environed with dignity, authority, and consideration, and it ought to lead to glory. The office of execution is an office of exertion. It is not from impotence we are to expect the tasks of power. What sort of person is a king to command executory service, who has no means whatsoever to reward it? Not in a permanent office; not in a grant of land; no, not in a pension of fifty pounds a year; not in the vainest and most

---

1. sergeants-at-mace：〈史〉手持权杖，引领仪仗队前行的低级士官
2. catchpoles：（旧时专司拘捕逃避债务者的）法警

trivial title. In France the king is no more the fountain of honour than he is the fountain of justice. All rewards, all distinctions, are in other hands. Those who serve the king can be actuated by no natural motive but fear — by a fear of everything except their master. His functions of internal coercion are as odious as those which he exercises in the department of justice. If relief is to be given to any municipality, the Assembly gives it. If troops are to be sent to reduce them to obedience to the Assembly, the king is to execute the order; and upon every occasion he is to be spattered over with the blood of his people. He has no negative; yet his name and authority is used to enforce every harsh decree. Nay, he must concur in the butchery of those who shall attempt to free him from his imprisonment, or show the slightest attachment to his person or to his ancient authority.

Executive magistracy ought to be constituted in such a manner that those who compose it should be disposed to love and to venerate those whom they are bound to obey. A purposed neglect, or, what is worse, a literal, but perverse and malignant obedience, must be the ruin of the wisest counsels. In vain will the law attempt to anticipate or to follow such studied neglects and fraudulent attentions. To make them act zealously is not in the competence of law. Kings, even such as are truly kings, may and ought to bear the freedom of subjects that are obnoxious to them. They may, too, without derogating from themselves, bear even the authority of such persons, if it promotes their service. Louis XIII mortally hated the Cardinal de Richelieu; but his support of that minister against his rivals was the source of all the glory of his reign, and the solid foundation of his throne itself. Louis XIV, when come to the throne, did not love the Cardinal Mazarin[1]; but for his interests he preserved him in power. When old, he detested

---

1. Cardinal Mazarin: 儒勒·马扎然枢机主教 (1602—1661), 路易十四时期接替黎塞留出任首相。他打破了法国封建贵族残存的特权, 大大增强了法国在欧洲的强权地位。

Louvois[1]; but for years, whilst he faithfully served his greatness, he endured his person. When George II took Mr. Pitt, who certainly was not agreeable to him, into his councils[2], he did nothing which could humble a wise sovereign. But these ministers, who were chosen by affairs, not by affections, acted in the name of and in trust for kings, and not as their avowed constitutional and ostensible masters. I think it impossible that any king, when he has recovered his first terrors, can cordially infuse vivacity and vigour into measures which he knows to be dictated by those who, he must be persuaded, are in the highest degree ill affected to his person. Will any ministers, who serve such a king (or whatever he may be called) with but a decent appearance of respect, cordially obey the orders of those whom but the other day in his name they had committed to the Bastille? Will they obey the orders of those whom, whilst they were exercising despotic justice upon them, they conceived they were treating with lenity, and for whom in a prison they thought they had provided an asylum? If you expect such obedience, amongst your other innovations and regenerations, you ought to make a revolution in nature, and provide a new constitution, for the human mind. Otherwise, your supreme government cannot harmonize with its executory system. There are cases in which we cannot take up with names and abstractions. You may call half a dozen leading individuals, whom we have reason to fear and hate, the nation. It makes no other difference than to make us fear and hate them the more. If it had been thought justifiable and expedient to make such a revolution by such means and through such persons as you have made yours, it would have been more wise to have completed the business of

---

1. Louvois：卢福瓦侯爵（1641—1691），路易十四时代的陆军国务大臣，对法国军队进行了大刀阔斧的改革。
2. George II ... into his councils：指 1756 年七年战争爆发，英国对法国正式宣战。英王乔治二世把老威廉·皮特纳入内阁，全权负责指挥战争和外交事务，尽管他本人很不喜欢皮特。

the fifth and sixth of October. The new executive officer would then owe his situation to those who are his creators as well as his masters; and he might be bound in interest, in the society of crime, and (if in crimes there could be virtues) in gratitude, to serve those who had promoted him to a place of great lucre and great sensual indulgence; and of something more: For more he must have received from those who certainly would not have limited an aggrandized creature as they have done a submitting antagonist.

A king circumstanced as the present, if he is totally stupefied by his misfortunes, so as to think it not the necessity, but the premium and privilege of life, to eat and sleep, without any regard to glory, can never be fit for the office. If he feels as men commonly feel, he must he sensible that an office so circumstanced is one in which he can obtain no fame or reputation. He has no generous interest that can excite him to action. At best, his conduct will be passive and defensive. To inferior people such an office might be matter of honour. But to be raised to it and to descend to it are different things, and suggest different sentiments. Does he *really* name the ministers? They will have a sympathy with him. Are they forced upon him? The whole business between them and the nominal king will be mutual counteraction. In all other countries the office of ministers of state is of the highest dignity. In France it is full of peril, and incapable of glory. Rivals, however, they will have in their nothingness, whilst shallow ambition exists in the world, or the desire of a miserable salary is an incentive to short-sighted avarice. Those competitors of the ministers are enabled by your Constitution to attack them in their vital parts, whilst they have not the means of repelling their charges in any other than the degrading character of culprits. The ministers of state in France are the only persons in that country who are incapable of a share in the national councils. What ministers! What councils! What a nation! — But they are responsible. It is a poor service that is to be had from responsibility. The elevation of mind to be derived from fear will never make a nation glorious. Responsibility prevents crimes. It makes all attempts against the laws dangerous. But for a principle of active and zealous service, none but idiots could think of it. Is the conduct of a war to be trusted to a man who may abhor its principle; who, in every step he may take to render it successful, confirms the power of those by whom he is oppressed? Will foreign states seriously treat with him who has no prerogative of peace or war? — No, not so much as in a single vote by himself or his ministers, or by any one whom he can possibly influence. A state of contempt is not a state for a prince: better get rid of him at once.

I know it will be said, that these humours in the court and executive government will continue only through this generation, and that the king has been brought to declare the dauphin[1] shall be educated in a conformity to his situation. If he is made to conform to his situation, he will have no education at all. His training must be worse even than that of an arbitrary monarch. If he reads, whether he reads or not, some good or evil genius will tell him his ancestors were kings. Thenceforward his object must be to assert himself and to avenge his parents. This you will say is not his duty. That may be; but it is Nature; and whilst you pique Nature against you, you do unwisely to trust to Duty. In this futile scheme of polity, the state nurses in its bosom, for the present, a source of weakness, perplexity, counteraction, inefficiency, and decay; and it prepares the means of its final ruin. In short, I see nothing in the executive force (I cannot call it authority) that has even an appearance of vigour, or that has the smallest degree of just correspondence or symmetry or amicable relation with the supreme power, either as it now exists, or as it is planned for the future government.

---

1. dauphin: 〈史〉王太子（1349 年至 1830 年法国王储的称谓）。详见"术语汇编与简释"中"爵士"条。

You have settled, by an oeconomy[1] as perverted as the policy, two establishments of government — one real, one fictitious. Both maintained at a vast expense; but the fictitious at, I think, the greatest. Such a machine as the latter is not worth the grease of its wheels. The expense is exorbitant; and neither the show nor the use deserve the tenth part of the charge. Oh! but I don't do justice to the talents of the legislators. I don't allow, as I ought to do, for necessity. Their scheme of executive force was not their choice. This pageant must be kept. The people would not consent to part with it. Right, I understand you. You do, in spite of your grand theories, to which you would have heaven and earth to bend, you do know how to conform yourselves to the nature and circumstances of things. But when you were obliged to conform thus far to circumstances, you ought to have carried your submission farther, and to have made, what you were obliged to take, a proper instrument, and useful to its end. That was in your power. For instance, among many others, it was in your power to leave to your king the right of peace and war. What! to leave to the executive magistrate the most dangerous of all prerogatives? I know none more dangerous; nor any one more necessary to be so trusted. I do not say that this prerogative ought to be trusted to your king, unless he enjoyed other auxiliary trusts along with it, which he does not now hold. But, if he did possess them, hazardous as they are undoubtedly, advantages would arise from such a constitution, more than compensating the risk. There is no other way of keeping the several potentates of Europe from intriguing distinctly and personally with the members of your Assembly, from intermeddling in all your concerns, and fomenting, in the heart of your country, the most pernicious of all factions — factions in the interest and under the direction of foreign powers. From that worst of evils, thank God, we

---

1. oeconomy：〈废〉经济，现已被 economy 取代。

are still free. Your skill, if you had any, would be well employed to find out indirect correctives and controls upon this perilous trust. If you did not like those which in England we have chosen, your leaders might have exerted their abilities in contriving better. If it were necessary to exemplify the consequences of such an executive government as yours, in the management of great affairs, I should refer you to the late reports of M. de Montmorin[1] to the National Assembly, and all the other proceedings relative to the differences between Great Britain and Spain[2]. It would be treating your understanding with disrespect to point them out to you.

I hear that the persons who are called ministers have signified an intention of resigning their places. I am rather astonished that they have not resigned long since. For the universe I would not have stood in the situation in which they have been for this last twelvemonth. They wished well, I take it for granted, to the Revolution. Let this fact be as it may, they could not, placed as they were upon an eminence, though an eminence of humiliation, but be the first to see collectively, and to feel each in his own department, the evils which have been produced by that revolution. In every step which they took, or forbore to take, they must have felt the degraded situation of their country, and their utter incapacity of serving it. They are in a species of subordinate servitude in which no men before them were ever seen. Without confidence from their sovereign on whom they were forced, or from the Assembly who forced them upon him, all the noble functions of their office are executed by committees of the assembly, without any regard whatsoever to their personal or their official authority. They are to execute, without power; they are to be responsible, without

---

1. de Montmorin：蒙莫兰伯爵（1745—1792），路易十六时期的法国外交和海军大臣。
2. differences between Great Britain and Spain：指 1789 年英国和西班牙为争夺北美洲西北部的殖民权而发生的冲突。

discretion; they are to deliberate, without choice. In their puzzled situation, under two sovereigns, over neither of whom they have any influence, they must act in such a manner as (in effect, whatever they may intend) sometimes to betray the one, sometimes the other, and always to betray themselves. Such has been their situation; such must be the situation of those who succeed them. I have much respect, and many good wishes, for Mr Necker. I am obliged to him for attentions. I thought, when his enemies had driven him from Versailles, that his exile was a subject of most serious congratulation — *sed multæ urbes et publica vota vicerunt*[1]. He is now sitting on the ruins of the finances and of the monarchy of France.

A great deal more might be observed on the strange constitution of the executory part of the new government; but fatigue must give bounds to the discussion of subjects which in themselves have hardly any limits.

As little genius and talent am I able to perceive in the plan of judicature formed by the National Assembly. According to their invariable course, the framers of your Constitution have begun with the utter abolition of the parliaments. These venerable bodies, like the rest of the old government, stood in need of reform, even though there should be no change made in the monarchy. They required several more alterations to adapt them to the system of a free constitution. But they had particulars in their constitution, and those not a few, which deserved approbation from the wise. They possessed one fundamental excellence: they were independent. The most doubtful circumstance attendant on their office, that of its being vendible, contributed, however, to this independency of character. They held for life. Indeed, they may be said to have held by inheritance. Appointed

---

1. *sed mult ... vicerunt*：〈拉〉引自古罗马讽刺诗人尤维纳利斯（Juvenal, 55—127）的《讽刺诗集》。英文大意是：Many cities and public votes of thanks had the best of him, 暗喻"集万千赞誉而自毁"。

by the monarch, they were considered as nearly out of his power. The most determined exertions of that authority against them only showed their radical independence[1]. They composed permanent bodies politic, constituted to resist arbitrary innovation; and from that corporate constitution, and from most of their forms, they were well calculated to afford both certainty and stability to the laws. They had been a safe asylum to secure these laws, in all the revolutions of humour and opinion. They had saved that sacred deposit of the country during the reigns of arbitrary princes and the struggles of arbitrary factions. They kept alive the memory and record of the constitution. They were the great security to private property; which might be said (when personal liberty had no existence) to be, in fact, as well guarded in France as in any other country. Whatever is supreme in a state ought to have, as much as possible, ifs judicial authority so constituted as not only not to depend upon it, but in some sort to balance it. It ought to give a security to its justice against its power. It ought to make its judicature, as it were, something exterior to the state.

These parliaments had furnished, not the best certainly, but some considerable corrective to the excesses and vices of the monarchy. Such an independent judicature was ten times more necessary when a democracy became the absolute power of the country. In that Constitution, elective, temporary, local judges, such as you have contrived, exercising their dependent functions in a narrow society, must be the worst of all tribunals. In them it will be vain to look for any appearance of justice towards strangers, towards the obnoxious rich, towards the minority of routed parties, towards all those who in the election have supported unsuccessful candidates. It will be impossible to keep the new tribunals clear of the worst spirit of faction.

----

1. radical independence：指 18 世纪法国法院多次与朝廷对峙事件，如 1771 年由于法院的抵制导致路易十五解散法院，1775 年路易十六又重新恢复了法院。

All contrivances by ballot we know experimentally to be vain and childish to prevent a discovery of inclinations. Where they may the best answer the purposes of concealment, they answer to produce suspicion, and this is a still more mischievous cause of partiality.

If the parliaments had been preserved, instead of being dissolved at so ruinous a change to the nation, they might have served in this new commonwealth, perhaps not precisely the same (I do not mean an exact parallel) but near the same purposes as the court and senate of Areopagus[1] did in Athens: that is, as one of the balances and correctives to the evils of a light and unjust democracy. Every one knows that this tribunal was the great stay of that state; every one knows with what care it was upheld, and with what a religious awe it was consecrated. The parliaments were not wholly free from faction, I admit; but this evil was exterior and accidental, and not so much the vice of their constitution itself as it must be in your new contrivance of sexennial[2] elective judicatories. Several English commend the abolition of the old tribunals, as supposing that they determined everything by bribery and corruption. But they have stood the test of monarchic and republican scrutiny. The court was well disposed to prove corruption on those bodies, when they were dissolved in 1771; those who have again dissolved them would have done the same, if they could; but both inquisitions having failed, I conclude that gross pecuniary corruption must have been rather rare amongst them.

It would have been prudent, along with the parliaments, to preserve their ancient power of registering, and of remonstrating at least upon, all the decrees of the National Assembly, as they did upon those which passed in the time of the monarchy. It would be a means of squaring the occasional decrees of a democracy to some principles

---

1. Areopagus: 亚略巴古，指雅典附近的一座小山丘，是古希腊雅典城邦的元老委员会和高等上诉法院所在地。
2. sexennial: 每六年一次的

of general jurisprudence. The vice of the ancient democracies, and one cause of their ruin, was, that they ruled, as you do, by occasional decrees, *psephismata*[1]. This practice soon broke in upon the tenor and consistency of the laws; it abated the respect of the people towards them, and totally destroyed them in the end.

Your vesting the power of remonstrance, which, in the time of the monarchy, existed in the parliament of Paris, in your principal executive officer, whom, in spite of common sense, you persevere in calling king, is the height of absurdity. You ought never to suffer remonstrance from him who is to execute. This is to understand neither council nor execution, neither authority nor obedience. The person whom you call king ought not to have this power, or he ought to have more.

Your present arrangement is strictly judicial. Instead of imitating your monarchy, and seating your judges on a bench of independence, your object is to reduce them to the most blind obedience. As you have changed all things, you have invented new principles of order. You first appoint judges, who, I suppose, are to determine according to law, and then you let them know, that, at some time or other, you intend to give them some law by which they are to determine. Any studies which they have made (if any they have made) are to be useless to them. But to supply these studies, they are to be sworn to obey all the rules, orders, and instructions which from time to time they are to receive from the National Assembly. These if they submit to, they leave no ground of law to the subject. They become complete and most dangerous instruments in the hands of the governing power, which, in the midst of a cause, or on the prospect of it, may wholly change the rule of decision. If these orders of the National Assembly come to be contrary to the will of the people who locally choose those judges, such

_____

1. *psephismata*：指经雅典公民大会投票通过后颁布的法令。

confusion must happen as is terrible to think of. For the judges owe their place to the local authority, and the commands they are sworn to obey come from those who have no share in their appointment. In the mean time they have the example of the court of *Châtelet*[1] to encourage and guide them in the exercise of their functions. That court is to try criminals sent to it by the National Assembly, or brought before it by other courses of delation. They sit under a guard to save their own lives. They know not by what law they judge, nor under what authority they act, nor by what tenure they hold. It is thought that they are sometimes obliged to condemn at peril of their lives. This is not perhaps certain, nor can it be ascertained; but when they acquit, we know they have seen the persons whom they discharge, with perfect impunity to the actors, hanged at the door of their court.

The Assembly, indeed, promises that they will form a body of law, which shall be short, simple, clear, and so forth. That is, by their short laws, they will leave much to the discretion of the judge, whilst they have exploded the authority of all the learning which could make judicial discretion (a thing perilous at best) deserving the appellation of a *sound* discretion.

It is curious to observe, that the administrative bodies are carefully exempted from the jurisdiction of these new tribunals. That is, those persons are exempted from the power of the laws who ought to be the most entirely submitted to them. Those who execute public pecuniary trusts ought of all men to be the most strictly held to their duty. One would have thought that it must have been among your earliest cares, if you did not mean that those administrative bodies should be real, sovereign, independent states, to form an awful tribunal, like your late parliaments, or like our King's Bench[2], where all corporate officers

---

1. the court of *Châtelet*：沙特雷法院是巴黎主要法院之一。1789 年夏天，国民议会授权该法院审判保皇派的阴谋家。
2. King's Bench：（英国高等法院的）王座法庭

might obtain protection in the legal exercise of their functions, and would find coercion, if they trespassed against their legal duty. But the cause of the exemption is plain. These administrative bodies are the great instruments of the present leaders in their progress through democracy to oligarchy[1]. They must therefore be put above the law. It will be said that the legal tribunals which you have made are unfit to coerce them. They are, undoubtedly. They are unfit for any rational purpose. It will be said, too, that the administrative bodies will be accountable to the general assembly. This, I fear, is talking without much consideration of the nature of that assembly or of these corporations. However, to be subject to the pleasure of that assembly is not to be subject to law, either for protection or for constraint.

This establishment of judges as yet wants something to its completion. It is to be crowned by a new tribunal. This is to be a grand state judicature; and it is to judge of crimes committed against the nation, that is, against the power of the Assembly. It seems as if they had something in their view of the nature of the high court of justice erected in England during the time of the great usurpation[2]. As they have not yet finished this part of the scheme, it is impossible to form a direct judgment upon it. However, if great care is not taken to form it in a spirit very different from that which has guided them in their proceedings relative to state offences, this tribunal, subservient to their inquisition, *the Committee of Research*[3], will extinguish the last sparks of liberty in France, and settle the most dreadful and arbitrary tyranny ever known in any nation. If they wish to give to this tribunal any appearance of liberty and justice, they must not evoke from or send

---

1. oligarchy：寡头政治
2. the high court ... great usurpation：作者可能是指 1649 年为审判查理一世而设立的特别法庭。
3. *the Committee of Research*："调查委员会"，指巴黎当局为应对失序状态，粉碎保王分子的阴谋而成立的一个特别机构，但是很快这一机构便背上了秘密调查局的名声。

to it the causes relative to their own members, at their pleasure. They must also remove the seat of that tribunal out of the republic of Paris.

Has more wisdom been displayed in the constitution of your army than what is discoverable in your plan of judicature? The able arrangement of this part is the more difficult, and requires the greater skill and attention, not only as a great concern in itself, but as it is the third cementing principle in the new body of republics which you call the French nation. Truly, it is not easy to divine what that army may become at last. You have voted a very large one, and on good appointments, at least fully equal to your apparent means of payment. But what is the principle of its discipline? or whom is it to obey? You have got the wolf by the ears, and I wish you joy of the happy position in which you have chosen to place yourselves, and in which you are well circumstanced for a free deliberation relatively to that army, or to anything else.

The minister and secretary of state for the War Department is M. de La Tour du Pin[1]. This gentleman, like his colleagues in administration, is a most zealous assertor of the revolution, and a sanguine admirer of the new constitution which originated in that event. His statement of facts relative to the military of France is important, not only from his official and personal authority, but because it displays very clearly the actual condition of the army in France, and because it throws light on the principles upon which the Assembly proceeds in the administration of this critical object. It may enable us to form some judgment how far it may be expedient in this country to imitate the martial policy of France.

M. de La Tour du Pin, on the 4th of last June, comes to give an account of the state of his department, as it exists under the auspices of the National Assembly. No man knows it so well; no man can express

---

1. de La Tour du Pin：德·拉图·杜·潘侯爵（1727—1794），法国贵族，大革命时期曾担任路易十六的战争部长，1794 年被送上断头台。

it better. Addressing himself to the National Assembly, he says:

"His Majesty has *this day* sent me to apprise you of the multiplied disorders of which *every day* he receives the most distressing intelligence. The army [*le corps militaire*] threatens to fall into the most turbulent anarchy. Entire regiments have dared to violate at once the respect due to the laws, to the King, to the order established by your decrees, and to the oaths which they have taken with the most awful solemnity. Compelled by my duty to give you information of these excesses, my heart bleeds when I consider who they are that have committed them. Those, against whom it is not in my power to withhold the most grievous complaints, are a part of that very soldiery which to this day have been so full of honour and loyalty, and with whom for fifty years I have lived the comrade and the friend.

"What incomprehensible spirit of delirium and delusion has all at once led them astray? Whilst you are indefatigable in establishing uniformity in the empire and moulding the whole into one coherent and consistent body, whilst the French are taught by you at once the respect which the laws owe to the rights of man and that which the citizens owe to the laws, the administration of the army presents nothing but disturbance and confusion. I see in more than one corps the bonds of discipline relaxed or broken; the most unheard-of pretensions avowed directly and without any disguise; the ordinances without force; the chiefs without authority; the military chest and the colours carried off; the authority of the King himself [*risum teneatis*[1]] proudly defied; the officers despised, degraded, threatened, driven away, and some of them prisoners in the midst of their corps, dragging on a precarious life in the bosom of disgust

---

1. *risum teneatis*：〈拉〉不应该笑

and humiliation. To fill up the measure of all these horrors, the commandants of places have had their throats out under the eyes and almost in the arms of their own soldiers.

"These evils are great; but they are not the worst consequences which may be produced by such military insurrections. Sooner or later they may menace the nation itself. *The nature of things requires that the army should never act but as an instrument.* The moment that, erecting itself into a deliberate body, it shall act according to its own resolutions, *the government, be it what it may, will immediately degenerate into a military democracy*; a species of political monster which has always ended by devouring those who have produced it.

"After all this, who must not be alarmed at the irregular consultations and turbulent committees formed in some regiments by the common soldiers and non-commissioned officers, without the knowledge, or even in contempt of the authority of their superiors; although the presence and concurrence of those superiors could give no authority to such monstrous democratic assemblies [*comices*][1]."

It is not necessary to add much to this finished picture: finished as far as its canvas admits, but, as I apprehend, not taking in the whole of the nature and complexity of the disorders of this military democracy, which, the minister at war truly and wisely observes, wherever it exists, must be the true constitution of the state, by whatever formal appellation it may pass. For, though he informs the assembly that the more considerable part of the army have not cast off their obedience, but are still attached to their duty, yet those travellers who have seen the corps whose conduct is the best rather observe in them the absence of mutiny than the existence of discipline.

I cannot help pausing here for a moment, to reflect upon the

---

1. *comices*：〈法〉（古罗马）民会，亦称"comitia（公民会议）"，即为通过法律、提名地方法官等目的而召开的民众大会。

expressions of surprise which this minister has let fall relative to the excesses he relates. To him the departure of the troops from their ancient principles of loyalty and honour seems quite inconceivable. Surely those to whom he addresses himself know the causes of it but too well. They know the doctrines which they have preached, the decrees which they have passed, the practices which they have countenanced. The soldiers remember the sixth of October. They recollect the French guards. They have not forgotten the taking of the king's castles in Paris and at Marseilles[1]. That the governors in both places were murdered with impunity is a fact that has not passed out of their minds. They do not abandon the principles, laid down so ostentatiously and laboriously, of the equality of men. They cannot shut their eyes to the degradation of the whole noblesse of France, and the suppression of the very idea of a gentleman. The total abolition of titles and distinctions is not lost upon them. But Mr du Pin is astonished at their disloyalty, when the doctors of the Assembly have taught them at the same time the respect due to laws. It is easy to judge which of the two sorts of lessons men with arms in their hands are likely to learn. As to the authority of the king, we may collect from the minister himself (if any argument on that head were not quite superfluous) that it is not of more consideration with these troops than it is with everybody else. "The king," says he, "has over and over again repeated his orders to put a stop to these excesses; but in so terrible a crisis, *your* [the Assembly's] concurrence is become indispensably necessary to prevent the evils which menace the state. *You* unite to the force of the legislative power *that of opinion*, still more important." To be sure, the army can have no opinion of the power or authority of the king. Perhaps the soldier has by this time learned, that the Assembly itself does not enjoy a much greater degree of liberty than that royal

---

1. Marseilles: 马赛（法国南部港口城市）

figure.

It is now to be seen what has been proposed in this exigency, one of the greatest that can happen in a state. The Minister requests the Assembly to array itself in all its terrors, and to call forth all its majesty. He desires that the grave and severe principles announced by them may give vigour to the King's proclamation. After this we should have looked for courts civil and martial, breaking of some corps, decimating of others, and all the terrible means which necessity has employed in such cases to arrest the progress of the most terrible of all evils; particularly, one might expect that a serious inquiry would be made into the murder of commandants in the view of their soldiers. Not one word of all this, or of anything like it. After they had been told that the soldiery trampled upon the decrees of the Assembly promulgated[1] by the King, the Assembly pass new decrees, and they authorize the King to make new proclamations. After the Secretary at War had stated that the regiments had paid no regard to oaths *prêtés avec la plus imposante solennité* — [2] they propose — what? More oaths. They renew decrees and proclamations as they experience their insufficiency, and they multiply oaths in proportion as they weaken in the minds of men the sanctions of religion. I hope that handy abridgments of the excellent sermons of Voltaire, D'Alembert[3], Diderot, and Helvétius, on the Immortality of the Soul, on a Particular Superintending Providence, and on a Future State of Rewards and Punishments, are sent down to the soldiers along with their civic oaths. Of this I have no doubt; as I understand that a certain description of reading makes no inconsiderable part of their military exercises, and that they are full as well supplied with the ammunition of pamphlets as of cartridges.

---

1. promulgated: 颁布
2. *prêtés avec ... solennité*: 〈拉〉英文大意是: sworn with the most imposing solemnity。
3. D'Alembert: 达朗贝尔 (1717—1783), 法国数学家, 哲学家。

To prevent the mischiefs arising from conspiracies, irregular consultations, seditious committees, and monstrous democratic assemblies [*comitia, comices*] of the soldiers, and all the disorders arising from idleness, luxury, dissipation, and insubordination, I believe the most astonishing means have been used that ever occurred to men, even in all the inventions of this prolific age. It is no less than this: — The king has promulgated in circular letters to all the regiments his direct authority and encouragement, that the several corps should join themselves with the clubs and confederations in the several municipalities, and mix with them in their feasts and civic entertainments! This jolly discipline, it seems, is to soften the ferocity of their minds, to reconcile them to their bottle companions of other descriptions, and to merge particular conspiracies in more general associations. That this remedy would be pleasing to the soldiers, as they are described by M. de La Tour du Pin, I can readily believe; and that, however mutinous otherwise, they will dutifully submit themselves to *these* royal proclamations. But I should question whether all this civic swearing, clubbing, and feasting would dispose them, more than at present they are disposed, to an obedience to their officers, or teach them better to submit to the austere rules of military discipline. It will make them admirable citizens after the French mode, but not quite so good soldiers after any mode. A doubt might well arise, whether the conversations at these good tables would fit them a great deal the better for the character of *mere instruments*, which this veteran officer and statesman justly observes the nature of things always requires an army to be.

Concerning the likelihood of this improvement in discipline by the free conversation of the soldiers with the municipal festive societies, which is thus officially encouraged by royal authority and sanction, we may judge by the state of the municipalities themselves, furnished to us by the war minister in this very speech. He conceives good hopes of the success of his endeavours towards restoring order *for the present* from the good disposition of certain regiments; but he finds something cloudy with regard to the future. As to preventing the return of confusion, "for this the administration" (says he) "cannot be answerable to you, as long as they see the municipalities arrogate to themselves an authority over the troops which your institutions have reserved wholly to the monarch. You have fixed the limits of the military authority and the municipal authority. You have bounded the action which you have permitted to the latter over the former to the right of requisition; but never did the letter or the spirit of your decrees authorize the commons in these municipalities to break the officers, to try them, to give orders to the soldiers, to drive them from the posts committed to their guard, to stop them in their marches ordered by the king, or, in a word, to enslave the troops to the caprice of each of the cities or even market-towns through which they are to pass."

Such is the character and disposition of the municipal society which is to reclaim the soldiery, to bring them back to the true principles of military subordination, and to lender them machines in the hands of the supreme power of the country! Such are the distempers of the French troops! Such is their cure! As the army is, so is the navy. The municipalities supersede the orders of the Assembly, and the seamen in their turn supersede the orders of the municipalities. From my heart I pity the condition of a respectable servant of the public, like this war minister, obliged in his old age to pledge the Assembly in their civic cups, and to enter with a hoary head into all the fantastic vagaries of these juvenile politicians. Such schemes are not like propositions coming from a man of fifty years' wear and tear amongst mankind. They seem rather such as ought to be expected from those grand compounders in politics who shorten the road to their degrees in the state, and have a certain inward fanatical assurance and illumination upon all subjects; upon the credit of which, one of their doctors has thought fit, with great applause, and greater success, to caution the Assembly not to attend to old men, or to any persons who value

248

themselves upon their experience. I suppose all the ministers of state must qualify, and take this test; wholly abjuring the errors and heresies of experience and observation. Every man has his own relish. But I think, if I could not attain to the wisdom, I would at least preserve something of the stiff and peremptory dignity of age. These gentlemen deal in regeneration, but at any price I should hardly yield my rigid fibres to be regenerated by them; nor begin, in my grand climacteric, to squall in their new accents, or to stammer, in my second cradle, the elemental sounds of their barbarous metaphysics. *Si isti mihi largiantur ut repuerascam, et in eorum cunis vagiam, valde recusem!*[1]

The imbecility of any part of the puerile and pedantic system which they call a constitution cannot be laid open without discovering the utter insufficiency and mischief of every other part with which it comes in contact, or that bears any the remotest relation to it. You cannot propose a remedy for the incompetence of the crown, without displaying the debility of the Assembly. You cannot deliberate on the confusion of the army of the state, without disclosing the worse disorders of the armed municipalities. The military lays open the civil, and the civil betrays the military anarchy. I wish everybody carefully to peruse the eloquent speech (such it is) of Mons. de La Tour du Pin. He attributes the salvation of the municipalities to the good behaviour of some of the troops. These troops are to preserve the well-disposed part of the municipalities, which is confessed to be the weakest, from the pillage of the worst disposed, which is the strongest. But the municipalities affect a sovereignty and will command those troops which are necessary for their protection. Indeed, they must command them or court them. The municipalities, by the necessity

---

1. *Si isti mihi ... valde recusem!*: 〈拉〉引自西塞罗的《论老年》。英文的大意是：If these people should offer me the chance of becoming a child again, and crying in a cradle of theirs, I should certainly refuse。作者的引述与原文稍有出入。

of their situation, and by the republican powers they have obtained, must, with relation to the military, be the masters, or the servants, or the confederates, or each successively, or they must make a jumble of all together, according to circumstances. What government is there to coerce the army but the municipality, or the municipality but the army? To preserve concord where authority is extinguished, at the hazard of all consequences, the Assembly attempts to cure the distempers by the distempers themselves; and they hope to preserve themselves from a purely military democracy by giving it a debauched interest in the municipal.

If the soldiers once come to mix for any time in the municipal clubs, cabals, and confederacies, an elective attraction will draw them to the lowest and most desperate part. With them will be their habits, affections, and sympathies. The military conspiracies which are to be remedied by civic confederacies, the rebellious municipalities which are to be rendered obedient by furnishing them with the means of seducing the very armies of the state that are to keep them in order — all these chimeras of a monstrous and portentous policy must aggravate the confusion from which they have arisen. There must be blood. The want of common judgment manifested in the construction of all their descriptions of forces, and in all their kinds of civil and judicial authorities, will make it flow. Disorders may be quieted in one time and in one part. They will break out in others; because the evil is radical and intrinsic. All these schemes of mixing mutinous soldiers with seditious citizens must weaken still more and more the military connection of soldiers with their officers, as well as add military and mutinous audacity to turbulent artificers and peasants. To secure a real army, the officer should be first and last in the eye of the soldier, first and last in his attention, observance, and esteem. Officers, it seems, there are to be, whose chief qualification must be temper and patience. They are to manage their troops by electioneering arts. They must bear themselves as candidates, not as commanders. But as by such means power may be occasionally in their hands, the authority by which they are to be nominated becomes of high importance[1].

What you may do finally does not appear: nor is it of much moment, whilst the strange and contradictory relation between your army and all the parts of your republic, as well as the puzzled relation of those parts to each other and to the whole, remain as they are. You seem to have given the provisional nomination of the officers, in the first instance, to the king, with a reserve of approbation by the National Assembly. Men who have an interest to pursue are extremely sagacious in discovering the true seat of power. They must soon perceive that those who can negative indefinitely in reality appoint. The officers must therefore look to their intrigues in the Assembly as the sole certain road to promotion. Still, however, by your new constitution, they must begin their solicitation at court. This double negotiation for military rank seems to me a contrivance, as well adapted as if it were studied for no other end, to promote faction in the Assembly itself relative to this vast military patronage; and then to poison the corps of officers with factions of a nature still more dangerous to the safety of government, upon any bottom on which it can be placed, and destructive in the end to the efficacy of the army itself. Those officers who lose the promotions intended for them by the crown must become of a faction opposite to that of the Assembly which has rejected their claims, and must nourish discontents in the heart of the army against the ruling powers. Those officers, on the other hand, who, by carrying their point through an interest in the Assembly, feel themselves to be at best only second in the good-will of the crown, though first in that of the Assembly, must slight an authority which would not advance and could not retard their promotion. If, to avoid these evils, you will have no other rule for command or promotion than seniority, you

---

1. the authority ... importance：法国大革命时期，国民卫队的军官是由士兵选举产生的。

will have an army of formality; at the same time it will become more independent and more of a military republic. Not they, but the king is the machine. A king is not to be deposed by halves. If he is not everything in the command of an army, he is nothing. What is the effect of a power placed nominally at the head of the army, who to that army is no object of gratitude or of fear? Such a cipher is not fit for the administration of an object of all things the most delicate, the supreme command of military men. They must be constrained (and their inclinations lead them to what their necessities require) by a real, vigorous, effective, decided, personal authority. The authority of the Assembly itself suffers by passing through such a debilitating channel as they have chosen. The army will not long look to an Assembly acting through the organ of false show and palpable imposition. They will not seriously yield obedience to a prisoner. They will either despise a pageant, or they will pity a captive king. This relation of your army to the crown will, if I am not greatly mistaken, become a serious dilemma in your politics.

It is besides to be considered, whether an Assembly like yours, even supposing that it was in possession of another sort of organ, through which its orders were to pass, is fit for promoting the obedience and discipline of an army. It is known that armies have hitherto yielded a very precarious and uncertain obedience to any senate or popular authority; and they will least of all yield it to an Assembly which is to have only a continuance of two years. The officers must totally lose the characteristic disposition of military men, if they see with perfect submission and due admiration the dominion of pleaders; especially when they find that they have a new court to pay to an endless succession of those pleaders, whose military policy, and the genius of whose command (if they should have any) must be as uncertain as their duration is transient. In the weakness of one kind of authority, and in the fluctuation of all, the officers of an army will remain for some time mutinous and full of faction, until some popular general, who understands the art of conciliating the soldiery, and who possesses the true spirit of command, shall draw the eyes of all men upon himself. Armies will obey him on his personal account. There is no other way of securing military obedience in this state of things. But the moment in which that event shall happen, the person who really commands the army is your master — the master (that is little) of your king, the master of your Assembly, the master of your whole republic.[1]

How came the Assembly by their present power over the army? Chiefly, to be sure, by debauching the soldiers from their officers. They have begun by a most terrible operation. They have touched the central point about which the particles that compose armies are at repose. They have destroyed the principle of obedience in the great, essential, critical link between the officer and the soldier, just where the chain of military subordination commences, and on which the whole of that system, depends. The soldier is told he is a citizen, and has the rights of man and citizen. The right of a man, he is told, is, to be his own governor, and to be ruled only by those to whom he delegates that self-government. It is very natural he should think that he ought most of all to have his choice where he is to yield the greatest degree of obedience. He will therefore, in all probability, systematically do what he does at present occasionally: that is, he will exercise at least a negative in the choice of his officers. At present the officers are known at best to be only permissive, and on their good behaviour. In fact, there have been many instances in which they have been cashiered by their corps. Here is a second negative on the choice of the king: a negative as effectual, at least, as the other of the Assembly. The soldiers know already that it has been a question, not ill received in the National Assembly, whether they ought not to have the direct choice of their officers, or some proportion of them. When such matters are

---

1. But the moment ... the master of your whole republic: 伯克逝世两年后的 1799 年，拿破仑发动了"雾月政变"，他的这一预言成为现实。

in deliberation, it is no extravagant supposition that they will incline to the opinion most favourable to their pretensions. They will not bear to be deemed the army of an imprisoned king, whilst another army in the same country, with whom too they are to feast and confederate, is to be considered as the free army of a free constitution. They will cast their eyes on the other and more permanent army: I mean the municipal. That corps, they well know, does actually elect its own officers. They may not be able to discern the grounds of distinction on which they are not to elect a Marquis de La Fayette[1] (or what is his new name?) of their own. If this election of a commander-in-chief be a part of the rights of men, why not of theirs? They see elective justices of peace, elective judges, elective curates, elective bishops, elective municipalities, and elective commanders of the Parisian army. Why should they alone be excluded? Are the brave troops of France the only men in that nation who are not the fit judges of military merit, and of the qualifications necessary for a commander-in-chief? Are they paid by the state, and do they therefore lose the rights of men? They are a part of that nation themselves, and contribute to that pay. And is not the king, is not the National Assembly, and are not all who elect the National Assembly, likewise paid? Instead of seeing all these forfeit their rights by their receiving a salary, they perceive that in all these cases a salary is given for the exercise of those rights. All your resolutions, you're your proceedings, all your debates, all the works of your doctors in religion and politics, have industriously been put into their hands; and you expect that they will apply to their own case just as much of your doctrines and examples as suits your pleasure.

Everything depends upon the army in such a government as yours; for you have industriously destroyed all the opinions and prejudices, and, as far as in you lay, all the instincts which support government.

---

1. Marquis de La Fayette：拉法耶特侯爵（1757—1834），法国将军、政治家，曾参与美国独立战争和法国大革命，被誉为"新旧两个世界的英雄"。

Therefore the moment any difference arises between your National Assembly and any part of the nation, you must have recourse to force. Nothing else is left to you; or rather, you have left nothing else to yourselves. You see, by the report of your war minister that the distribution of the army is in a great measure made with a view of internal coercion. You must rule by an army; and you have infused into that army by which you rule, as well as into the whole body of the nation, principles which after a time must disable you in the use you resolve to make of it. The king is to call out troops to act against his people, when the world has been told, and the assertion is still ringing in our ears, that troops ought not to fire on citizens. The colonies assert to themselves an independent constitution and a free trade. They must be constrained by troops. In what chapter of your code of the rights of men are they able to read that it is a part of the rights of men to have their commerce monopolized and restrained for the benefit of others? As the colonists rise on you, the Negroes rise on them. Troops again — massacre, torture, hanging! These are your rights of men! These are the fruits of metaphysic declarations wantonly made and shamefully retracted! It was but the other day that the farmers of land in one of your provinces refused to pay some sorts of rents to the lord of the soil. In consequence of this, you decree that the country-people shall pay all rents and dues, except those which as grievances you have abolished[1]; and if they refuse, then you order the king to march troops against them. You lay down metaphysic propositions which infer universal consequences, and then you attempt to limit logic by despotism. The leaders of the present system tell them of their rights, as men, to take fortresses, to murder guards, to seize on kings without the least appearance of authority even from the Assembly, whilst, as the sovereign legislative body, that Assembly

---

1. grievances you have abolished: 指被取消了的、不合理的封建税费制度。

was sitting in the name of the nation; and yet these leaders presume to order out the troops which have acted in these very disorders, to coerce those who shall judge on the principles and follow the examples which have been guarantied by their own approbation.

The leaders teach the people to abhor and reject all feudality as the barbarism of tyranny; and they tell them afterwards how much of that barbarous tyranny they are to bear with patience. As they are prodigal of light with regard to grievances, so the people find them sparing in the extreme with regard to redress. They know that not only certain quit-rents and personal duties, which you have permitted them to redeem, (but have furnished no money for the redemption) are as nothing to those burdens for which you have made no provision at all; they know that almost the whole system of landed property in its origin is feudal — that it is the distribution of the possessions of the original proprietors made by a barbarous conqueror to his barbarous instruments; and that the most grievous effects of the conquest axe the land-rents of every kind, as without question they are.

The peasants, in all probability, are the descendants of these ancient proprietors, Romans or Gauls[1]. But if they fail, in any degree, in the titles which they make on the principles of antiquaries and lawyers, they retreat into the citadel of the rights of men. There they find that men are equal; and the earth, the kind and equal mother of all, ought not to be monopolized to foster the pride and luxury of any men, who by nature are no better than themselves, and who, if they do not labour for their bread, are worse. They find, that, by the laws of Nature, the occupant and subduer of the soil is the true proprietor; that there is no prescription against Nature; and that the agreements (where any there are) which have been made with the landlords during the time of slavery are only the effect of duresse[2] and force, — and that, when the

---

1. Romans or Gauls: 罗马人或高卢人
2. duress(e): 强迫，胁迫

people re-entered into the rights of men, those agreements were made as void as everything else which had been settled under the prevalence of the old feudal and aristocratic tyranny. They will tell you that they see no difference between an idler with a hat and a national cockade and an idler in a cowl or in a rochet[1]. If you ground the title to rents on succession and prescription, they tell you from the speech of Mr Camus[2], published by the National Assembly for their information, that things ill begun cannot avail themselves of prescription; that the title of those lords was vicious in its origin; and that force is at least as bad as fraud. As to the title by succession, they will tell you that the succession of those who have cultivated the soil is the true pedigree of property, and not rotten parchments and silly substitutions; that the lords have enjoyed their usurpation too long; and that, if they allow to these lay monks any charitable pension, they ought to be thankful to the bounty of the true proprietor, who is so generous towards a false claimant to his goods.

When the peasants give you back that coin of sophistic reason on which you have set your image and superscription, you cry it down as base money, and tell them you will pay for the future with French guards, and dragoons, and hussars[3]. You hold up, to chastise them, the second-hand authority of a king, who is only the instrument of destroying, without any power of protecting either the people or his own person. Through him, it seems, you will make yourselves obeyed. They answer, "You have taught us that there are no gentlemen; and which of your principles teach us to bow to kings whom we have not elected? We know, without your teaching, that lands were given

---

1. rochet: （主教等高级牧师穿的）白色法衣
2. Camus: 卡缪（Armand Gaston Camus, 1740—1804），法国大革命时期杰出的档案活动家和法学家，法国国家档案馆的创建者和首任馆长。
3. French guards, and dragoons, and hussars: 法国近卫军、龙骑兵和轻骑兵

for the support of feudal dignities, feudal titles, and feudal offices. When you took down the cause as a grievance, why should the more grievous effect remain? As there are now no hereditary honours and no distinguished families, why are we taxed to maintain what you tell us ought not to exist? You have sent down our old aristocratic landlords in no other character and with no other title but that of exactors under your authority. Have you endeavoured to make these your rent-gatherers respectable to us? No. You have sent them to us with their arms reversed, their shields broken, their impresses defaced, and so displumed, degraded, and metamorphosed, such unfeathered two-legged things, that we no longer know them. They are strangers to us. They do not even go by the names of our ancient lords. Physically they may be the same men, though we are not quite sure of that, on your new philosophic doctrines of personal identity. In all other respects they are totally changed. We do not see why we have not as good a right to refuse them their rents as you have to abrogate all their honours, titles, and distinctions. This we have never commissioned you to do; and it is one instance among many, indeed, of your assumption of undelegated power. We see the burghers of Paris, through their clubs, their mobs, and their national guards, directing you at their pleasure, and giving that as law to you, which, under your authority, is transmitted as law to us. Through you, these burghers dispose of the lives and fortunes of us all. Why should not you attend as much to the desires of the laborious husbandman with regard to our rent, by which we are affected in the most serious manner, as you do to the demands of these insolent burghers relative to distinctions and titles of honour, by which neither they nor we are affected at all? But we find you pay more regard to their fancies than to our necessities. Is it among the rights of man to pay tribute to his equals? Before this measure of yours we might have thought we were not perfectly equal; we might have entertained some old, habitual, unmeaning prepossession in favour of those landlords; but we cannot conceive with what other view than that of destroying all respect to them you could have made the law that degrades them. You have forbidden us to treat them with any of the old formalities of respect; and now you send troops to sabre and to bayonet us into a submission to fear and force which you did not suffer us to yield to the mild authority of opinion."

The ground of some of these arguments is horrid and ridiculous to all rational ears; but to the politicians of metaphysics, who have opened schools for sophistry, and made establishments for anarchy, it is solid and conclusive. It is obvious, that, on a mere consideration of the right, the leaders in the Assembly would not in the least have scrupled to abrogate the rents along with the titles and family ensigns. It would be only to follow up the principle of their reasonings, and to complete the analogy of their conduct. But they had newly possessed themselves of a great body of landed property by confiscation. They had this commodity at market; and the market would have been wholly destroyed, if they were to permit the husbandmen to riot in the speculations with which they so freely intoxicated themselves. The only security which property enjoys in any one of its descriptions is from the interests of their rapacity with regard to some other. They have left nothing but their own arbitrary pleasure to determine what property is to be protected and what subverted.

Neither have they left any principle by which any of their municipalities can be bound to obedience; or even conscientiously obliged not to separate from the whole, to become independent, or to connect itself with some other state. The people of Lyons[1], it seems, have refused lately to pay taxes. Why should they not? What lawful authority is there left to exact them? The king imposed some of them. The old states, methodized by orders, settled the more ancient. They may say to the Assembly, "Who are you, that are not our kings, nor

---

1. Lyons：里昂（法国城市名）

the states we have elected, nor sit on the principles on which we have elected you? And who are we, that when we see the gabelles[1] which you have ordered to be paid wholly shaken off, when we see the act of disobedience afterwards ratified by yourselves, who are we, that we are not to judge what taxes we ought or ought not to pay, and are not to avail ourselves of the same powers the validity of which you have approved in others?" To this the answer is, "We will send troops." The last reason of kings is always the first with your Assembly. This military aid may serve for a time, whilst the impression of the increase of pay remains, and the vanity of being umpires in all disputes is flattered. But this weapon will snap short, unfaithful to the hand that employs it. The Assembly keep a school, where, systematically, and with unremitting perseverance, they teach principles and form regulations destructive to all spirit of subordination, civil and military — and then they expect that they shall hold in obedience an anarchic people by an anarchic army.

The municipal army, which, according to their new policy, is to balance this national army, if considered in itself only, is of a constitution much more simple, and in every respect less exceptionable. It is a mere democratic body, unconnected with the crown or the kingdom, armed and trained and officered at the pleasure of the districts to which the corps severally belong; and the personal service of the individuals who compose, or the fine in lieu of personal service, are directed by the same authority. Nothing is more uniform. If, however, considered in any relation to the crown, to the National Assembly, to the public tribunals, or to the other army, or considered in a view to any coherence or connection between its parts, it seems a monster, and can hardly fail to terminate its perplexed movements in some great national calamity. It is a worse

---

1. gabelles：（法国大革命前征收的）盐税

preservative of a general constitution than the systasis of Crete[1], or the confederation of Poland, or any other ill-devised corrective which has yet been imagined, in the necessities produced by an ill-constructed system of government.

* * * * *

Having concluded my few remarks on the constitution of the supreme power, the executive, the judicature, the military, and on the reciprocal relation of all these establishments, I shall say something of the ability showed by your legislators with regard to the revenue.

In their proceedings relative to this object, if possible, still fewer traces appear of political judgment or financial resource. When the states met, it seemed to be the great object to improve the system of revenue, to enlarge its collection, to cleanse it of oppression and vexation, and to establish it on the most solid footing. Great were the expectations entertained on that head throughout Europe. It was by this grand arrangement that France was to stand or fall; and this became, in my opinion very properly, the test by which the skill and patriotism of those who ruled in that Assembly would be tried. The revenue of the state is the state. In effect, all depends upon it, whether for support or for reformation. The dignity of every occupation wholly depends upon the quantity and the kind of virtue that may be exerted in it. As all great qualities of the mind which operate in public, and are not merely suffering and passive, require force for their display, I had almost said for their unequivocal existence, the revenue, which is the spring of all power, becomes in its administration the sphere of every active virtue. Public virtue, being of a nature magnificent

---

1. the systasis of Crete, or the confederation of Poland: 指古希腊克里特岛城邦国为对付入侵者而结成的松散联盟，以及 18 世纪一些半独立的封地结成的波兰联盟。历史证明，这些联盟是行不通的，也是靠不住的。

and splendid, instituted for great things, and conversant about great concerns, requires abundant scope and room, and cannot spread and grow under confinement, and in circumstances straitened, narrow, and sordid. Through the revenue alone the body politic can act in its true genius and character; and therefore it will display just as much of its collective virtue, and as much of that virtue which may characterize those who move it, and are, as it were, its life and guiding principle, as it is possessed of a just revenue. For from hence not only magnanimity, and liberality, and beneficence, and fortitude, and providence, and the tutelary protection of all good arts derive their food, and the growth of their organs, but continence, and self-denial, and labour, and vigilance, and frugality, and whatever else there is in which the mind shows itself above the appetite, are nowhere more in their proper element than in the provision and distribution of the public wealth. It is therefore not without reason that the science of speculative and practical finance, which must take to its aid so many auxiliary branches of knowledge, stands high in the estimation not only of the ordinary sort, but of the wisest and best men; and as this science has grown with the progress of its object, the prosperity and improvement of nations has generally increased with the increase of their revenues; and they will both continue to grow and flourish as long as the balance between what is left to strengthen the efforts of individuals and what is collected for the common efforts of the state bear to each other a due reciprocal proportion, and are kept in a close correspondence and communication. And perhaps it may be owing to the greatness of revenues, and to the urgency of state necessities, that old abuses in the constitution of finances are discovered, and their true nature and rational theory comes to be more perfectly understood; insomuch that a smaller revenue might have been more distressing in one period than a far greater is found to be in another, the proportionate wealth even remaining the same. In this state of things, the French Assembly found something in their revenues to preserve, to secure, and wisely to administer, as well as to abrogate and alter. Though their proud assumption might justify the severest tests, yet in trying their abilities on their financial proceedings, I would only consider what is the plain obvious duty of a common finance minister, and try them upon that, and not upon models of ideal perfection.

The objects of a financier are, then, to secure an ample revenue; to impose it with judgment and equality; to employ it economically; and when necessity obliges him to make use of credit, to secure its foundations in that instance, and forever, by the clearness and candour of his proceedings, the exactness of his calculations, and the solidity of his funds. On these heads we may take a short and distinct view of the merits and abilities of those in the National Assembly who have taken to themselves the management of this arduous concern. Far from any increase of revenue in their hands, I find, by a report of M. Vernier[1], from the Committee of Finances, of the second of August last, that the amount of the national revenue, as compared with its produce before the Revolution, was diminished by the sum of two hundred millions, or *eight millions sterling*, of the annual income, considerably more than one-third of the whole!

If this be the result of great ability, never surely was ability displayed in a more distinguished manner or with so powerful an effect. No common folly, no vulgar incapacity, no ordinary official negligence, even no official crime, no corruption, no peculation, hardly any direct hostility, which we have seen in the modern world, could in so short a time have made so complete an overthrow of the finances, and with them, of the strength of a great kingdom. — *Cedo quî vestram rempublicam tantam amisistis tam cito?*[2]

---

1. Vernier：西奥多·韦尼耶（Theodre Vernier，1731—1818），法国贵族，国民议会财政专家之一。
2. *Cedo quî ... amisistis tam cito?*〈拉〉引自西塞罗的《论老年》。英文大意是：Come tell me how you ruined your great state so quickly?

The sophisters and declaimers, as soon as the Assembly met, began with decrying the ancient constitution of the revenue in many of its most essential branches, such as the public monopoly of salt. They charged it, as truly as unwisely, with being ill-contrived, oppressive, and partial. This representation they were not satisfied to make use of in speeches preliminary to some plan of reform; they declared it in a solemn resolution or public sentence, as it were judicially passed upon it; and this they dispersed throughout the nation. At the time they passed the decree, with the same gravity they ordered the same absurd, oppressive, and partial tax to be paid, until they could find a revenue to replace it. The consequence was inevitable. The provinces which had been always exempted from this salt monopoly, some of whom were charged with other contributions, perhaps equivalent, were totally disinclined to bear any part of the burden, which by an equal distribution was to redeem the others. As to the Assembly, occupied as it was with the declaration and violation of the rights of men, and with their arrangements for general confusion, it had neither leisure nor capacity to contrive, nor authority to enforce, any plan of any kind relative to the replacing the tax, or equalizing it, or compensating the provinces, or for conducting their minds to any scheme of accommodation with the other districts which were to be relieved. The people of the salt provinces, impatient under taxes damned by the authority which had directed their payment, very soon found their patience exhausted. They thought themselves as skilful in demolishing as the Assembly could be. They relieved themselves by throwing off the whole burden. Animated by this example, each district, or part of a district, judging of its own grievance by its own feeling, and of its remedy by its own opinion, did as it pleased with other taxes.

We are next to see how they have conducted themselves in contriving equal impositions, proportioned to the means of the citizens, and the least likely to lean heavy on the active capital employed in the generation of that private wealth from whence the public fortune must be derived. By suffering the several districts, and several of the individuals in each district, to judge of what part of the old revenue they might withhold, instead of better principles of equality, a new inequality was introduced of the most oppressive kind. Payments were regulated by dispositions. The parts of the kingdom which were the most submissive, the most orderly, or the most affectionate to the commonwealth, bore the whole burden of the state. Nothing turns out to be so oppressive and unjust as a feeble government. To fill up all the deficiencies in the old impositions, and the new deficiencies of every kind which were to be expected, what remained to a state without authority? The National Assembly called for a voluntary benevolence; for a fourth part of the income of all the citizens, to be estimated on the honour of those who were to pay. They obtained something more than could be rationally calculated, but what was far indeed from answerable to their real necessities, and much less to their fond expectations. Rational people could have hoped for little from this their tax in the disguise of a benevolence; a tax weak, ineffective, and unequal; a tax by which luxury, avarice, and selfishness were screened, and the load thrown upon productive capital, upon integrity, generosity, and public spirit — a tax of regulation upon virtue. At length the mask is thrown off, and they are now trying means (with little success) of exacting their benevolence by force.

This benevolence, the rickety offspring of weakness, was to be supported by another resource, the twin brother of the same prolific imbecility. The patriotic donations were to make good the failure of the patriotic contribution. John Doe was to become security for Richard Roe[1]. By this scheme they took things of much price from the giver, comparatively of small value to the receiver; they ruined several trades; they pillaged the crown of its ornaments, the churches

---

1. John Doe ... Richard Roe：两个虚构人物，用来泛指"某人"。如同中文常用张三李四来泛指某人。

of their plate, and the people of their personal decorations. The invention of those juvenile pretenders to liberty was in reality nothing more than a servile imitation of one of the poorest resources of doting despotism. They took an old, huge, full-bottomed periwig out of the wardrobe of the antiquated frippery of Louis the Fourteenth, to cover the premature baldness of the National Assembly. They produced this old-fashioned formal folly, though it had been so abundantly exposed in the Memoirs of the Duke de Saint-Simon[1], if to reasonable men it had wanted any arguments to display its mischief and insufficiency. A device of the same kind was tried in my memory by Louis XV, but it answered at no time. However, the necessities of ruinous wars were some excuse for desperate projects. The deliberations of calamity are rarely wise. But here was a season for disposition and providence. It was in a time of profound peace, then enjoyed for five years, and promising a much longer continuance, that they had recourse to this desperate trifling. They were sure to lose more reputation by sporting, in their serious situation, with these toys and playthings of finance, which have filled half their journals, than could possibly be compensated by the poor temporary supply which they afforded. It seemed as if those who adopted such projects were wholly ignorant of their circumstances, or wholly unequal to their necessities. Whatever virtue may be in these devices, it is obvious that neither the patriotic gifts nor the patriotic contribution can ever be resorted to again. The resources of public folly are soon exhausted. The whole, indeed, of their scheme of revenue is to make, by any artifice, an appearance of a full reservoir for the hour, whilst at the same time they cut off the springs and living fountains of perennial supply. The account not long since furnished by Mr Necker was meant, without question,

---

1. Duke de Saint-Simon：圣西蒙公爵（1675—1755），法国贵族、军人、外交家，著有展现路易十四最后几年及摄政时期法国宫廷和政坛情况的回忆录。

to be favourable. He gives a flattering view of the means of getting through the year; but he expresses, as it is natural he should, some apprehension for that which was to succeed. On this last prognostic, instead of entering into the grounds of this apprehension, in order by a proper foresight, to prevent the prognosticated evil, Mr Necker receives a sort of friendly reprimand from the President of the Assembly.

As to their other schemes of taxation, it is impossible to say anything of them with certainty, because they have not yet had their operation; but nobody is so sanguine as to imagine they will fill up any perceptible part of the wide gaping breach which their incapacity has made in their revenues. At present the state of their treasury sinks every day more and more in cash, and swells more and more in fictitious representation. When so little within or without is now found but paper, the representative not of opulence, but of want, the creature not of credit, but of power, they imagine that our flourishing state in England is owing to that bank-paper, and not the bank-paper to the flourishing condition of our commerce, to the solidity of our credit, and to the total exclusion of all idea of power from any part of the transaction. They forget that in England not one shilling of paper money of any description is received but of choice; that the whole has had its origin in cash actually deposited; and that it is convertible at pleasure, in an instant, and without the smallest loss, into cash again. Our paper is of value in commerce, because in law it is of none. It is powerful on Change[1], because in Westminster Hall[2] it is impotent. In payment of a debt of twenty shillings a creditor may refuse all the paper of the Bank of England. Nor is there amongst us a single public security, of any quality or nature whatsoever, that is enforced by authority. In fact, it might be easily shown that our paper wealth,

---

1. Change：指当时的伦敦货币市场。
2. Westminster Hall：威斯敏斯特议会厅，是英国议会大厦群落中最古老的建筑，也曾是英国最高法院所在地。

instead of lessening the real coin, has a tendency to increase it; instead of being a substitute for money, it only facilitates its entry, its exit, and its circulation — that it is the symbol of prosperity, and not the badge of distress. Never was a scarcity of cash and an exuberance of paper, a subject of complaint in this nation.

Well! but a lessening of prodigal expenses, and the economy which has been introduced by the virtuous and sapient Assembly, make amends for the losses sustained in the receipt of revenue. In this at least they have fulfilled the duty of a financier. Have those, who say so, looked at the expenses of the National Assembly itself? of the municipalities? of the city of Paris? of the increased pay of the two armies? of the new police? of the new judicatures? Have they even carefully compared the present pension-list with the former? These politicians have been cruel, not economical. Comparing the expenses of the former prodigal government and its relation to the then revenues with the expenses of this new system as opposed to the state of its new treasury, I believe the present will be found beyond all comparison more chargeable.

It remains only to consider the proofs of financial ability furnished by the present French managers when they are to raise supplies on credit. Here I am a little at a stand; for credit, properly speaking, they have none. The credit of the ancient government was not, indeed, the best; but they could always, on some terms, command money, not only at home, but from most of the countries of Europe where a surplus capital was accumulated; and the credit of that government was improving daily. The establishment of a system of liberty would of course be supposed to give it new strength: and so it would actually have done, if a system of liberty had been established. What offers has their government of pretended liberty had from Holland, from Hamburg[1], from Switzerland, from Genoa[2], from England, for a

---

1. Hamburg：汉堡（德国北部城市名）
2. Genoa：热那亚，意大利重要商港和工业中心

dealing in their paper? Why should these nations of commerce and economy enter into any pecuniary dealings with a people who attempt to reverse the very nature of things; amongst whom they see the debtor prescribing at the point of the bayonet the medium of his solvency to the creditor; discharging one of his engagements with another; turning his very penury into his resource; and paying his interest with his rags?

Their fanatical confidence in the omnipotence of church plunder has induced these philosophers to overlook all care of the public estate, just as the dream of the philosopher's stone induces dupes, under the more plausible delusion of the hermetic art, to neglect all rational means of improving their fortunes. With these philosophic financiers, this universal medicine made of church mummy[1] is to cure all the evils of the state. These gentlemen perhaps do not believe a great deal in the miracles of piety; but it cannot be questioned that they have an undoubting faith in the prodigies of sacrilege. Is there a debt which presses them? — Issue *assignats*. Are compensations to be made or a maintenance decreed to those whom they have robbed of their freehold in their office or expelled from their profession? — *Assignats*. Is a fleet to be fitted out? — *Assignats*. If sixteen millions sterling of these *assignats* forced on the people leave the wants of the state as urgent as ever — issue, says one, thirty millions sterling of *assignats* — says another, issue fourscore millions more of *assignats*. The only difference among their financial factions is on the greater or the lesser quantity of *assignats* to be imposed on the public sufferance. They are all professors of *assignats*. Even those, whose natural good sense and knowledge of commerce, not obliterated by philosophy, furnish decisive arguments against this delusion, conclude their arguments, by proposing the emission of *assignats*. I suppose they must talk of *assignats*, as no other language would be understood. All experience of their inefficacy does

---

1. church mummy：指把教堂内存放的木乃伊制成药材。直到 20 世纪初，欧洲人都一直相信木乃伊可以制药，医治各种疾病。

not in the least discourage them. Are the old *assignats* depreciated at market? What is the remedy? Issue new *assignats*. — *Mais si maladia opiniatria non vult se garire, quid illi facere? Assignare; postea assignare; ensuita assignare.*[1] The word is a trifle altered. The Latin of your present doctors may be better than that of your old comedy; their wisdom and the variety of their resources are the same. They have not more notes in their song than the cuckoo; though, far from the softness of that harbinger of summer and plenty, their voice is as harsh and as ominous as that of the raven.

Who but the most desperate adventurers in philosophy and finance could at all have thought of destroying the settled revenue of the state, the sole security for the public credit, in the hope of rebuilding it with the materials of confiscated property? If, however, an excessive zeal for the state should have led a pious and venerable prelate[2] (by anticipation a father of the church) to pillage his own order, and, for the good of the church and people, to take upon himself the place of grand financier of confiscation and comptroller-general of sacrilege, he and his coadjutors were, in my opinion, bound to show, by their subsequent conduct, that they knew something of the office they assumed. When they had resolved to appropriate to the *Fisc*[3] a certain portion of the landed property of their conquered country, it was their business to render their bank a real fund of credit, as far as such a bank was capable of becoming so.

To establish a current circulating credit upon any *land-bank*, under

---

1. *Mais si maladia ... ensuita assignare*：〈拉〉作者此处采用法国喜剧作家莫里哀在其作品《无病呻吟》中的嘲讽手法，以一段蹩脚的拉丁文挖苦法国新政府发行纸币的行为。英文的大意是：But if diseased opinion does not wish to cure itself, what's to be done? Issue assignats — and then more assignats; and yet more assignats。
2. led a pious and venerable prelate：指 1789 年秋法国就财政问题举行的一场辩论，奥顿主教在辩论中起到主导作用。
3. *Fisc*：国库

any circumstances whatsoever, has hitherto proved difficult at the very least.[1] The attempt has commonly ended in bankruptcy. But when the Assembly were led, through a contempt of moral, to a defiance of economical principles, it might at least have been expected that nothing would be omitted on their part to lessen this difficulty, to prevent any aggravation of this bankruptcy. It might be expected, that, to render your land-bank tolerable, every means would be adopted that could display openness and candour in the statement of the security, everything which could aid the recovery of the demand. To take things in their most favourable point of view, your condition was that of a man of a large landed estate which he wished to dispose of for the discharge of a debt and the supply of certain services. Not being able instantly to sell, you wished to mortgage. What would a man of fair intentions and a commonly clear understanding do in such circumstances? Ought he not first to ascertain the gross value of the estate; the charges of its management and disposition; the incumbrances perpetual and temporary of all kinds that affect it; then, striking a net surplus, to calculate the just value of the security? When that surplus (the only security to the creditor) had been clearly ascertained, and properly vested in the hands of trustees; then he would indicate the parcels to be sold, and the time and conditions of sale; after this he would admit the public creditor, if he chose it, to subscribe his stock into this new fund; or he might receive proposals for an *assignat* from those who would advance money to purchase this species of security.

This would be to proceed like men of business, methodically and rationally, and on the only principles of public and private credit that have an existence. The dealer would then know exactly what he

---

1. To establish ... least: 文中提到的 land-bank 是指为土地开发和农业抵押贷款提供融资的地产银行。威廉三世时期的英国也做过类似的尝试，但最终以惨败收场。

purchased; and the only doubt which could hang upon his mind would be the dread of the resumption of the spoil, which one day might be made (perhaps with an addition of punishment) from the sacrilegious gripe of those execrable wretches who could become purchasers at the auction of their innocent fellow-citizens.

An open and exact statement of the clear value of the property, and of the time, the circumstances, and the place of sale, were all necessary, to efface as much as possible the stigma that has hitherto been branded on every kind of land-bank. It became necessary on another principle, that is, on account of a pledge of faith previously given on that subject, that their future fidelity in a slippery concern might be established by their adherence to their first engagement. When they had finally determined on a state resource from Church booty, they came, on the 14th of April, 1790, to a solemn resolution on the subject, and pledged themselves to their country, "that in the statement of the public charges for each year there should be brought to account a sum sufficient for defraying the expenses of the R.C.A. religion[1], the support of the ministers at the altars, the relief of the poor, the pensions to the ecclesiastics, secular as well as regular, of the one and of the other sex, *in order that the estates and goods which are at the disposal of the nation may be disengaged of all charges, and employed by the representatives, or the legislative body, to the great and most pressing exigencies of the state.*" They further engaged, on the same day, that the sum necessary for the year 1791 should be forthwith determined.

In this resolution they admit it their duty to show distinctly the expense of the above objects, which, by other resolutions, they had before engaged should be first in the order of provision. They

---

1. the R.C.A. religion: 美国归正会 (Reformed Church in America) 是美国新教主流教派之一。该教派起源于荷兰，曾经用名荷兰归正会 (Dutch Reformed Church)。

admit that they ought to show the estate clear and disengaged of all charges, and that they should show it immediately. Have they done this immediately, or at any time? Have they ever furnished a rent-roll of the immovable estate, or given in an inventory of the movable effects, which they confiscate to their assignats? In what manner they can fulfil their engagements of holding out to public service "an estate disengaged of all charges," without authenticating the value of the estate or the quantum of the charges, I leave it to their English admirers to explain. Instantly upon this assurance, and previously to any one step towards making it good, they issue, on the credit of so handsome a declaration, sixteen millions sterling of their paper. This was manly. Who, after this masterly stroke, can doubt of their abilities in finance? — But then, before any other emission of these financial *indulgences*, they took care at least to make good their original promise! — If such estimate, either of the value of the estate or the amount of the incumbrances, has been made, it has escaped me. I never heard of it.

At length they have spoken out, and they have made a full discovery of their abominable fraud in holding out the church lands as a security for any debts or any service whatsoever. They rob only to enable them to cheat; but in a very short time they defeat the ends both of the robbery and the fraud, by making out accounts for other purposes, which blow up their whole apparatus of force and of deception. I am obliged to M. de Calonne for his reference to the document which proves this extraordinary fact: it had by some means escaped me. Indeed, it was not necessary to make out my assertion as to the breach of faith on the declaration of the 14th of April, 1790. By a report of their committee it now appears that the charge of keeping up the reduced ecclesiastical establishments, and other expenses attendant on religion, and maintaining the religious of both sexes, retained or pensioned, and the other concomitant expenses of the same nature, which they have brought upon themselves by this convulsion in property, exceeds the income of the estates acquired by it in the enormous sum of two millions sterling annually; besides a debt of seven millions and upwards. These are the calculating powers of imposture! This is the finance of philosophy! This is the result of all the delusions held out to engage a miserable people in rebellion, murder, and sacrilege, and to make them prompt and zealous instruments in the ruin of their country! Never did a state, in any case, enrich itself by the confiscations of the citizens. This new experiment has succeeded like all the rest. Every honest mind, every true lover of liberty and humanity, must rejoice to find that injustice is not always good policy, nor rapine the high-road to riches. I subjoin with pleasure, in a note, the able and spirited observations of M. de Calonne on this subject.

In order to persuade the world of the bottomless resource of ecclesiastical confiscation, the Assembly have proceeded to other confiscations of estates in offices, which could not be done with any common colour without being compensated out of this grand confiscation of landed property. They have thrown upon this fund, which was to show a surplus disengaged of all charges, a new charge, namely, the compensation to the whole body of the disbanded judicature, and of all suppressed offices and estates: a charge which I cannot ascertain, but which unquestionably amounts to many French millions. Another of the new charges is an annuity of four hundred and eighty thousand pounds sterling, to be paid (if they choose to keep faith) by daily payments, for the interest of the first assignats. Have they ever given themselves the trouble to state fairly the expense of the management of the church lands in the hands of the municipalities, to whose care, skill, and diligence, and that of their legion of unknown under-agents, they have chosen to commit the charge of the forfeited estates, and the consequence of which had been so ably pointed out by the Bishop of Nancy[1]?

---

1. Bishop of Nancy: 天主教南锡（教区）主教

But it is unnecessary to dwell on these obvious heads of incumbrance. Have they made out any clear state of the grand incumbrance of all, I mean the whole of the general and municipal establishments of all sorts, and compared it with the regular income by revenue? Every deficiency in these becomes a charge on the confiscated estate, before the creditor can plant his cabbages on an acre of church property. There is no other prop than this confiscation to keep the whole state from tumbling to the ground. In this situation they have purposely covered all, that they ought industriously to have cleared, with a thick fog; and then, blindfold themselves, like bulls that shut their eyes when they push, they drive, by the point of the bayonets, their slaves, blindfolded indeed no worse than their lords, to take their fictions for currencies, and to swallow down paper pills by thirty-four millions sterling at a dose. Then they proudly lay in their claim to a future credit, on failure of all their past engagements, and at a time when (if in such a matter anything can be clear) it is clear that the surplus estates will never answer even the first of their mortgages, I mean that of the four hundred millions (or sixteen millions sterling) of *assignats*. In all this procedure I can discern neither the solid sense of plain dealing nor the subtle dexterity of ingenious fraud. The objections within the Assembly to pulling up the flood-gates for this inundation of fraud are unanswered; but they are thoroughly refuted by an hundred thousand financiers in the street. These are the numbers by which the metaphysic arithmeticians compute. These are the grand calculations on which a philosophical public credit is founded in France. They cannot raise supplies; but they can raise mobs. Let them rejoice in the applauses of the club at Dundee[1], for their wisdom and patriotism in having thus applied the plunder of the citizens to the service of the state. I hear of no address upon this subject from the directors of the

---

1. the club at Dundee：敦提为苏格兰东南部的港口城市。该俱乐部亦称为 "自由之友（The Friends of Liberty）"。

Bank of England, though their approbation would be of a *little* more weight in the scale of credit than that of the club at Dundee. But to do justice to the club, I believe the gentlemen who compose it to be wiser than they appear, that they will be less liberal of their money than of their addresses, and that they would not give a dog's-ear of[1] their most rumpled and ragged Scotch paper for twenty of your fairest assignats.

Early in this year the Assembly issued paper to the amount of sixteen millions sterling. What must have been the state into which the assembly has brought your affairs, that the relief afforded by so vast a supply has been hardly perceptible? This paper also felt an almost immediate depreciation of five per cent, which in a little time came to about seven. The effect of these assignats on the receipt of the revenue is remarkable. Mr Necker found that the collectors of the revenue, who received in coin, paid the treasury in *assignats*. The collectors made seven per cent by thus receiving in money, and accounting in depreciated paper. It was not very difficult to foresee that this must be inevitable. It was, however, not the less embarrassing. Mr Necker was obliged (I believe, for a considerable part, in the market of London) to buy gold and silver for the mint, which amounted to about twelve thousand pounds above the value of the commodity gained. That minister was of opinion, that, whatever their secret nutritive virtue might be, the state could not live upon *assignats* alone; that some real silver was necessary, particularly for the satisfaction of those who, having iron in their hands, were not likely to distinguish themselves for patience, when they should perceive, that, whilst an increase of pay was held out to them in real money, it was again to be fraudulently drawn back by depreciated paper. The minister, in this very natural distress, applied to the Assembly, that they should order the collectors to pay in specie what in specie they had received. It could not escape

---

1. give a dog's-ear of: 把书页折角（用来标记某人认为书中重要或有意义的章节或短语）

him, that, if the treasury paid three per cent for the use of a currency which should be returned seven per cent worse than the minister issued it, such a dealing could not very greatly tend to enrich the public. The assembly took no notice of his recommendation. They were in this dilemma: If they continued to receive the assignats, cash must become an alien to their treasury; if the treasury should refuse those paper *amulets*[1], or should discountenance them in any degree, they must destroy the credit of their sole resource. They seem then to have made their option, and to have given some sort of credit to their paper by taking it themselves; at the same time, in their speeches, they made a sort of swaggering declaration, something, I rather think, above legislative competence; that is, that there is no difference in value between metallic money and their assignats. This was a good, stout, proof article of faith, pronounced under an anathema by the venerable fathers of this philosophic synod. *Credat* who will — certainly not *Judæus Apella*[2].

A noble indignation rises in the minds of your popular leaders, on hearing the magic-lantern in their show of finance compared to the fraudulent exhibitions of Mr. Law[3]. They cannot bear to hear the sands of his Mississippi compared with the rock of the Church, on which they build their system. Pray let them suppress this glorious spirit, until they show to the world what piece of solid ground there is for their assignats, which they have not preoccupied by other charges. They do injustice to that great mother fraud, to compare it with their degenerate imitation. It is not true that Law built solely on a speculation concerning the Mississippi. He added the East India

---

1. *amulets*：护身符
2. *Judæus Apella*：〈拉〉引自贺拉斯的《讽刺诗集》。英文的大意是：Let the Jew Apella believe it, not me。Judaeus Apella 是轻易相信别人的代名词。
3. Mr. Law：指约翰·罗（John Law，1671—1729），苏格兰财务专家，摄政王时期担任法国财政总监，密西西比计划的策划者。泡沫破裂后，公司倒闭，他逃离了法国。

trade; he added the African trade; he added the farms of all the farmed revenue of France. All these together unquestionably could not support the structure which the public enthusiasm, not he, chose to build upon these bases. But these were, however, in comparison, generous delusions. They supposed, and they aimed at, an increase of the commerce of France. They opened to it the whole range of the two hemispheres. They did not think of feeding France from its own substance. A grand imagination found in this flight of commerce something to captivate. It was wherewithal to dazzle the eye of an eagle. It was not made to entice the smell of a mole, nuzzling and burying himself in his mother earth, as yours is. Men were not then quite shrunk from their natural dimensions by a degrading and sordid philosophy, and fitted for low and vulgar deceptions. Above all, remember, that, in imposing on the imagination, the then managers of the system made a compliment to the freedom of men. In their fraud there was no mixture of force. This was reserved to our time, to quench the little glimmerings of reason which might break in upon the solid darkness of this enlightened age.

On recollection, I have said nothing of a scheme of finance which may be urged in favour of the abilities of these gentlemen, and which has been introduced with great pomp, though not yet finally adopted in the National Assembly. It comes with something solid in aid of the credit of the paper circulation; and much has been said of its utility and its elegance. I mean the project for coining into money the bells of the suppressed churches. This is their alchemy. There are some follies which baffle argument, which go beyond ridicule, and which excite no feeling in us but disgust; and therefore I say no more upon it.

It is as little worth remarking any farther upon all their drawing and re-drawing, on their circulation for putting off the evil day, on the play between the Treasury and the *Caisse d'Escompte*, and on all these old, exploded contrivances of mercantile fraud, now exalted into policy of state. The revenue will not be trifled with. The prattling about the rights of men will not be accepted in payment of a biscuit or a pound of gunpowder. Here, then, the metaphysicians descend from their airy speculations, and faithfully follow examples. What examples? the examples of bankrupts. But defeated, baffled, disgraced, when their breath, their strength, their inventions, their fancies desert them, their confidence still maintains its ground. In the manifest failure of their abilities, they take credit for their benevolence. When the revenue disappears in their hands, they have the presumption, in some of their late proceedings, to value *themselves* on the relief given to the people. They did not relieve the people. If they entertained such intentions, why did they order the obnoxious taxes to be paid? The people relieved themselves, in spite of the Assembly.

But waiving all discussion on the parties who may claim the merit of this fallacious relief, has there been, in effect, any relief to the people in any form? Mr Bailly[1], one of the grand agents of paper circulation, lets you into the nature of this relief. His speech to the National Assembly contained a high and laboured panegyric on the inhabitants of Paris, for the constancy and unbroken resolution with which they have borne their distress and misery. A fine picture of public felicity! What! great courage and unconquerable firmness of mind to endure benefits and sustain redress! One would think, from the speech of this learned Lord Mayor, that the Parisians, for this twelvemonth past, had been suffering the straits of some dreadful blockade; that Henry IV had been stopping up the avenues to their supply, and Sully[2] thundering with his ordnance at the gates of Paris, when in reality they are besieged by no other enemies than their own madness and folly, their own credulity and perverseness. But Mr Bailly will sooner thaw the eternal ice of his Atlantic regions than restore the central

---

1. Bailly：指当时的巴黎市长（Jean Sylvain Bailly，1736—1793）。作为巴黎市长，他经常在国民议会上发表演讲。
2. Sully：苏利公爵。详见第 33 页的脚注。

heat to Paris, whilst it remains "smitten with the cold, dry, petrifick mace" [1] of a false and unfeeling philosophy. Some time after this speech, that is, on the thirteenth of last August, the same magistrate, giving an account of his government at the bar of the same Assembly, expresses himself as follows: "In the month of July, 1789, [the period of everlasting commemoration] the finances of the city of Paris were *yet* in good order; the expenditure was counterbalanced by the receipt, and she had at that time a million [forty thousand pounds sterling] in bank. The expenses which she has been constrained to incur, *subsequent to the revolution*, amount to 2,500,000 livres. From these expenses, and the great falling off in the product of the *free gifts*, not only a momentary but a *total* want of money has taken place." This is the Paris upon whose nourishment, in the course of the last year, such immense sums, drawn from the vitals of all France, have been expended. As long as Paris stands in the place of ancient Rome, so long she will be maintained by the subject provinces. It is an evil inevitably attendant on the dominion of sovereign democratic republics. As it happened in Rome, it may survive that republican domination which gave rise to it. In that case despotism itself must submit to the vices of popularity. Rome, under her emperors, united the evils of both systems; and this unnatural combination was one great cause of her ruin.

To tell the people that they are relieved by the dilapidation of their public estate is a cruel and insolent imposition. Statesmen, before they valued themselves on the relief given to the people by the destruction of their revenue, ought first to have carefully attended to the solution of this problem: — Whether it be more advantageous to the people to pay considerably and to gain in proportion, or to gain little or nothing and to be disburdened of all contribution? My mind is made

---

1. "smitten with the cold, dry, petrifick mace": 引自英国诗人约翰·弥尔顿的《失乐园》。原句是: The aggregated Soyle | Death with Mace petrific, cold and dry。

up to decide in favour of the first proposition. Experience is with me, and, I believe, the best opinions also. To keep a balance between the power of acquisition on the part of the subject and the demands he is to answer on the part of the state is the fundamental part of the skill of a true politician. The means of acquisition are prior in time and in arrangement. Good order is the foundation of all good things. To be enabled to acquire, the people, without being servile, must be tractable and obedient. The magistrate must have his reverence, the laws their authority. The body of the people must not find the principles of natural subordination by art rooted out of their minds. They must respect that property of which they cannot partake. They must labour to obtain what by labour can be obtained; and when they find, as they commonly do, the success disproportioned to the endeavour, they must be taught their consolation in the final proportions of eternal justice. Of this consolation whoever deprives them deadens their industry, and strikes at the root of all acquisition as of all conservation. He that does this is the cruel oppressor, the merciless enemy of the poor and wretched; at the same time that by his wicked speculations he exposes the fruits of successful industry and the accumulations of fortune to the plunder of the negligent, the disappointed, and the unprosperous.

Too many of the financiers by profession are apt to see nothing in revenue but banks, and circulations, and annuities on lives, and tontines[1], and perpetual rents, and all the small wares of the shop. In a settled order of the state, these things are not to be slighted, nor is the skill in them to be held of trivial estimation. They are good, but then only good when they assume the effects of that settled order, and are built upon it. But when men think that these beggarly contrivances may supply a resource for the evils which result from breaking up

---

1. tontines：联合养老金制。所有参与这种养老保险者需集体共同投保，领取年金的份额随参与投保者逐一离世而递增，最后一个生存者获得剩下的全部储蓄金。本质上，这是一种彩票化了的养老金制。

the foundations of public order, and from causing or suffering the principles of property to be subverted, they will, in the ruin of their country, leave a melancholy and lasting monument of the effect of preposterous politics, and presumptuous, short-sighted, narrow-minded wisdom.

The effects of the incapacity shown by the popular leaders in all the great members of the commonwealth are to be covered with the "all-atoning name" of Liberty. In some people I see great liberty, indeed; in many, if not in the most, an oppressive, degrading servitude. But what is liberty without wisdom and without virtue? It is the greatest of all possible evils; for it is folly, vice, and madness, without tuition or restraint. Those who know what virtuous liberty is cannot bear to see it disgraced by incapable heads, on account of their having high-sounding words in their mouths. Grand, swelling sentiments of liberty, I am sure I do not despise. They warm the heart; they enlarge and liberalize our minds; they animate our courage in a time of conflict. Old as I am, I read the fine raptures of Lucan and Corneille[1] with pleasure. Neither do I wholly condemn the little arts and devices of popularity. They facilitate the carrying of many points of moment; they keep the people together; they refresh the mind in its exertions; and they diffuse occasional gayety over the severe brow of moral freedom. Every politician ought to sacrifice to the graces, and to join compliance with reason. But in such an undertaking as that in France, all these subsidiary sentiments and artifices are of little avail. To make a government requires no great prudence. Settle the seat of power, teach obedience, and the work is done. To give freedom is still more easy. It is not necessary to guide; it only requires to let go the rein. But to form a *free government*, that is, to temper together these opposite

---

1. Lucan and Corneille: 卢坎 (Marcus Annaeus Lucanus, 39—65), 古罗马诗人。皮埃尔·高乃依 (Pierre Corneille, 1606—1684), 17 世纪上半叶法国古典主义悲剧的代表作家之一。

elements of liberty and restraint in one consistent work, requires much thought, deep reflection, a sagacious, powerful, and combining mind. This I do not find in those who take the lead in the National Assembly. Perhaps they are not so miserably deficient as they appear. I rather believe it. It would put them below the common level of human understanding. But when the leaders choose to make themselves bidders at an auction of popularity, their talents, in the construction of the state, will be of no service. They will become flatterers instead of legislators, the instruments, not the guides of the people. If any of them should happen to propose a scheme of liberty soberly limited, and defined with proper qualifications, he will be immediately outbid by his competitors, who will produce something more splendidly popular. Suspicions will be raised of his fidelity to his cause. Moderation will be stigmatized as the virtue of cowards, and compromise as the prudence of traitors; until, in hopes of preserving the credit which may enable him to temper and moderate on some occasions, the popular leader is obliged to become active in propagating doctrines and establishing powers that will afterwards defeat any sober purpose at which he ultimately might have aimed.

*　*　*　*　*

But am I so unreasonable as to see nothing at all that deserves commendation in the indefatigable labours of this Assembly? I do not deny, that, among an infinite number of acts of violence and folly, some good may have been done. They who destroy everything certainly will remove some grievance. They who make everything new have a chance that they may establish something beneficial. To give them credit for what they have done in virtue of the authority they have usurped, or to excuse them in the crimes by which that authority has been acquired, it must appear that the same things could not have been accomplished without producing such a revolution. Most assuredly they might; because almost every one of the regulations made by them, which is not very equivocal, was either in the cession of the king, voluntarily made at the meeting of the States, or in the concurrent instructions to the orders. Some usages have been abolished on just grounds; but they were such, that, if they had stood as they were to all eternity, they would little detract from the happiness and prosperity of any state. The improvements of the National Assembly are superficial, their errors fundamental.

Whatever they are, I wish my countrymen rather to recommend to our neighbours the example of the British constitution than to take models from them for the improvement of our own. In the former they have got an invaluable treasure. They are not, I think, without some causes of apprehension and complaint; but these they do not owe to their constitution, but to their own conduct. I think our happy situation owing to our constitution, but owing to the whole of it, and not to any part singly; owing in a great measure to what we have left standing in our several reviews and reformations, as well as to what we have altered or superadded. Our people will find employment enough for a truly patriotic, free, and independent spirit, in guarding what they possess from violation. I would not exclude alteration neither; but even when I changed, it should be to preserve. I should be led to my remedy by a great grievance. In what I did, I should follow the example of our ancestors. I would make the reparation as nearly as possible in the style of the building. A politic caution, a guarded circumspection, a moral rather than a complexional timidity, were among the ruling principles of our forefathers in their most decided conduct. Not being illuminated with the light of which the gentlemen of France tell us they have got so abundant a share, they acted under a strong impression of the ignorance and fallibility of mankind. He that had made them thus fallible rewarded them for having in their conduct attended to their nature. Let us imitate their caution, if we wish to deserve their fortune or to retain their bequests. Let us add, if we please, but let us preserve what they have left; and standing on the firm ground of the British constitution, let us be satisfied to admire, rather than attempt to follow in their desperate flights, the aeronauts of France.

I have told you candidly my sentiments. I think they are not likely to alter yours. I do not know that they ought. You are young; you cannot guide, but must follow, the fortune of your country. But hereafter they may be of some use to you, in some future form which your commonwealth may take. In the present it can hardly remain; but before its final settlement, it may be obliged to pass, as one of our poets says, "through great varieties of untried being," [1] and in all its transmigrations to be purified by fire and blood.

I have little to recommend my opinions but long observation and much impartiality. They come from one who has been no tool of power, no flatterer of greatness, and who in his last acts does not wish to belie the tenor of his life. They come from one almost the whole of whose public exertion has been a struggle for the liberty of others; from one in whose breast no anger durable or vehement has ever been kindled, but by what he considered as tyranny; and who snatches from his share in the endeavours which are used by good men to discredit opulent oppression the hours he has employed on your affairs; and who in so doing persuades himself he has not departed from his usual office. They come from one who desires honours, distinctions, and emoluments, but little; and who expects them not at all; who has no contempt for fame, and no fear of obloquy; who shuns contention, though he will hazard an opinion; from one who wishes to preserve consistency, but who would preserve consistency by varying his means

---

1. "through ... being": 引自英国散文家、剧作家约瑟夫·艾迪生 (Joseph Addison, 1672—1719) 的剧作《卡托》。原文为：Eternity! thou pleasing dreadful Thought! | Through what Variety of untry'd Being, | Through what new Scenes and Changes must we pass!

to secure the unity of his end; and, when the equipoise[1] of the vessel in which he sails may be endangered by overloading it upon one side, is desirous of carrying the small weight of his reasons to that which may preserve its equipoise.

FINIS.

---

1. equipoise: 平衡

术语汇编与简释

artificial：人为

指由人类智慧和技能造就，人为设定，如"由人设立的典章制度（artificial institutions）"，"人为限制（artificial limitation）"；与之相对应的是天然、天赋、与生俱来（natural），如"天赋权利（natural rights）"。

Assignat：指券

指 1789 年至 1796 年法国革命时期发行的、可作货币流通的有价证券，其价值与从神职人员手中没收的土地价值挂钩。

cabal：阴谋小集团

伯克在书中多处用"阴谋集团"和"阴谋家"来形容那些鼓吹法国革命的团体和其中的积极分子，称他们是一小撮密谋分子（caballer）。

constitution：宪法

简而言之，宪法从法律上对一个国家及其政府的基本框架和结构作出明确规定和保证。就形式而言，英国宪法与世界上大多数国家实行的不同。伯克认为，1215 年的大宪章及其后来的宪法性文件、法律条文、议会通过的宣言、法院先前的判例，以及习俗惯例，代表英国过往先辈们世代因袭的智慧，构成了英国神圣的宪法。伯克宣称，宪法不可被推翻，只能予以继承和改良。

伯克在颂扬英国君主立宪政体的同时，对英国通过继承法规定的世袭罔替（inherited succession），实行朝代更迭、王位继替的做法赞不绝口；对法国抛弃旧规、拥立新法、建设民主制度、让民众投票选举政府、弹劾政府官员的做法，不遗余力地予以抨击。伯克认为，在国王以及世袭贵族、拥有土地财产的达官贵族所组成的议会统治下的英国，其优越性远胜于由人民选举代表治理的法国。他认为"民主同暴政有许多惊人的相似点"。

事实上，法国 1791 年通过的宪法并没有废除波旁王朝，仍

然保留了路易十六的王位。法国国民议会中的大多数议员仍希望
与路易十六合作，共同分享国家统治权。因此，法国革命时期建
立的是君主立宪制度，而不是民主共和制。

Department：（法国的）省

法国革命时期整个国家被划分成 83 个整齐划一的大城区，称
为省（Department），属一级行政区划单位。省下面的行政单位
是公社（Commune），相当于郡县，管辖的区域也相当整齐，共
1 720 个。再下面是乡镇（Canton），总共 6 400 个。伯克在书中提
到的这些数据和划分方法是大革命初期国民议会为议会选举而拟
定的行政区划方案，与 1791 年最后公布实施的行政划分有所不同。

Dissenter：不顺从国教者

指基督教教派中主张背离英国国教的新教徒。伯克在书中多
处使用 dissent，dissenting 及 non-conformity 等词，均指信仰背离
或不信奉英国国教的意思。

entailed inheritance：限嗣继承

1285 年英国《限嗣继承条例》规定，土地持有人不得出售土
地，死后只能由其直系卑亲属继承。继承人不一定是长子，除长
子外还可以是特别指定的其他直系后裔。若没有在世的后嗣，限
嗣继承的土地产即告终止。限嗣继承的目的是要确保土地永远留
在本族内。

Estates-General：三级会议

指 1789 年革命前由僧侣（第一等级）、贵族（第二等级）和
平民（第三等级）的代表分别组成的法国议事会，亦称 States-
General。三个等级的议事会各自独立，由法兰西国王随意召集和
遣散。1789 年 5 月，国王路易十六下令召开三级会议，寻找解救
法国财政危机的方案。这是自 1614 年以来法国首次召开这样的

会议。当时，教士和贵族的势力在法国已经开始衰落，第三等级特别是其中的资产阶级正在壮大。他们的代表提出改革税制，要求取消第一、第二等级的税务特权。由于第三等级提出的要求迟迟没得到满足，同时第一、第二等级的一些代表也加入第三等级的阵营，遂自行组成代表全体法国人民的国民议会。路易十六起先试图通过调动军队予以压制，但 7 月 14 日巴士底狱被攻占后，他最终屈服，承认革命，三级会议就此名存实亡。

Glorious Revolution：光荣革命

指 1688 年在英国发生的废黜天主教国王詹姆斯二世（James II）、确立信仰新教的詹姆斯二世的长女玛丽（Queen Mary）及其夫婿荷兰奥兰治的威廉（King William）作为共同君主联合统治英国的历史事件。作者在书中提及的 our revolution，The Revolution of 1688 等，均指这一事件。

job：舞弊、假公济私的勾当

指假借为公众服务、利用受公众信任的有利条件，以舞弊、假公济私等非法手段为个人或小集团谋利的人或行为。伯克在书中多处用到这一词语，如"倒腾货币的奸商（money-jobber）"，"炒买炒卖股票（stock-jobbing）"，"侵吞公共资产（the jobbing of the public funds）"等。

landed property：地产

因地皮而受益、以土地价值为基础所构建的财产。相对应的是以金钱为后盾的财产（moneyed property）。

legislative election：立法议会选举

大革命初期，法国立法议会选举采取三级间接选举制，即由最基层的乡镇地区进行初选，按人口比例选出代表（deputy）进入公社（郡县）议会，再从他们中间选出代表进入省级议会，然后按规定数额选出代表组成国民议会。按伯克的说法，乡镇一级的初选时，每 4 000 名居民大致上会有 360 名投票人（只有纳税的"积极公民"才有选举和被选举权），而每 200 名投票人产生 1 名代表进入公社议会。每个公社下面有 9 个乡镇。公社议会以上的选举所产生的代表还要根据"区域（territory）"和"捐献（contribution）"的原则作调整。伯克把这种立法会议选举的模式称为"选举人团（electoral college）"制度。当时的法国宪法规定，国王拥有行政权，立法权则属于议会。国王不得解散议会，但可以采纳或拒绝议会通过的法令。

liberty：自由

对于法国革命中提出的"自由、平等、博爱"的口号，伯克认为反叛者的自由概念是抽象的、模糊的、无意义的。他认为，自由不能一蹴而就，必须经过很长一段时间才能实现。自由是一种"需要得到的财产"，而不是一种"需要争夺的奖品"。自由作为一种权利，犹如王位继承一样，需要"世袭传承"。

National Assembly：国民议会

指 1789 年 6 月 17 日法国第三等级的代表在三级会议期间脱离该议事会后自行组建的立法会议。同年 7 月 9 日改名为"制宪会议（National Constituent Assembly）"，并于 8 月 26 日颁布《人权和公民权宣言》（Declaration of the Rights of Man and of the Citizen）。1791 年 10 月 1 日制宪会议被立法会议（Legislative Assembly）取代，随后至 1792 年 8 月 9 日巴黎公社（Paris Commune）成立，国民议会宣告终结。

Orders：（社会）等级；阶级

指法国旧制度下，由国王召集的三级议事会议中代表各自阶级利益、显示主次尊卑特征的三种等级，亦称"states"，如 Third Estate（法文为 *Tiers État*）。详见"三级会议"。

parlement：（法国大革命前的）最高法院

最高法院是法国旧制度中的省级上诉法院。1789 年，法国共有 13 个最高法院，而其中巴黎最高法院有着举足轻重的作用，其司法管辖权涉及法国近三分之一的国土。最高法院的法官皆具有贵族身份。最高法院并非立法机构，而是司法系统中的终审法院，就连国王颁布的敕令，只有经最高法院正式认可、颁发后才可在各法院的司法辖区内具有法律效力。最高法院于 1790 年 9 月法国革命期间被正式废除。英语 parliament 一词与法文 parlement 同源，有时也作"最高法院"解。

Parliament：（英国）议会

英国议会（Parliament of the United Kingdom），又称威斯敏斯特议会，是英国最高立法机关。英国议会实行两院制，分上院（House of Lords）和下院（House of Commons）两部分。上院又称"贵族院"，由王室后裔、离任首相、神职主教以及终身贵族（世袭贵族于 20 世纪末被取消担任上院议员资格）等各色上流人士组成，无任期限制。下院也称"平民院"，议员由选举产生。时至今日，上院已无立法和否决法案的权力，下院成为英国议会中单一的国家立法机关。

popular：民众的，人数众多的

伯克在书中使用这一词语时，大多取其"民众的""人数众多的"意思，并不包含"被大多数人喜欢的"词义。

positive law：实在法

指与自然法则相对的、由人（或国家权力机关）制定或认可、实证的法规。同样，伯克在书中提到 positive authority，positive institutions 等词语时，也包含类似的内涵。

prejudice：先入之见

伯克在书中使用这一术语时，撷取该词"根据以往经验对某事物所形成的固有看法"的词义，并无"偏见"的含义。作者把"先入之见"与"未验证的理性（naked reason）"作对比，认为成见远比理性主义革命更可靠，可为改革提供更牢靠的基础。

prescription：因袭成俗

根据法学理论，人们对某物长期有效占用，因袭成俗，最终将取得对该物的权利。基于因袭为所有权确立之基础这一观点，伯克认为，一个家族如几个世纪以来一直持有一块土地的使用权和控制权，这个家族便因此拥有了这块土地；因袭成俗也会成为政府合法化的基础，"一个以暴力起家的政府，经过长期执政将融入合法化的佳境"。

Prince：亲王

在伯克撰写本书的年代，Prince 不只是表示某君主之子，也是一种爵位，即亲王，通常被视为某领地之君主；与此相对应的女性则被称为"公主（Princess）"。君主王位的指定继承者叫"王储（Crown Prince）"，在英国则被称为"威尔士亲王（Prince of Wales）"，一国之君的长女叫"大公主（Princess Royal）"。

rights of man：人权

法国国民议会于 1789 年通过《人权宣言》法案，把伏尔泰和卢梭等法国启蒙运动领袖所宣扬的"人人生而平等""人民主权""天赋人权"等主张变成法律。伯克对此大张挞伐，断然否定《人权宣言》提出的人人都应享有自由和平等的权利这一主张。他在书中写道，"他们对一切拥有权利时就会索要一切"。他推崇祖先传承下来的"英国人的权利（rights of Englishmen）"，而不是理论上的"人权"概念："我们有可继位承袭的君主，可继位承袭的贵族院和下议院，以及从远祖那儿承继了特权、选举权和自由的人民"。

Sir：爵士

英国贵族的尊称之一，用于爵位等级最低的爵士和从男爵的名字或姓名前面。公爵以下的侯爵、伯爵、子爵、男爵以及公爵之子则称为"勋爵（Lord）"。

欧洲贵族的爵位制度等级森严，爵位由国王或女王册封、褫夺。以下是 18 世纪英法两国的君主和贵族爵位等级排列对照表及其中文译名：

英国	法国	中文译名
Emperor	Empereur	皇帝
King/Queen	Roi/Reine	国王 / 女王
Prince of Wales	Dauphin	王储 / 王太子
Prince	Prince	亲王
Duke	Duc	公爵
Marquess	Marquis	侯爵
Earl	Comte	伯爵
Viscount	Vicomte	子爵
Baron/Lord	Baron	男爵
Baronet		从男爵
Knight	Chevalier	爵士

同贵族说话时，不得直呼其名。对勋爵必须称"阁下"（Your Lordship），对公爵称"大人（Your Grace）"，对亲王及其他王室成员称"殿下（Your Highness）"，对国王和女王称"陛下（Your Majesty）"。

Edmund Burke
Reflections on the Revolution in France

图书在版编目（CIP）数据

评法国革命：导读注释版=Reflections on the
Revolution in France：英、汉 /（英）埃德蒙·伯克
（Edmund Burke）著；林骧华，任建国注释. — 上海：
上海译文出版社，2021.11
（世界学术经典系列）
ISBN 978-7-5327-8829-3

Ⅰ.①评… Ⅱ.①埃… ②林… ③任… Ⅲ.①法国大
革命—英、汉 Ⅳ.①K565.41

中国版本图书馆 CIP 数据核字（2021）第 161006 号

评法国革命（导读注释版）
［英］埃德蒙·伯克　著　林骧华　导读　任建国　注释
责任编辑 / 吴梦菡　装帧设计 / 张志全工作室

上海译文出版社有限公司出版、发行
网址：www.yiwen.com.cn
200001　上海福建中路 193 号
江阴市机关印刷服务有限公司印刷

开本 890×1240　1/32　印张 10.25　插页 6　字数 289,000
2022 年 1 月第 1 版　2022 年 1 月第 1 次印刷
印数：0,001—2,000 册

ISBN 978-7-5327-8829-3/D·143
定价：118.00 元

World Academic Classics
世界学术经典·英文版

Marxism
马克思主义

The Communist Manifesto（Marx & Engels）
共产党宣言（马克思、恩格斯）

Chinese Classics
中国经典

论语（汉英对照）
Confucius' Analects

道德经（汉英对照）
Dao De Jing

孟子（汉英对照）
Mencius

庄子（汉英对照）
Zhuangzi

孙子兵法（汉英对照）
Sun Tzu on the Art of War

大学·中庸（汉英对照）
The Great Learning & The Doctrine of the Mean

Philosophy
哲 学

Republic（Plato）
理想国（柏拉图）

Metaphysics（Aristotle）
形而上学（亚里士多德）

Meditations on First Philosophy（René Descartes）
第一哲学沉思录（笛卡尔）

A Discourse on Method（René Descartes）
方法论（笛卡尔）

Pascal's Pensées（Blaise Pascal）
思想录（帕斯卡尔）

A Treatise of Human Nature（David Hume）
人性论（休谟）

Critique of Pure Reason（Kant）
纯粹理性批判（康德）

Critique of Judgement（Kant）
判断力批判（康德）

The Phenomenology of Mind（Hegel）
精神现象学（黑格尔）

The Logic of Hegel（Hegel）
小逻辑（黑格尔）

The World as Will and Representation（Schopenhauer）
作为意志与表象的世界（叔本华）

Thus Spake Zarathustra（Nietzsche）
查拉图斯特拉如是说（尼采）

Either / Or（Kierkegaard）
非此即彼（克尔凯郭尔）

Ideas: General Introduction to Pure Phenomenology（Husserl）
纯粹现象学导论（胡塞尔）

On First Philosophy（Husserl）
论第一哲学（胡塞尔）

Tractatus Logico-Philosophicus（Wittgenstein）
逻辑哲学论（维特根斯坦）

Philosophical Investigations（Wittgenstein）
哲学研究（维特根斯坦）

Pragmatism（William James）
实用主义（威廉·詹姆斯）

Reconstruction in Philosophy（John Dewey）
哲学的改造（杜威）

Time and Free Will（Henri Bergson）
时间与自由意志（柏格森）

A Discourse on the Positive Spirit（Auguste Comte）
论实证精神（孔德）

Novum Organum（Francis Bacon）
新工具（培根）

Ethics
伦理学

The Nicomachean Ethics of Aristotle (Aristotle)
尼各马可伦理学（亚里士多德）

Critique of Practical Reason (Kant)
实践理性批判（康德）

The Theory of Moral Sentiments (Adam Smith)
道德情操论（亚当·斯密）

Utilitarianism (Mill)
功利主义（密尔）

A Discourse on Inequality (Rousseau)
论人类不平等的起源与基础（卢梭）

Principia Ethica (Moore)
伦理学原理（摩尔）

Religion
宗教学

Confessions (St. Augustine)
忏悔录（圣·奥古斯丁）

The Courage to Be (Paul Tillich)
存在的勇气（蒂利希）

Basic Writings of Saint Thomas Aquinas (Thomas Aquinas)
圣托马斯基本著作（阿奎那）

The Essence of Christianity (Ludwig Feuerbach)
基督教的本质（费尔巴哈）

Basic Theological Writings (Martin Luther)
路德基本著作选（马丁·路德）

Politics
政治学

The Politics of Aristotle (Aristotle)
政治学（亚里士多德）

The Federalist Papers (Hamilton)
联邦党人文集（汉密尔顿）

The Prince (Machiavelli)
君主论（马基雅维利）

The Ancien Régime and the Revolution (Tocqueville)
旧制度与大革命（托克维尔）

The Social Contract (Rousseau)
社会契约论（卢梭）

Utopia (Thomas More)
乌托邦（莫尔）

Leviathan (Thomas Hobbes)
利维坦（霍布斯）

On Liberty (Mill)
论自由（密尔）

Two Treatises of Government (John Locke)
政府论（洛克）

Reflections on the Revolution in France (Edmund Burke)
评法国革命（伯克）

The Spirit of the Laws (Montesquieu)
论法的精神（孟德斯鸠）

The Will to Power (Nietzsche)
权力意志（尼采）

Democracy in America (Tocqueville)
论美国民主（托克维尔）

On War (Carl von Clausewitz)
战争论（克劳塞维茨）

Considerations on Representative Government (Mill)
代议制政府（密尔）

Mutual Aid: A Factor of Evolution (Kropotkin)
互助论（克鲁泡特金）

Economics
经济学

The Economics of Welfare (Pigou)
福利经济学（庇古）

Principles of Economics (Alfred Marshall)
经济学原理（马歇尔）

The General Theory of Employment, Interest and Money (Keynes)
就业、利息与货币通论（凯恩斯）

Capitalism, Socialism and Democracy (Schumpeter)
资本主义、社会主义与民主（熊彼特）

The Theory of Economic Development (Schumpeter)
经济发展理论（熊彼特）

An Essay on Population (Thomas Robert Malthus)
人口原理（马尔萨斯）

An Inquiry into the Nature and Causes of the Wealth of Nations (Adam Smith)
国民财富的性质和原因的研究（亚当·斯密）

The Principles of Scientific Management (Frederick Winslow Taylor)
科学管理原理（泰勒）

Sociology
社会学

Suicide: A Study in Sociology (Durkheim)
自杀：社会学研究（迪尔凯姆）

Ideology and Utopia (Mannheim)
意识形态与乌托邦（曼海姆）

The Protestant Ethic and the Spirit of Capitalism (Max Weber)
新教伦理与资本主义精神（韦伯）

First Principles (Herbert Spencer)
基本原理（斯宾塞）

The Philosophy of Money (Georg Simmel)
货币哲学（西美尔）

The Theory of the Leisure Class (Thorstein B. Veblen)
论闲逸阶级（凡勃伦）

A Treatise on General Sociology (Vilfredo Pareto)
社会学总论（帕累托）

Anthropology
人类学

The Golden Bough (James George Frazer)
金枝（詹姆斯·乔治·弗雷泽）

Race, Language and Culture (Franz Boas)
种族、语言与文化（弗朗茨·博厄斯）

Argonauts of the Western Pacific (Malinowski)
西太平洋的航海者（马林诺夫斯基）

The Savage Mind (Claude Lévi-Strauss)
野性思维（克劳德·列维-斯特劳斯）

Structure and Function in Primitive Society (Radcliffe-Brown)
原始社会的结构和功能（拉德克利夫-布朗）

Psychology
心理学

The Principles of Psychology (William James)
心理学原理（威廉·詹姆斯）

The Interpretation of Dreams (Sigmund Freud)
梦的解析（弗洛伊德）

Principles of Physiological Psychology (Wundt)
生理心理学原理（冯特）

The Archetypes and the Collective Unconscious (Jung)
原型与集体无意识（荣格）

Law
法　学

Ancient Law (Maine)
古代法（梅因）

Lectures on Jurisprudence (Austin)
法理学演讲录（奥斯丁）

English Law and the Renaissance (Maitland)
英国法律与文艺复兴（梅特兰）

Fundamental Principles of the Sociology of Law (Ehrlich)
法律社会学基本原理（埃利希）

History
历史学

The Histories (Herodotus)
历史（希罗多德）

The Peloponnesian War (Thucydides)
伯罗奔尼撒战争史（修昔底德）

The Annals of Imperial Rome (Tacitus)
编年史（塔西佗）

The City of God (St. Augustine)
上帝之城（圣·奥古斯丁）

On Heroes, Hero Worship, and the Heroic in History
(Thomas Carlyle)
论历史上的英雄、英雄崇拜和英雄业绩（卡莱尔）

The Idea of History (Collingwood)
历史的观念（科林伍德）

History of Civilization in Europe (Francois Guizot)
欧洲文明史（基佐）

The Influence of Sea Power (Alfred T. Mahan)
海权对历史的影响（马汉）

Theory & History of Historiography (Benedetto Croce)
史学理论与史学史（克罗齐）

A Short Account of the Destruction of the Indies
(Bartolomé de Las Cases)
西印度毁灭述略（卡萨斯）

Literary Theory and Aesthetics
文学理论与美学

On the Art of Poetry (Aristotle)
诗学（亚里士多德）

On the Art of Poetry (Horace)
诗艺（贺拉斯）

On the Sublime (Longinus)
论崇高（朗吉努斯）

Theory of Aesthetic / History of Aesthetic (Benedetto Croce)
美学理论 / 美学史（克罗齐）

Hegel's Aesthetics Lectures on Fine Art (Hegel)
黑格尔美学讲演录（黑格尔）

The Birth of Tragedy (Friedrich Nietzsche)
悲剧的诞生（尼采）

Linguistics
语言学

Course in General Linguistics (Saussure)
普通语言学教程（索绪尔）

On Language (Wilhelm von Humboldt)
论语言（威廉·冯·洪堡特）

Scientific Philosophy
自然科学哲学

On the Origin of Species (Charles Darwin)
物种起源（查尔斯·达尔文）

*Mathematical Principles of Natural Philosophy and Its
System of the World* (Issac Newton)
自然哲学的数学原理（牛顿）

Natural History (Pliny the Elder)
自然史（老普林尼）